TEACHING
READING IN THE
CONTENT
AREAS

Vicki Urquhart | Dana Frazee

TEACHING READING IN THE
CONTENT AREAS

If not me, then who?

3RD EDITION

ASCD®

LEARN. TEACH. LEAD.

Alexandria, Virginia USA

McREL

Mid-continent Research for Education and Learning

Denver, Colorado USA

1703 N. Beauregard St. • Alexandria, VA 22311-1714 USA
Phone: 800-933-2723 or 703-578-9600 • Fax: 703-575-5400
Website: www.ascd.org • E-mail: member@ascd.org
Author guidelines: www.ascd.org/write

Gene R. Carter, *Executive Director;* Ed Milliken, *Chief Program Development Officer;* Carole Hayward, *Publisher;* Laura Lawson, *Acquisitions Editor;* Julie Houtz, *Director, Book Editing & Production;* Jamie Greene, *Editor;* Louise Bova, *Senior Graphic Designer;* Mike Kalyan, *Production Manager;* Keith Demmons, *Typesetter;* Kyle Steichen, *Production Specialist.*

MꞒREL®

Mid-continent Research for Education and Learning
4601 DTC Boulevard, Suite 500
Denver, CO 80237 USA
Phone: 303-337-0990 • Fax: 303-337-3005
Website: www.mcrel.org • E-mail: info@mcrel.org

All web links in this book are correct as of the publication date below but may have become inactive or otherwise modified since that time. If you notice a deactivated or changed link, please e-mail books@ascd.org with the words "Link Update" in the subject line. In your message, please specify the web link, the book title, and the page number on which the link appears.

PAPERBACK ISBN: 978-1-4166-1421-0   ASCD product #112024   n7/12

Also available as an e-book (see Books in Print for the ISBNs).

Quantity discounts for the paperback edition only: 10–49 copies, 10%; 50+ copies, 15%; for 1,000 or more copies, call 800-933-2723, ext. 5634, or 703-575-5634. For desk copies: member@ascd.org.

Library of Congress Cataloging-in-Publication Data

Urquhart, Vicki, 1950-
  Teaching reading in the content areas : if not me, then who? / Vicki Urquhart, Dana Frazee. — 3rd ed.
    p. cm.
  Includes bibliographical references and index.
  ISBN 978-1-4166-1421-0 (pbk. : alk. paper)
  1. Content area reading. 2. Reading (Secondary) I. Frazee, Dana. II. Title.
  LB1050.455.U77 2012
  428.4071'2—dc23
                        2012007967

20 19 18 17 16 15 14 13 12   1 2 3 4 5 6 7 8 9 10 11 12

TEACHING READING IN THE CONTENT AREAS

If not me, then who?

3rd Edition

Acknowledgments

Special thanks to our colleagues at McREL: Heather Hein for her editing expertise on this edition; Maura McGrath for her oversight of copyright permissions; and Greg Cameron, Bryan Goodwin, and Monette McIver for their quality assurance review.

In addition, we acknowledge Rachel Billmeyer and Mary Lee Barton, the authors of *Teaching Reading in the Content Areas: If Not Me, Then Who? 2nd edition*, upon which this book is based, and the authors of the other manuals in the series: *Teaching Reading in Science,* by Mary Lee Barton and Deborah L. Jordan; *Teaching Reading in Mathematics,* by Mary Lee Barton and Clare Heidema; and *Teaching Reading in Social Studies,* by Jane K. Doty, Gregory N. Cameron, and Mary Lee Barton.

Introduction

"New focus on reading, writing: Improving literacy offers gains in all subjects."

—Taryn Plumb, *The Boston Globe*

As a middle school or high school teacher, or even as a parent of a "tween" or teen, it's likely that you are not shocked by any part of the above news headline; however, you certainly may be dismayed. How and when did we stop expecting students to go to school and read and write in all of their classes?

Rediscovering the impact that reading in the content areas has on learning is the primary goal of this book. The second goal is to provide the latest research, tools, and guidance necessary to ensure that reading is a part of every young person's daily learning experience.

Rationale: An Abundance of Compelling Reasons

The following short anecdote comes from the previous version of this book, which was written in 1998. We return to it now because, in many ways, students' attitudes about reading haven't changed much in the intervening years. This exchange is just as likely—and relevant—today as it was then. Perhaps you can sense the alarm one of the authors felt after hearing this response from her daughter's boyfriend, Brian, when she asked him about reading: "No, I don't read much; actually, I haven't read a book all summer. . . ." Knowing that he was valedictorian of the senior class, she asked him about the reading involved with his assignments in school. "Oh, I read what I need to in order to get by, but nothing more. I know I should read," he admitted, "but I just don't get into it."

The authors of the second edition of this book had plenty of data showing Brian to be a typical student. A long-term assessment of academic progress, the *NAEP 1998 Reading Report Card for the Nation and the States*, had found that nearly half of the 9-, 13-, and 17-year-old students they surveyed reported reading ten or fewer pages each day, including material read in school and for homework (Donahue, Voekl, Campbell, & Mazzeo, 1998). The same report revealed 36 percent of 9-year-olds, 48 percent of 13-year-olds, and 39 percent of 17-year-olds watched three to five hours of television per day.

More data analysis revealed that a shocking percentage of our adult population—from 15 to 30 percent—had difficulty reading common print material such as news articles, report cards, coupons, recipes, or even the directions on prescription medicine bottles (Barton, 1997; Stedman & Kaestle, 1991). There was also the stark pronouncement that some adults, much like Brian, simply chose not to read. According to Bernice Cullinan (1987) of New York University, approximately 80 percent of the books read in the United States were read by about 10 percent of the people. This was a startling revelation about the reading habits of one of the most advanced countries in the world. Could it be that the American intellect was in free fall? These kinds of statistics suggested to some that it was. Finally, two Kent State University education professors came to the disturbing conclusion that many preservice teachers disliked reading and avoided it whenever possible (Manna & Misheff, 1987).

Fast forward to 2012, and although there are still many students who opt out of reading, there are many others who choose to opt in. Key findings from consumer research provide a hopeful glimpse into young readers' attitudes and behaviors (Scholastic, 2008):

- A majority of kids say they like to read books for fun, and reading books for fun is important.

- Most kids perceive a correlation between reading and success.

- One in four kids aged 5–17 reads books for fun every day (high-frequency reader), and more than half of all kids read books for fun at least two to three times a week.

These findings are reportedly based on more than 1,000 interviews, including 501 children aged 5–17 and their parents or guardians, in 25 cities across the country. In another report, however, we can see the other side of the proverbial coin—a return to the belief that most young people are choosing not to read.

The authors of *To Read or Not To Read* (National Endowment for the Arts [NEA], 2007) describe their data collection and analysis process as encompassing data from large, national studies regularly conducted by federal agencies and supplemented by academic, foundation, and business surveys. NEA chairman Dana Gioia considers the findings especially important because they go beyond literary implications to social, economic, and cultural ones. "Although there has been measurable progress in recent years in reading ability at the elementary school level, all progress appears to halt as children enter their teenage years. There is a general decline in reading among teenage and adult Americans. Most alarming, both reading ability and the habit of regular reading have greatly declined among college graduates" (NEA, 2007, p. 5).

Although the question of whether today's students are reading seems to depend on whom you ask, Gioia suggests that there are a few "truths" that emerge from the data:

- Reading is declining as an activity among teenagers.

- College attendance no longer guarantees active reading habits.

- Even when reading does occur, it competes with other media.

- American families are spending less money on books than at almost any other time during the past two decades.

- Among high school seniors, the average reading proficiency score has declined for virtually all levels of reading.

- Reading proficiency rates are stagnant or declining among all adults.

The young people you know and teach probably fall somewhere between the extremes; they might not openly profess to a love of reading, but they do sometimes love a particular book or series of books—as witnessed by the way many adolescents (and adults) have devoured the *Twilight* and *Harry Potter* books. Although some young people may not be reading the so-called classics, they are finding and reading funny, contemporary stories about people their own age.

However, no one can deny that data shine a spotlight on real and legitimate concerns. We know, for instance, that reading for pleasure correlates strongly with academic achievement; that employers rank reading and writing as top deficiencies in new hires; and that good readers generally have more financially rewarding jobs, whereas less-advanced readers report fewer opportunities for career growth (NEA, 2007). It is, in the eyes of some, a crisis of epic proportions. Nevertheless, as within every crisis, cooler heads and calmer voices do exist. Vicki Jacobs sees "opportunities ahead for researchers, policymakers, and practitioners who are positioned to respond to the adolescent literacy crisis and improve adolescent literacy achievement" (2008, p. 7). There are opportunities enough to go around, but perhaps none is as great as the opportunity (and challenge) the classroom offers.

New Challenges

"There are approximately 8.7 million 4th through 12th graders in America whose chances for academic success are dismal because they are unable to read and comprehend the material in their textbooks" (Kamil, 2003, p. 1). To help all students become better readers, educators must understand the premise that guides the teaching of reading in their discipline, how to choose the best reading strategies from the vast array available, and how to put it all together and positively impact student learning. The greatest challenge, though, may be in understanding the learning process from a wider perspective, especially as it relates to variables such as technology, changing student demographics, and a national set of common standards for academic achievement.

Technology promotes skimming, scanning, and flipping

Technology's explosive growth over the past few decades has fueled much speculation about the future of the book as we know it and, of course, of reading. In the early 1990s, Microsoft, Hewlett-Packard, and IBM conducted web usability studies, some of which included an examination of how people read while online. Their conclusion was . . . they don't. Instead, when they look at text on a screen, people tend to skim, scan, and flip—they don't read deeply or for an extended period of time. Some Internet users even warn others that content is long and takes too much time to read, simply by communicating "tl;dr," which stands for "too long; don't read" (Fernando, 2011).

Even the perception of reading is changing. This is becoming more and more evident as we find that when we mention an interesting book to colleagues, many respond along the lines of "I'm really a Kindle kind of person," suggesting that "Kindling" and reading are distinctly different activities. Although e-readers now sit among the stacks of hardbacks, paperbacks, and magazines in many homes, some people no longer think of themselves as "book readers." This situation sounds fairly ominous, but even Jeff Bezos, founder of Amazon and a passionate Kindle promoter, remains a fan of the printed book, calling it an "incredible device" that is "highly evolved" (Levy, 2007). In truth, the only thing certain about the future of reading is that it is changing—new rituals (sitting down at your computer, searching the e-library, and downloading your e-book) replace existing ones (sitting in your favorite chair, adjusting the light, and turning to a dog-eared page), but reading remains an active and demanding process that requires effort on our parts.

The question is whether our students see it this way. If they don't, what can we do about it? They are, after all, "digital natives," which is how Marc Prensky (2001) refers to the generation of students who have been exposed to technology since birth. For them, it is completely natural to skim, scan, and flip through reading materials.

Therefore, it should come as no surprise that parents still worry about the effects of all this technology use. The *2010 Kids and Family Reading Report* (Scholastic, 2010), based on a nationally representative sample of 1,045 children aged 6–17 and their parents, reports that parents believe the use of electronic or digital devices negatively affects the time children spend reading books, doing physical activity, and engaging with family. In addition, when asked about the one device parents would like their children to stop using for a one- or two-week period, parents most often cite television, video game systems, and cell phones.

Not surprisingly, the kids surveyed see things a little differently. It appears that they even define the term *reading* differently than their parents do; for example, they expand it to include reading text messages. Nonetheless, 66 percent of children aged 9–17 report in the Scholastic study that they won't abandon printed books, even though e-books are available. Faced with the ubiquity of technology, what's a teacher or parent to do?

One suggestion is simply to reembrace the maxim "if you can't beat 'em, join 'em." After all, there is some research to support such an approach. For example, in an effort to identify adolescents' motivation to read, 11 researchers (who also happen to be college and university teachers) interviewed teens from various school settings at eight sites (Pitcher et al., 2007). Aware of adolescents' use of technology, they adapted their questions and prompts in an effort to better understand how preteens and teens see themselves as readers. Here is a typical exchange with a 6th grader:

> Interviewer: How much time do you spend on the computer a day?
> Adolescent: Two hours every day.
> Interviewer: What do you usually do?
> Adolescent: Search and play games on the Internet. I go to Ask Jeeves and ask questions. Draw things and write e-mails, print them out and hang them up. Shop for my mother so she can go to the store and buy things. Read about things that are going on around the world. I read magazines and music on the Internet and about getting into college and things. (Pitcher et al., 2007, p. 378)

The researchers in this study concluded that these adolescents were reading and writing for many hours each day in "multiple, flexible, and varied ways and formats" (Ibid., p. 394), yet they didn't see themselves as readers or writers because they were using computer literacies, which they considered to be different from more traditional, school-based reading and writing skills. The primary recommendation for teachers, then, is to get to know your students, including their personal uses of literacy and what's important to them. Furthermore, the research team suggests that teachers model their own enjoyment of reading; find ways to incorporate multiple literacies into their classrooms; embrace engaging and interactive activities (e.g., book clubs, literature circles); include reading material that represents a variety of formats, levels, and topics; and incorporate elements of choice in reading and project assignments (Ibid.). The key point of this study is something most teachers agree with: by increasing students' motivations to read, you increase the odds of improving reading outcomes.

Consider also the striking headline that recently ran in *The Denver Post*: "It's old school—and it's the future" (Nix, 2011). The article profiles Thomas MacLaren School in Colorado Springs, where single-sex classes, Latin classes, and reading the classics are the norm. All of the school's 110 students follow the same liberal arts curriculum, which includes learning how to play a stringed instrument. This is not an elite school, curriculum, or group of students. One-third of the students benefit from free or reduced lunch, and one-third belong to an ethnic minority group. School leaders say they simply aim to attract and keep students for whom the curriculum and approach are a good fit. Although a focus on liberal arts might sound "old school" to some, it is hard to believe that today's generation will be ready to lead globally until it has mastered the skills we most often need and use—not the ability to multitask with numerous electronic devices but the ability to read widely, think deeply, and question courageously.

An ELL population booms

You have probably heard statistics about how English language learners (ELLs) form the fastest growing segment of the U.S. school-aged population, yet many of these students continue to lag behind their peers on state and national achievement measures. "The students' levels of exposure to English, their educational histories, the socioeconomic levels of their families, and the number of books in their homes all play a role in their readiness to learn—and learn *in*—a new language" (Hill & Flynn, 2006, p. 3). Further complicating the situation, rigorous research into the instructional practices that target ELL literacy and language development remains scarce (Barker, 2010).

The National Clearinghouse for English Language Acquisition (n.d.) reports that in 2008–2009, approximately five million ELLs were enrolled in grades pre-K through 12. We can imagine the frustration teachers in general education classrooms must feel as they try to meet the needs of this growing population in their classes, knowing they should differentiate their instruction for ELLs yet not knowing how. With the right assistance and models, though, teachers can learn to integrate reading, writing, and content into their ELL instruction. Margarita Calderón, senior research scientist and professor at Johns Hopkins University, acknowledges that limited English language skills is a major contributor to low student performance. However, after conducting three five-year studies on expediting reading comprehension in ELLs, she confidently asserts that teachers can learn to craft their instruction in a way that accelerates ELLs' achievement and addresses their lack of background knowledge and vocabulary. "Teaching subject matter to ELLs requires direct, explicit instruction in the strategies students need to build vocabulary and comprehend grade-level texts" (Calderón, 2007, p. viii).

The really good news here is that the type of instruction Calderón proposes works for *all* students. Whenever instruction is intentional, research-based, and integrated, students benefit. Better still, teachers can learn which reading strategies are best suited to each discipline, how and why they work, and specific ways to adapt those strategies for their students, content, and classroom. Not surprisingly, "quality teaching is critically important to ELL language development (and maintenance), regardless of program model" (Barker, 2010, p. 3).

The Common Core makes its entrance

In the summer of 2009, armed with and alarmed by data about a nationwide decrease in graduation rates, and resulting from an outcry among many in the business community that they were spending huge sums of money to remediate new hires in basic reading and writing competencies, three organizations came together united by one goal: build upon the most advanced current thinking on how to prepare all students for success in college and their careers. The Council of Chief State School Officers, a nonpartisan organization of the heads of departments of elementary and secondary education, together with the National Governors Association, the bipartisan organization of the nation's governors, joined to form the Common Core State Standards Initiative. By June 2010, this group had published two documents: *Common Core State Standards for English Language Arts & Literacy in History/Social Studies, Science, and Technical Subjects* and *Common Core State Standards for Mathematics.*

A closer look at the English language arts and literacy standards reveals four strands that comprise the College and Career Readiness anchor standards: (1) reading, (2) writing, (3) speaking and listening, and (4) language. Within each strand, standards are organized under a set of topics that apply across all grades (Kendall, 2011). The example in Figure A is based on the anchor standards for reading.

The new common core standards require students to read considerably less fiction. Two objectives emphasized are: (1) engage students in increasingly complex texts as they move through school, and (2) help students conquer literacy skills specific to disciplines such as history and science (Gewertz, 2011). In general, research evidence supports this change, since there is a significant difficulty gap between texts used at the end of high school and those used at the beginning of college. One reason for the gap in students' ability to readily comprehend higher-level texts is that as college and workplace texts have become more complex, K–12 reading texts have become easier. Consequently, students leave high school without having developed the skills to comprehend challenging text, particularly when it comes to discipline-specific texts. In addition, K–12 reading usually favors narrative fiction over expository texts, yet the majority of reading required in college and the workplace is expository prose. According to David Coleman, one of the lead writers of the common core standards for English/Language Arts, by preparing students to succeed in college and build solid careers, text complexity and disciplinary/literacy skills become inseparable (Gewertz, 2011).

FIGURE A → Excerpt from the Common Core English Language Arts Anchor Standards for Reading

Key Ideas and Details

- Read closely to determine what the text says explicitly and to make logical inferences from it; cite specific textual evidence when writing or speaking to support conclusions drawn from the text.

Craft and Structure

- Analyze the structure of texts, including how specific sentences, paragraphs, and larger portions of the text (e.g., a section, chapter, scene, or stanza) relate to each other and the whole.

Integration of Knowledge and Ideas

- Delineate and evaluate the argument and specific claims in a text, including the validity of the reasoning as well as the relevance and sufficiency of the evidence.

Range of Reading and Level of Text Complexity

- Read and comprehend complex literary and informational texts independently and proficiently.

Source: From *Common Core State Standards: English Language Arts Standards*, 2010, Washington, DC: National Governors Association Center for Best Practices, Council of Chief State School Officers. Retrieved from http://www.corestandards.org

For students who may need reading remediation in college, the outlook is grim; they are the least likely to complete a degree (Kendall, 2011). Therefore, many experts agree that the goal of connecting K–12 standards with postsecondary education is the right one, as long as the standards are consistently revisited and updated according to students' education needs.

The Current Literacy Landscape

Although researchers began to scrutinize literacy practices in the 1970s, and they continued to do so throughout the 1980s and 1990s, it was the 2000s that some called, perhaps ironically, the "literacy decade." Although reading skills are only improving minimally, greater worldwide interest in the topic clearly has emerged. The United Nations, for example, proclaimed 2003–2012 the Literacy Decade and has stated its intent "to increase literacy levels and to empower all people everywhere" (United Nations Educational, Scientific, and Cultural Organization, n.d.).

The Programme for International Student Assessment (PISA) and the Progress in International Reading Literacy Study are the two leaders in global comparative studies in reading comprehension. Since 2000, PISA has administered standardized tests in reading, mathematics, and science to more than one million 15-year-old students in 41 countries, and it continues to collect and share test results. In reading, for example, questions focus on the ability to read written text in real-life situations. These two organizations partnered to make the resulting test data available to countries around the world. In so doing, they ushered in an era of global literacy, during which a common foundation in reading comprehension instruction shone a spotlight on foundational instructional strategies (Block & Parris, 2008). However, according to national assessments, the reading skills of many U.S. students in general, and of high school students in particular, have shown little or no improvement, despite regular and substantial increases in federal and state funding over the past several decades for elementary and secondary education. According to a 2011 report on state test score trends from 2002–2009, high school scores on state English language arts and mathematics tests have risen modestly in most states since 2002, but progress made by high school students has been markedly less than progress made by students in 4th through 8th grades (Center on Education Policy [CEP], 2011). Furthermore, the authors of the study observe that "many states show a troubling lack of progress among high school students at the advanced achievement level" (CEP, 2011, p. 2).

Various skills-related issues contribute to the difficulties students have with reading and writing in the content areas. Many students have trouble understanding concepts in a science, history, or mathematics text because they haven't learned how to mentally organize information as they read or because they have little or no experience with the topic and don't know how to make meaningful and personal connections to new ideas while reading. When students lack the effective reading and self-regulation skills needed to persevere and succeed, they sometimes simply label an assignment as "too hard" or "boring." Additionally, research on school-level, teacher-level, and student-level influences on student achievement identifies vocabulary as a pivotal component of a student's background knowledge (Marzano, 2003). A lack of background knowledge is a hurdle for many students, and because vocabulary is a significant component of background knowledge, it is a particularly tough challenge for ELLs.

Timothy and Cynthia Shanahan, who prefer the term *disciplinary literacy*, have identified something of a catch-22 for teachers when it comes to teaching reading in the content areas: literacy professionals don't know enough about the content areas to help teachers in those subjects teach students with appropriate literacies, and teachers in the content areas don't know enough about the literacy demands of their specialized content areas to know what literacies to teach students (Shanahan & Shanahan, 2008). To successfully read texts in different content areas, students must develop discipline-specific skills and strategies along with knowledge of that discipline, including knowledge of the authors, the genres they use to reach their audiences, and their purposes for writing (Ibid.).

By focusing on the differences of how content-area experts read and reason, teachers can be better prepared to help students understand that the ways they read in biochemistry are different from the ways they read in English, European history, or mathematics.

In English, for example, students might read a short story in its entirety, then go back and analyze its theme and structure for further discussion. In mathematics, though, they would benefit from learning to read as mathematicians do—reading and rereading the same few lines of text, which requires tolerance for the intensity of "close reading." (Gewertz, 2011)

There is no doubt that teachers continue to face tough odds in the ongoing effort to improve literacy nationwide. Given the complexities of the reading process, teachers deserve clear, research-based answers to their overarching questions about teaching reading in the content areas:

- What are the specific skills students need in order to read effectively in a particular content area?

- What strategies should I use to help my students become more effective readers and independent learners?

- What type of learning environment promotes effective reading and learning?

As with earlier editions of *Teaching Reading in the Content Areas*, this third edition aims to help you—the content-area teacher—by answering these questions. Before going any further, however, we want to assure you that an emphasis on reading and writing in your daily instruction works to strengthen students' ability to access and grasp the key concepts of your content area. Consider the story of Brockton High School in Brockton, Massachusetts, where 4,400 students from 50 countries—70 percent of whom are from low-income households and one-third of whom speak a language other than English—come to learn. And learn they do. In 2009, the Achievement Gap Initiative at Harvard University recognized the school as one of 15 exemplary schools in the United States. Thirteen years ago, though, Brockton High School had quite another story.

In 1998, when Massachusetts implemented standardized testing in reading and mathematics and tied it to graduation requirements, the administrators at Brockton High School received reports showing their students' abysmally low test scores and were told that more than 75 percent of their students would not graduate. In response, they joined forces with a small group of interested teachers at the school who wanted to spearhead a schoolwide literacy program to reinforce reading and writing in every class—including mathematics, science, and even band and physical education. This group, which eventually became a restructuring committee, asked one question: "What are the skills we want our students to have by the time they leave Brockton High School? Their answer: reading, writing, speaking, and reasoning (Ferguson, Hackman, Hanna, & Ballantine, 2010).

The restructuring group believed the path to success for their students would be through a schoolwide literacy initiative. Their first goal was to make the four core skills—reading writing, speaking, and reasoning—an integral part of the curriculum. They began by outlining the elements of each skill and displaying the elements on charts posted in every classroom. They decided to focus on one of the elements every year, and the administration set up a calendar to reflect this expectation. The school provided professional development, and all teachers were asked to learn and use literacy strategies. One year, for example, the school tenaciously focused on active-reading strategies.

After one year, students' failure rate on the English language arts (ELA) portion of the state test dropped from 43 to 23 percent, and they continue to drop. "The transformation at Brockton has been remarkable: Failure rates for that state test have dropped to 6 percent for English" (Murthy & Weber, 2011). According to Jennifer Morgan, an instructional resource specialist and teacher coach at the school, after seeing such powerful results, teachers were willing to implement the next element of the literacy initiative. Results continue to impress. In 2008, students' ELA test score gains from 8th to 10th grade ranked the school above the 90th percentile when compared to other high schools in Massachusetts (Ferguson et al., 2010). In 2009, 77 percent of the 882 graduates planned to attend two- or four-year colleges (Bolton, 2010).

Five Research-Based Recommendations for Content-Area Teachers

In the report *Bringing Literacy Strategies into Content Instruction*, Kosanovich, Reed, and Miller (2010) make five scientifically based recommendations they consider pivotal to improving adolescent literacy. Their recommendations provide an instructional focus and suggest improvements that content-area teachers can make to improve reading comprehension among adolescents. They call for the recommendations to be implemented in a thoughtful, planned, and systematic manner: "When implemented widely and effectively, [the five recommendations] will likely lead to significant long-term improvement in adolescents' literacy abilities" (Kosanovich et al., 2010, p. 9). In addition, they realistically point out that teachers and administrators may need high-quality professional development to successfully implement the recommendations. As you continue through the rest of this book, you will likely recognize the recommendations reflected in the various literacy-related topics we discuss.

Recommendation 1:
All teachers should provide explicit instruction and supportive practice in effective comprehension strategies throughout the school day

Graphic organizers and questioning techniques are two comprehension strategies used across content areas that have been studied broadly. Newer findings suggest that some comprehension strategies are specific to a content area or even a specific course. Even though science, mathematics, and social studies all demand distinct reading and writing skills, common features of strategy instruction that are particularly important for adolescent readers include

- Discussions to help students become more aware of their own cognitive processes and to help them set a purpose for using comprehension strategies.

- Teacher modeling of explanations for when, how, and why to use particular comprehension strategies.

- Many meaningful opportunities for students to use comprehension strategies and receive teacher feedback.

- A gradual transfer of responsibility for implementing comprehension strategies from teacher to student.

Recommendation 2:
Increase the amount and quality of open, sustained discussion of reading content

Research supports the frequent use of both teacher-led and small group discussions. Rich discussions about text have the potential to increase students' abilities to analyze what they read, to think critically, to engage students, and to improve students' conceptual understanding and learning—all of which can lead to improved reading comprehension over time. Discussing texts is a way to mine the shared knowledge of the class while simultaneously supporting students as they independently construct meaning. The impact of these experiences extends beyond a single lesson; it ultimately supports comprehension when students read text independently.

Recommendation 3:
Set and maintain high standardsfor text, conversation, questions, and vocabulary

Teachers need to use instructional methods that support student growth toward meeting the literacy standards of the school, district, and state. Regardless of how high the literacy standards might be, they will nevertheless have minimal impact if teachers do not buy in and are not "on board." For all students to reach high literacy standards, schools and districts need to implement evidenced-based instructional techniques such as those covered in this book.

Recommendation 4:
Increase students' motivation and engagement with reading

Although research does not identify specific motivational techniques for particular types of students, it does support using the following techniques:

- Give students more choices of text and assignments to build their autonomy.

- Create opportunities for students to interact with each other in pairs or in small groups with a shared focus on understanding text.

- Provide students with a variety of interesting texts that reflect the diverse interests of adolescents.
- Focus students on personally important and interesting learning goals.

Recommendation 5:
Teach essential content knowledge so students can master critical concepts

As students improve their knowledge in a specific area, their ability to understand the associated reading material also improves. As a content-area teacher, you are much more likely to improve your students' ability to independently comprehend relevant reading material when you use instructional routines that support their understanding of content-area vocabulary, concepts, and facts.

Three Interlocking Gears of Disciplinary Literacy

At its most basic, teaching reading in the content areas is about helping learners make connections between what they already know and new information presented in written form—either in a textbook or electronically. As students make connections, they create meaning and better comprehend what they are reading. Teaching reading in the content areas, therefore, is not about teaching basic reading skills; rather, it is about teaching students how to use reading as a tool for thinking and learning.

An approach that some literacy experts recommend is for content-area teachers to plan lessons that, initially, do not require extensive reading (e.g., Lee & Spratley, 2010). Teachers should introduce a variety of on-level texts that will allow students to use what they already know to tackle discipline-related problems presented in the text. Over time, teachers can steadily increase the complexity of the texts, moving students from on-level texts to above-level texts. You might find the information in Figure B to be a helpful reference when preparing lessons or units of study.

A dynamic relationship

The previous edition of this book identified three elements that work together to determine the meaning readers construct from content-area text: the reader, and what he or she brings to the situation; the learning climate, or the environment in which the reading occurs; and the text features, or specific characteristics of the written text. A simple Venn diagram illustrates this approach (see Figure C).

It is true that the interaction of reader, climate, and text is in play whenever readers read, but more recent studies describe the need to move beyond content-area reading and toward content literacy that reflects the essential literacy skills of a particular academic discipline (e.g., Lee & Spratley, 2010; Shanahan & Shanahan, 2008; Vacca & Vacca, 2005). With this in mind, we revisit and redefine the three interactive elements as follows:

FIGURE B ⇢   Needs of Adolescent Struggling Readers

Instructional Foci for Supporting Adolescent Struggling Readers in the Content Areas
Apply both generic and discipline-focused strategies and knowledge to the comprehension and evaluation of • Textbooks • Full-length books • Book chapters • Journal and magazine articles • Newspaper articles • Historically situated primary documents • Multimedia and digital texts

Generic Reading Strategies	Discipline-Specific Reading Strategies
• Monitor Comprehension • Preread • Set Goals • Use Prior Knowledge • Ask Questions • Make Predictions • Test Predictions • Reread • Summarize	• Build Prior Knowledge • Build Specialized Vocabulary • Deconstruct Complex Sentences • Predict Main and Subordinate Ideas *(based on text structures and genres)* • Map Graphic Representations *(against explanations in the text)* • Pose Discipline-Relevant Questions • Compare Claims and Propositions Across Texts • Use Norms for Reasoning within the Discipline to Evaluate Claims *(i.e., What counts as evidence?)*

Source: From *Reading in the Disciplines: The Challenges of Adolescent Literacy* (p.16), by C. D. Lee and A. Spratley, 2010, New York: Carnegie Corporation. Copyright 2010 by the Carnegie Corporation of New York. Reprinted with permission.

FIGURE C ⇢   Three Interactive Elements of Reading

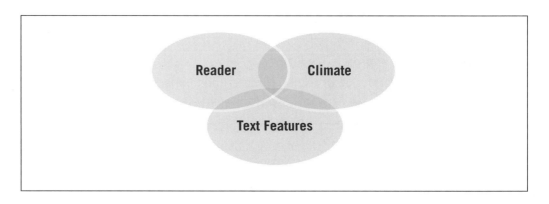

- The reader's **knowledge**, including experiences students bring to the classroom and the multiple ways in which they learn, in addition to how readers construct meaning while reading in specific disciplines.

- The reader's use of **strategies**, or ways of thinking and doing that reflect how experts in particular disciplines read and think.

- The reader's **goals and dispositions**, which include engagement, motivation, metacognitive skills, and teachers' expectations.

To fully understand how these elements affect the reading process, we examine them in light of findings and research results from the field of cognitive science.

About This Resource

This book should be a resource for expanding and refining your repertoire of teaching strategies as they apply to your subject. It also can serve as a guide for instructional planning and decision making as you meet with colleagues to consider your school's or district's curriculum objectives, the nature and needs of your students, and your personal teaching style.

In this book, we will

- Examine the dynamic relationship among three elements of the reading process that influence comprehension: knowledge, strategies, and goals and dispositions. These elements work together, much like the way that individual gears function as one assembly and for one purpose—to create forward movement.

- Explain how you can create a literacy-rich environment in your classroom and help expand that environment throughout the school and district. With a solid background in place, we look at the practical implications of integrating strategies on a daily basis and help you plan for instruction.

- Present teaching strategies that are proven to work best in certain content areas. Some strategies are most effective when they are adapted to a particular discipline by teachers who are experts in those fields. Teachers are able to maximize the effectiveness of the strategies they use by customizing those strategies with discipline-specific questions, vocabularies, purposes, and audiences (Shanahan, 2010). Thus, the strategies section of this edition has been fully revised to reflect this understanding.

FIGURE D ⇢   Interlocking Gears of Disciplinary Literacy

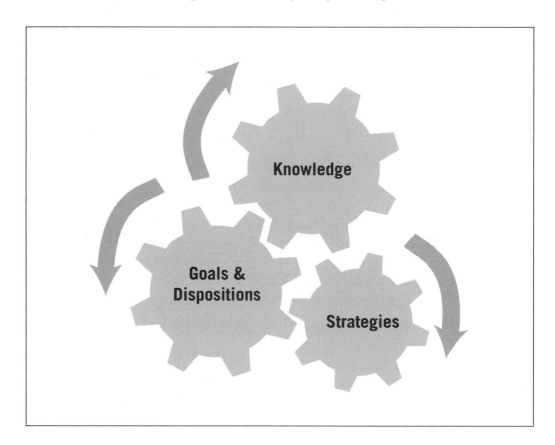

PART

I

The Knowledge Gear

"We are evolving from being cultivators of personal knowledge to being hunters and gatherers in the electronic data forest."

—Nicholas Carr, *The Shallows: What the Internet is Doing to Our Brains*

Twenty-first century science offers a new way of looking at and understanding the workings of the human brain. We now know, for example, which areas of the brain activate when we decipher a written word, that a genetic variation might be at the root of dyslexia, and that the recycling of neural networks in our brains may be what allows us the uniquely human abilities of reading and writing. Neuroscientist Stanislas Dehaene (2009) refers to this new way of looking at reading and learning as the "neurocultural approach." Although these theories and understandings are just now materializing, there have long been five basic principles with implications not only for the learner but also for the content-area teacher who wants to plan instruction that helps students improve both their reading comprehension and their content learning.

Revisiting the Five Basic Premises of Teaching Reading

As columnist, author, and cultural observer David Brooks observes, we experienced a scientific revolution during the last 30 years that revealed more about the human brain than had had been discovered in the previous 3,000 years. He asserts, "Brain research rarely creates new philosophies, but it does validate some old ones" (2011, p. xiii), and we agree. Using today's lens of brain-based research to look at the five premises that cognitive science previously identified as basic to teaching content-area reading skills, we find they still hold true.

Premise 1: The reader constructs the meaning of a text

A reader actively constructs meaning by making seemingly logical, sensible connections between new information and existing knowledge about a topic (Duke & Pearson, 2002). Researchers believe that what we know from prior knowledge and past experience is stored in knowledge "frameworks" called schemata. One way to think of schemata is to visualize mental maps that provide a structure or guide for understanding new material. Schemata are not distinct from one another; rather, they are highly interrelated and significantly impact comprehension. Learners draw on these schemata to make inferences and predictions, to organize and reflect on new information, and to elaborate on that content (Vacca & Vacca, 1993).

The brain is a dynamic organ, shaped to a great extent by our experiences. When learners are confronted with new information, they try to make sense of it by seeing how it fits with what they already know. For example, we use the schema of "driving a car" the first time we try to operate a boat, jet ski, or snowmobile. Alternatively, we might use the familiar schema of our local neighborhood's grid of streets to get our bearings in a new city. To further illustrate the power of these schemata, try reading the following passage:

> I cdnuolt blveiee that I cluod aulaclty uesdnatnrd what I was rdanieg. The phaonmneal pweor of the hmuan mnid, aoccdrnig to a rscheearch at Cmabrigde Uinervtisy, it dseno't mtaetr in what oerdr the ltteres in a word are, the olny iproamtnt tihng is that the frsit and last ltteer be in the rghit pclae.

How did you do? This simple exercise illustrates the fact that deriving meaning is not just a matter of reading words on a page. In order to comprehend, the reader selects a schema that seems appropriate and connects it with the new information, filling in gaps so the text makes sense. "Teachers have a critical role in assisting learners to engage their understanding, building on learners' understandings, correcting misconceptions, and observing and engaging with learners during the processes of learning" (Bransford, Brown, & Cocking, 2004).

An interesting display of this phenomenon is in the experiments of Dutch clinical psychologist Christof van Nimwegen. In 2003, while studying computer-aided learning, he found that participants using "helpful" software programs with features that provided lots of clues designed to more easily solve a puzzle did not do as well as participants who struggled to solve the puzzle with a "bare-bones" program. After eight months of repeated experiments, van Nimwegen concluded that participants who did not rely on their computers to handle cognitive tasks built knowledge structures, or schemata, in their brains to apply to new situations (van Nimwegen, 2008). In the long run, the home-grown schemata beat out the fancy manmade technology. There isn't always a "winner" in technology versus human brain competitions. In February 2011, IBM's supercomputer Watson handily beat two former *Jeopardy!* champions on the nightly quiz show, providing not only entertainment but also further encouragement to learn more about the brain's machinations.

Premise 2: Prior knowledge plays an important role in learning

Prior knowledge includes the content knowledge and personal experiences that readers bring to any learning task. According to Vacca and Vacca, "the single most important variable in learning with texts is a reader's prior knowledge" (1993, p.13). By activating prior knowledge and generating interest, a teacher creates a context for students to approach reading with purpose and anticipation (Vacca & Vacca, 2005). Strategies that help readers "take out and dust off" prior knowledge before reading enable them to make more connections and learn more while they read. Those readers whose prior knowledge is accessible and well developed remember more from their reading than do readers whose prior knowledge of the topic is limited. Research and common sense tell us that the more a reader brings to a text in terms of knowledge and skills, the more he or she will learn and remember from it (Anthony & Raphael, 1989; Dole, Valencia, Greer, & Wardrop, 1991).

Nevertheless, accessing prior knowledge is not always easy. If information in the text is unclear, disorganized, or does not make sense to students, they may struggle to call up relevant prior knowledge. In addition, their purpose for reading will influence how they use their prior knowledge to make connections to the new information; this, in turn, affects comprehension. In one study, students who were told to read a description of a house as if they were home buyers were able to recall its location and number of bathrooms, whereas students who were told to read the selection from the perspective of a burglar remembered information about security systems and the number and location of windows (Jones, Palincsar, Ogle, & Carr, 1987).

Students may also have difficulty activating prior knowledge if that knowledge is what some researchers refer to as "inert knowledge"—knowledge students have but can't access because they lack the appropriate strategies that help learners retrieve what they know (Bransford, Sherwood, Vye, & Rieser; 1986). As classrooms grow more diverse, it's important to remember that no two students bring the same backgrounds and experiences to class, and no two students will comprehend a text passage in the same way. The same classroom may include students whose families are highly educated and encourage reading of all kinds from an early age, students whose experience of the world is limited to what they see on television, and students for whom English is a second—or even a third—language. You can help all students prepare for reading by incorporating prereading strategies, such as brainstorming, providing analogies, or using advance organizers, all of which serve to activate and assess learners' prior knowledge. Eliciting this knowledge gives readers a structure on which to attach new knowledge. Building and activating prior knowledge, particularly in a content-area classroom, is a powerful predictor of comprehension.

Premise 3: Reader comprehension depends heavily on metacognition

Metacognition is the ability to think about and control the thinking process before, during, and after reading. Students who have learned metacognitive skills can plan and monitor their comprehension, adapting and modifying their reading accordingly. Depending on the type of written material, the delivery medium (electronic or print), and their reasons for reading, students will decide whether to skip, skim, and flip or to read carefully. Throughout this process, students monitor the meaning they are constructing, and when the text (e.g., an editorial in an online news magazine) does not meet their purposes—such as reading for evidence to support their own opinion or argument—they may switch to another text that fits their needs and allows them to complete their assignment.

Ineffective readers, on the other hand, often don't realize they should be doing something while reading except moving their eyes across the page. They are unaware of the complexities of reading and have never been taught to think about what they are reading, create mental pictures, or ask questions (e.g., *Do I understand this? What should I do if I don't understand? Do I get the author's point? How does it fit with what I already know? What do I think the author will discuss next?*).

A student who hasn't been taught how to think about what he or she is learning might say something such as, "No, I didn't finish reading the homework. It was way too hard. I mean, I have no clue about chromosomes, or whatever the chapter was about. How can you expect me to read the chapter if it doesn't make any sense?" Alternatively, you might hear something such as, "What did we read yesterday? Well . . . uh . . . I think it was something about . . . Bosnia, no, wait . . . um . . . maybe it was Botswana? I don't know . . . it was about some foreign country that started with a *B*." Of course, there is always this all-too-familiar comment: "But I *did* read the assignment. I just don't remember it. I never do. I can read something three times and still not remember what I read."

Students who struggle while reading often give up and lose confidence. To them, reading comprehension is something of a mystery. Unaware that they have an active role to play in their learning, these students think comprehension simply happens, and when they aren't successful at understanding what they read, they tend to blame the text or themselves. The key to helping students take control of their own processes while reading involves deliberate attention to text content. McKeown and Beck (2009) suggest that teachers deliberately ask questions, use prompts, and encourage students to elaborate on what they read. Low-achieving students, in particular, need to be taught appropriate methods to monitor their understanding and how to select and use appropriate "fix-up" strategies when needed (Caverly, Mandeville, & Nicholson, 1995; Pogrow, 1993). Fix-up strategies include the think aloud, wherein students practice verbalizing their thoughts, and text coding, whereby students use symbols to mark up materials while reading (see Strategy 35 in Part II). The former helps students recognize their reading and thought processes; the latter helps them track their thinking.

One of the most important things a teacher can do to increase student readiness to learn is plan prereading activities. A particularly apt term for this method of prereading instruction is *frontloading*. By practicing frontloading techniques (e.g., building background knowledge of the topic, preteaching critical vocabulary concepts, setting a purpose for reading, focusing students' attention on the topic, cueing students about relevant reading strategies), we not only help increase readiness to learn but also foster strategic reading behavior.

Premise 4: Reading and writing are integrally related

Despite a decades-long debate about the specific connections between reading and writing processes, researchers agree they are inherently connected. Laflamme (1997) describes the reading and writing processes as being analogous and complementary because each involves generating ideas, logically organizing them, revisiting them several times until they make sense, and then revising or rethinking them as needed. Given this connection, it's easier to understand why avid readers tend to be good writers, and vice versa.

Teachers should know about this connection because they will, without question, have students who don't like to do either one—read or write. This situation presents the perfect teachable moment. When students resist reading and writing, you have an opportunity to share your knowledge and show them how to think like readers. Demonstrate how effective readers use a repertoire of strategies, such as reading aloud, rereading, and asking questions, to clarify ideas and make sure they understand what they read.

Of course, writers also contribute to how well readers are able to read and understand a text. Describing the relationship between reading and writing, Harvey and Goudvis simply say, "The reader *is* part writer" (2000, p. 5). They therefore advise teachers to have students read with a pencil or pen in hand in order to take notes, create individualized symbols and codes, and write down questions that arise as part of the process. By interacting with a text in these ways, students begin to grasp that reading and writing are active processes that require them to be engaged with the text if they are to comprehend, remember, and apply their learning. Harvey and Goudvis (2007) also, somewhat radically, recommend that students throw out their highlighters, which can fool them into thinking they are reading actively when they, in fact, are not.

Several researchers have found that improving students' writing skills, in addition to their reading skills, improves their capacity to learn (e.g., Buerger, 1997; National Survey of Student Engagement, 2008; Report of the National Commission on Writing, 2006; Tierney & Shanahan, 1991; Tynjala, Mason, & Lonka, 2001). A writer's language choices and knowledge of the topic, as well as his or her skill in using written language for a particular purpose, influence the reader's ability to construct meaning.

> The degree to which readers and writers share the same understanding of the language and the topic of the text influences how well they communicate

with each other. . . . For example, through reading readers learn the power of a strong introduction and eventually use such knowledge as they write their own pieces. Conversely, writing develops awareness of the structures of language, the organization of text, and spelling patterns which in turn contributes to reading proficiency. (Commission on Reading of the National Council of Teachers of English, n.d., para. 6, 14)

Graham and Hebert call writing an "often-overlooked tool for improving students' reading, as well as their learning from text" (2010, p. 4). They recommend that students write about the texts they read, teachers teach the skills and processes that go into creating text, and schools increase the amount of time students write. The results of their studies suggest that writing has the potential to enhance reading in at least three ways:

1. As functional activities, when reading and writing are combined, they facilitate learning (e.g., writing about information in a science text requires a student to record, connect, analyze, personalize, and manipulate key ideas in the text).

2. They each draw upon common knowledge and cognitive processes; therefore, improving students' writing skills should lead to improved reading skills.

3. They both are communication activities and vehicles for better comprehension (i.e., writers gain insight about reading by creating their own texts, which leads to better comprehension of other texts).

Indeed, teachers who integrate reading and writing in content-area instruction often view it as a natural fit:

- They are reciprocal processes, where writers learn from reading, and vice versa.
- They are parallel processes—both are purposeful and dependent on background knowledge, and both focus on the construction of meaning.
- They naturally intersect in the process of learning.
- Both are social activities driven by a need for communication.

Further underscoring this connection is research that shows students who are taught how to write and edit different forms of expository text demonstrate improved comprehension of content-area textbooks (Pressley, Mohan, Raphael, & Fingeret, 2007; Raphael, Kirschner, & Englert, 1988). Research also has shown that when students have opportunities to write in conjunction with reading, such as when they write summaries of material they just read, they are better able to think critically about what they read (Marzano, 2010).

Similarly, many related writing skills, such as grammar and spelling, reinforce reading skills. However, research also indicates grammar instruction is not effective and may actually be harmful to writing development. Grammar, when taught in isolation, tends to stay in isolation; students fail to integrate the rules of grammar into their writing. When they view grammar as a tool for writing, however, they are more apt to find the rules useful and will more readily apply them to achieve their writing purpose. Alternatively, teaching students sentence structure, summarizing techniques, and writing strategies (e.g., brainstorming, outlining) significantly improves their writing (Kolln & Hancock, 2005). Many teachers have success teaching students the multistep learning process (i.e., discovering, drafting, revising, editing, proofreading), and Biancarosa and Snow (2006) concur that learning the writing process is helpful, as long as the practice writing tasks are similar to those students will encounter and be expected to perform in high school, college, and future careers.

Donna Alvermann (2002), an expert in adolescent literacy, urges all teachers, regardless of their content-area expertise, to encourage students to read and write in different ways. Doing so, she believes, challenges students to solve problems and think critically, thus raising the so-called cognitive bar. There are many creative ways teachers can connect reading, writing, and content. The best part, of course, is that you are limited only by your imagination. Here are a few examples of assignments that help students make reading-writing-content connections:

- Students read about, analyze, and write about one of their favorite athlete's abilities and achievements.

- Students read biographies of historians, scientists, and artists to understand the genre, and then each student interviews a family member and writes a biography about that person.

- Students read primary source documents about a specific historical event from the National Archives website, and then each student writes a story as if he or she were present at and part of that event.

- Students read the scientific explanation for how planets form, identify and read a myth (from any number of various cultures) that explains how Earth was formed, and then write their own myths about the birth of a planet.

- Students research and read about a famous painting, sculpture, or building and then write about the feelings it evokes in themselves and others.

Researchers agree that improving students' reading and writing skills improves their capacity to learn (National Institute for Literacy, 2007). Therefore, effective adolescent literacy programs must include an element that helps students improve their writing skills, but it is not enough simply to ask students to do more writing. Students must receive intensive writing instruction that has clear objectives and expectations and consistently challenges them, regardless of their ability, to engage with academic content at high levels of reasoning (Biancarosa & Snow, 2006). Harvey and Goudvis recommend that teachers should encourage students to jot down their thinking in logs or notebooks (or e-logs or e-notebooks) as they read. Their point is that "writing about reading should enhance engagement and understanding, not interrupt it and bring it to a halt" (2007, p. 59).

A final thought—and perhaps the most concisely stated one about the reading-writing-learning connection—comes from Vacca and Vacca (2005), who observe that when students write, they explore, clarify, and think deeply about the ideas they read. This, ultimately, is the essence of the reading–writing connection.

Premise 5: Learning increases when students collaborate

Students learn by interacting with others in the classroom, by generating and asking questions, and by discussing their ideas freely with the teacher or one another. Conversation not only sparks new ideas but also provides an opportunity for the speaker to deepen his or her understanding of an idea or topic. Well-known literacy expert Judith Langer (2000) notes that in schools where students outperform expectations, learning English (both content and skills) is a social activity with a depth and complexity of understanding that results from skillful conversations and interactions with others.

Class discussions—large group, small group, or online group—are chances for students to compare their thinking with others'. Teachers can provide support during group discussion by moving from group to group, modeling questions and comments that deepen the analysis, and encouraging the use of challenging questions that cause students to think deeply (Langer, 2000). As students begin to teach one another, they assume more responsibility for their own learning and for the learning of others in the class.

Over the years, specific structures and elements have been developed to foster the positive effects of social learning while avoiding the negative effects, such as uneven student participation. These structures are realized as cooperative learning, a subset of collaboration. A new research synthesis further supports the same positive effects found within many previous studies that looked at both academic and emotional outcomes of cooperative learning. Specifically, researchers who conducted a meta-analysis of 20 studies found the average effect size was 0.44 (Dean, Hubbell, Pitler, & Stone, 2012).

Of course, simply putting students into cooperative learning groups is not enough to improve learning. Understanding the following three implementation principles is key to making cooperative learning work:

1. **Teach group processing and interpersonal skills.** Skills that effective teachers model for students include making eye contact, asking probing or clarifying questions, using wait time effectively, and using summary statements as comprehension checks. How teachers and students respond to one another is also vitally important. Giving and receiving constructive criticism is a skill students can learn by focusing on the quality of the work, rather than on the individual, and by identifying in equal measure the strengths and weaknesses of another student's work.

2. **Establish cooperative goal structures within groups**. One way teachers can establish cooperative goal structures in their classrooms is by linking outcomes among group members. Grades should not be considered outcomes; instead, an outcome can be as simple as the successful completion of an experiment.

3. **Provide mechanisms for individual accountability.** There are several ways to establish individual accountability. One technique is to keep groups small (i.e., three to five students). Small groups often police themselves since loafing by any single member puts larger burdens on the others. Another technique is to have groups determine nonredundant roles and responsibilities upfront. Each group member might learn a particular aspect of the lesson and teach it to teammates, or each may take on a particular role within the group, such as materials manager or timekeeper.

Intriguingly, brain imaging studies have shown that the amygdala, a portion of the brain associated with memory and emotions, is active and engaged when we learn new material. For example, students who struggle to solve a problem or deduce an answer independently will experience heightened anxiety and a reduction in the flow of new information. When working with others, however, the anxiety level is much lower and allows for free flow of information (Willis, 2007).

Lessened anxiety is one of the reasons cooperative learning groups are beneficial for ELLs. In addition, such groups "allow for the repetition of key words and phrases; require functional, context-relevant speech; and are 'feedback-rich'" (Hill & Flynn, 2006, p. 56). Working in small groups not only provides ELLs with opportunities to speak but also requires them to adjust their meaning as they speak, so other members of the group comprehend what they are saying.

A Final Thought on the Knowledge Gear

Couple what we are now learning with what we have long known about reading, and the power of reading grows exponentially. Take, for instance, the results of a recent study in which researchers, who wanted to know what really happens inside people's brains when they read fiction, examined brain scans and discovered that as readers encountered new situations, their brains captured the text and integrated it with their personal knowledge and past experiences (Speer, Reynolds, Swallow, & Zacks, 2009). Furthermore, the activated regions of the brain mirrored those involved when people see, perform, or imagine real-world activities. Such findings confirm that reading is anything but a passive process. Indeed, writer Nicholas Carr seems to agree; he describes a particular point many people experience when they become fully immersed in the reading matter and "the reader becomes the book" (2010, p. 74). That idea, in itself, is fascinating.

02
The Strategies Gear

"However beautiful the strategy, you should occasionally look at the results."

—Winston Churchill

We think the National Reading Panel would agree with Churchill—they took quite a serious look at strategy instruction, and in their final report, they described it as being highly successful overall: "Readers acquire these strategies informally to some extent, but explicit or formal instruction in the application of comprehension strategies has been shown to be highly effective in enhancing understanding" (National Institute of Child Health and Human Development [NICHD], 2000, p. 14).

One of the seven questions guiding the research of the panel and its subgroups was *Does comprehension strategy instruction improve reading? If so, how is this instruction best provided?* To answer the second part of the question, panel members closely examined the findings of two major approaches: direct explanation (when a teacher explicitly explains the reasoning and mental processes behind a reading strategy) and transactional strategy instruction (when a teacher explicitly explains the thinking process and further emphasizes it by facilitating student discussions and collaboration). Among the panel's salient findings is the revelation that teachers can learn these methods, but they need extensive formal instruction in teaching reading comprehension, modeling thinking processes, encouraging student inquiry, and keeping students engaged.

The larger message here is that all teachers can learn these skills, and content-area teachers must consciously plan to teach reading. This book contains several strategies to help you do just that. Before introducing and using these strategies in the classroom, however, we suggest discussing the benefits of strategy use directly with your students.

We know students are more motivated to learn when they recognize personal value in the material or lesson. Consequently, it's helpful to explain that all students can benefit from using reading strategies, especially if they have had trouble with reading comprehension in the past (Barton, 1997). As for students like Brian, our non-reading valedictorian from the introduction of this book, it can be best to address the issue directly, asking a student his or her reasons for not reading. If, for instance, students tell you they begin reading but eventually "get bored" and set the reading assignment aside, you might probe a little further. Alternatively, you could ask them to journal about their reading experience and identify the point at which they get bored. Together, you can then brainstorm some ways to continue reading. Through journaling, students gain insight into their reading hurdles, and teachers gain insight into their students' needs, whether it's for structured reading assignments or the need for greater variety in reading materials.

Instructional Frameworks

Instructional frameworks are particularly helpful tools that provide structure to teaching and the learning environment (Richardson, Morgan, & Fleener, 2009). Over the years, several such frameworks, all of which share similar assumptions, have emerged. Richardson and Morgan (1994) developed a simple three-phase framework for content reading instruction known as PAR, which stands for

- **Preparation:** Before reading, teachers motivate students by arousing their curiosity and need to know. In this phase, teachers should anticipate text problems and consider students' background knowledge.

- **Assistance:** During reading, teachers help students make connections and monitor their understanding. In this phase, teachers should select strategies that will guide students as they read and maintain their motivation to read.

- **Reflection:** After reading, teachers encourage students to reflect on the key concepts and ideas they read about. In this phase, teachers should provide students with thinking, talking, and writing opportunities in order to fully understand the material they are learning.

The PAR approach suggests that teachers incorporate learning activities at each stage and explain to students why each activity is essential for reading comprehension. For example, during the first phase, you might use techniques to activate and assess prior knowledge and to build background. During the second phase, you would select and model reading comprehension strategies for students. In the third phase, you might ask students to use the Learning Log strategy to encourage reflection on what they have read and how well they have understood it (see Strategy 16 in Part II). Alternatively, you could have students talk in small groups about the reading passage and why they think the content is important to learn. Though all three PAR phases are important and should be completed, the second one—assistance—is the most critical in aiding student reading comprehension (Richardson et al., 2009).

Strategy instruction is particularly important for those students who are completely unprepared to read and understand printed text; invariably, there are always students who match this description. These students aren't likely to develop effective cognitive and metacognitive strategies on their own, so they need numerous opportunities to practice and apply the strategies you introduce. Of course, some students will already have and use some efficient strategies for learning a skill or given type of content. If students are confidently using strategies—but in ways that are different from how you might recommend—then allow them to continue using their methods. There is no reason to inhibit students' success if they have identified an approach that is comfortable and works for them.

After all, the ultimate goal of strategy instruction is independence. We want students to recognize which strategies work best for them in the different content areas, and we want them to practice those strategies until they can use them naturally while reading, much like this former Brockton High School graduate who is now in college: "You wouldn't think I'd still be using the literacy strategies I learned [at Brockton], but I am" (Murthy & Weber, 2011). Anything you do to foster this kind of independence will benefit your students.

In Part II of this book, we have categorized strategies according to when they are the most effective: before, during, or after reading. We've done this to reflect the underlying concept of PAR and other instructional frameworks that acknowledge learning occurs in phases. For example, one such framework refers to the three phases this way (Buehl, 1995; Costa & Garmston, 1994):

- Phase 1: Preactive thought, or preparing for learning
- Phase 2: Interactive thought, or processing that occurs during learning
- Phase 3: Reflective thought to integrate, extend, refine, and apply what has been learned

The preactive phase sets the stage for learning. During this phase, students prepare for learning by activating prior knowledge. They may preview a text to determine its organizational structure and identify which subject-specific reading skills might be needed; skim the text, prewrite about the topic, or mentally review what they already know; or identify a purpose for reading (e.g., to take away information or to imagine oneself as a character in an unfolding story) and approach the text with that purpose in mind. During this phase, students may also make predictions (see Strategy 20) and use anticipation guides (see Strategy 2).

During the interactive phase, learners are actively engaged in processing what they read. For example, while reading a social studies text, they select what they think is most important—the main causes of the Cold War—and undertake some method to organize this information, such as chronologically ordering major events that led up to the Cold War. They evaluate their earlier predictions in light of new information read, revising them as needed. What Jones and colleagues (1987) term the "start/pause" nature of the learning process is especially evident during this phase. That is, readers monitor their comprehension and adjust their progress, sometimes rereading and reviewing material for clarification or developing a mental summary of what was read and evaluating new information in light of prior knowledge. Just as you might rewind a television show or movie and then rewatch a scene to make sure you understood it before moving forward, readers literally pause to think of questions, look back for answers to those questions, and think ahead to possible upcoming topics. Thus, although learning occurs in phases, it is not a neatly linear process.

Rather than simply describe the reflective phase, we'd like for you to do some reflecting of your own. Because you are an experienced reader, the three phases are probably second nature to you, and you may not even be aware that you are strategically processing information before you read, as you read, and after you finish reading. Take a few minutes to look over and answer the following questions. You might gain new insights into your own reading practices.

Reflective Questions for Strategic Processing

Before you begin a reading assignment, what do you do to develop a plan of action? Do you

- Understand the purpose for reading the text selection?
- Ask yourself what you might already know about this topic?
- Preview the text by looking at headings, bold print, illustrations, graphics, and maps?
- Make any predictions about what this selection is about?
- Consider what skills you will need to read and comprehend the text?
- Think about how to eliminate any distractions that would impact your reading?

When you are reading, do you monitor your thinking by asking yourself the following questions?

- Does the information make sense to me?
- Am I revising my predictions as I read?
- Am I using a graphic organizer to take notes on important information as I read?

---

continued

- Am I asking questions or writing down questions to ask later?
- Am I looking for patterns in the text that will help me understand what I have read?
- Do I know what to do when I come to a word I do not understand?
- Do I stop and think about passages I have just finished?
- Do I think about my attitude and habits of mind as I am reading, and do I adjust them to successfully complete the work?

After you finish reading, do you

- Know if you learned what you were supposed to?
- Reread or review to seek clarity?

After you finish reading, are you able to

- Summarize the major ideas?
- Give your opinion of the selection?
- Discuss how the text supported your prior knowledge?
- Discuss how reading in this class is different from reading in other classes?
- Find more resources about this topic?

Source: From *Teaching Reading In Social Studies: A Supplement To Teaching Reading in the Content Areas Teacher's Manual* (2nd ed.) by J. K. Doty, G. N. Cameron, and M. L. Barton, 2003, p. 44. Aurora, CO: McREL. © 2003 McREL.

We encourage you to use these questions with your students and to lead a discussion about your own reading awareness, sharing what you've discovered about your reading behaviors. Because you will want students to use these questions while they read, this is a great opportunity to model how to use them. Using a think aloud, tell your students that you *always* preview the text and that you like to read acknowledgments and dedications when reading a book for pleasure because it helps you feel like you personally know the author, which heightens your interest. You might explain that you visit author websites and read online book reviews—all before you ever read a word in the book, which not only prepares you to read but also heightens your enjoyment once you begin reading and motivates you to continue reading. You might tell students that you read with a dictionary or computer nearby or that you use the dictionary feature on your e-book. You also might describe your frustration at not understanding a difficult passage and describe how rereading it helps you. Finally, you might explain that you'll read several books and articles on the same topic once you've gotten interested in it. Let's now take a closer look at the differences among the three phases or categories of strategies.

Prereading Strategies

Using prereading strategies in science, history, or mathematics classrooms can benefit all students—both those whose prior knowledge is well developed and those whose backgrounds are more limited. When students work together to apply prereading strategies, such as making predictions or creating concept maps, they learn from one another. For example, while using the PLAN strategy (see Strategy 19), students begin by creating a graphic organizer using titles and subtitles from a chapter. During the next step, they use check marks or other symbols to identify which concepts, names, and facts they already know something about. At this point, it becomes clear to students, whether they are working alone or in small groups, that their prior knowledge (as a group or on their own) is either strong or limited. By incorporating prereading strategies into your instruction, you not only help students access prior knowledge but also gain valuable information to use while planning further instruction.

When preparing your students to read, it's best to keep in mind that what seems straightforward to you may seem complex to them, especially if you have any students in your classroom with limited English skills. As students talk about what they already know, you should listen carefully to determine which students need a more thorough grounding in a specific topic before reading. In addition, prereading strategies can reveal whether the information students think they know is accurate. Studies show that readers who have misperceptions about a topic often do so because they have overlooked, misinterpreted, or didn't remember information that contradicted their preexisting—though incorrect—background information (Barton, 1997). Prereading strategies provide teachers with opportunities to correct misunderstandings before exposing students to new knowledge and ideas. For example, in the KNFS strategy (see Strategy 15), students first identify the facts they know from a mathematics problem they are trying to solve. Before moving on to the next three steps (identifying information that isn't relevant, asking what the problem wants them to find, and selecting a strategy to use to solve the problem), the math teacher can see whether students successfully identified information from the problem or if they transferred inaccurate information or faulty assumptions to the new problem.

When explaining to students the impact prior knowledge has on learning, you might also discuss how people's experiences shape perceptions and influence judgment. Literature, history, current events, and even television programs contain a wealth of illustrations—both comic and tragic—of how people's past experiences color the way they view the world. Students can reflect on times when their own background and experience caused them to misjudge another person, group, or situation. When students recognize that perceptions are not facts and that schema can be revised as they learn new information, they also recognize that they have the power to control what they think and learn.

Reader aids

Vision trumps all other senses. According to brain researcher John Medina (2008), when we receive information orally, we only remember about 10 percent of the content three days later. Pair that information with a picture, and we remember 65 percent of it. Thus, it is crucial that students inspect texts or reading selections before reading, looking for reader aids—pictorial, typographical, graphic, and structural elements that represent and reinforce content.

Reader aids aren't just limited to pictures and other graphics. They also include lists, maps, charts, sidebars (information that is adjacent to, but graphically separated from, the main content), and quotes. Previewing texts for reader aids reveals clues about important concepts and provides a mental framework for organizing ideas, which helps with retention and recall. For example, to prepare students for reading, you can ask them to locate and read sidebars that include author-provided questions or reading tips in the textbook. Frequently, such questions and tips appear as eye-catching, colorful graphics. Learning to pay special attention to bold print, heading size, italics, bulleted material, colored textboxes, and lists helps students become more effective readers (Ficca, 1997).

Science textbooks, in particular, can be problematic for students (Broughton & Sinatra, 2010). They commonly use lists to present related topics (e.g., plants, animals, cells) in a discrete manner. Although the topics are related, many textbooks fail to provide any supporting information to help learners connect them. A science text might provide a list and drawings of three types of protozoa, for example, but the language on the page may broadly describe microorganisms. If the relationship is not explicit in the discussion on the page, or if there is not a clear statement explaining that protozoa are single-celled organisms, students might not make the connection. For students who lack sufficient background knowledge, this approach practically guarantees they will not comprehend the main ideas of the text. However, if students outline a chapter using only the headings and subheadings or turn headings and subheadings into questions, then they are required to notice and work with text features before they begin reading. As they identify these types of reader aids, they recognize the simple concept that if a heading is bigger and more pronounced, it must be more important. Another conclusion they might reach is that lists appearing within the same section or chapter of a science text have something in common. This common feature can become a springboard for understanding new knowledge. A student might then ask whether the things discussed in that section or chapter are classified together, what type of classification system is used, and how that system can be applied to other material.

Regardless of what subject you teach—chemistry, business, history, or language arts—it is important to teach students not to skip over text features and reader aids. Emphasize the importance of this step by having students work together to paraphrase graphics from the textbook before they read the relevant section or chapter. Alternatively, as a way of broaching the topic of being a savvy reader, you might ask students to complete the Metacognitive Reading Awareness Inventory (see Appendix A). One way to think about this inventory is as an informal data collection tool or formative assessment. Once students answer the questions, they could work in pairs or small groups to analyze the results and then, as a whole group, create a chart that shows the most popular responses. Identify students' responses that are different than the suggested ones, then solicit and discuss possible reasons why they might be different. Students can then write a summary of the results along with their explanations, and the class could develop an action plan to address needed areas of improvement.

Vocabulary

Vocabulary is terminology the author uses to express ideas and concepts. Robert Marzano (2003) conducted a meta-analysis of influences affecting student achievement, and he noted that much of the variance was attributable to three broad factors: home environment, background knowledge, and student motivation. Vocabulary is a pivotal component of a student's background knowledge, and research indicates direct instruction in vocabulary can effectively increase background knowledge in the content areas (Dean et al., 2012; Stone & Urquhart, 2008). Moreover, vocabulary instruction has been shown to play a major role in improving comprehension (Laflamme, 1997). Even though each content area has its own unique vocabulary or lexicon, there are many all-purpose words used within and across disciplines. These include words for thinking (*hypothesize*, *evidence*, *criterion*), classifying (*vehicle*, *utensil*, *process*), communicating (*emphasize*, *affirm*, *negotiate*), and expressing relationships (*dominate*, *correspond*, *locate*). So-called Tier Two words, which are useful across content areas and in many learning situations, "are high-frequency words for mature language users—*coincidence*, *absurd*, *industrious*—and thus instruction in these words can add productively to an individual's language ability" (Beck, McKeown, & Kucan, 2002, p. 16). By contrast, Tier One includes basic words (e.g., *baby*, *clock*, *happy*), and Tier Three includes content-specific words (e.g., *peninsula*, *habitat*, *metamorphic*).

Beyond the all-purpose words, however, is terminology that distinguishes disciplines, particularly labels that identify important content-area concepts—the Tier Three words. Armbruster and Nagy (1992) identify three aspects of content-area vocabulary that differentiate it from vocabulary used in literature-based lessons. First, content-area vocabulary often consists of words for major concepts that undergird a lesson or unit; therefore, it is critical students have a clear understanding of what these concepts mean. A student who cannot explain the meaning of *perspective* after an art lesson on that drawing technique has failed to grasp an essential portion of the lesson. By contrast, if a student does not understand a word such as *desultory* in a short story, his or her understanding of the story might not be affected. Second, content-area vocabulary is rarely associated with concepts that students already know. For example, a student who encounters the word *photosynthesis* for the first time while reading a science text is confronting an entirely new concept. Without prior knowledge, the student has no context for understanding the word, and nothing in his or her experience can provide a synonym or related idea. Third, content-area terms are often semantically related. Students studying a unit on weather might encounter the words *cirrus*, *cumulus*, and *stratus*. How thoroughly a student understands the concept of cirrus clouds will affect what he or she understands cumulus clouds to be.

Students in the upper elementary grades and beyond encounter more than 10,000 new words, most of them multisyllabic, in content-area texts each year (Nagy, Berninger, & Abbott, 2006). Therefore, content-area teachers must incorporate systematic vocabulary instruction into their planning and instruction. Content-area vocabulary words often represent major concepts in a unit, so instruction needs to go beyond simple definitions. Many teachers would like to do more vocabulary instruction in their content-area classrooms but are unsure about how to tackle it. Prereading vocabulary strategies can help students learn the meaning of new concepts and recognize the connections between and among them. Rote memorization, on the other hand, will not provide students with any practical means of making logical connections.

Even though it is a common practice to preteach vocabulary at the beginning of a unit of study, researchers disagree about whether vocabulary terms should be taught prior to, during, or after students' exposure to text passages that contain them. Several studies have shown that intensive preteaching of vocabulary can improve comprehension (e.g., Blachowicz & Fisher, 2000; Harmon, Hedrick, & Wood, 2006; Laflamme, 1997; Merkley & Jeffries, 2000/2001). Others advocate teaching target vocabulary during or after reading: "An important goal of content area lessons is to help students learn how to learn from reading so that they can independently acquire information from text" (Armbruster & Nagy, 1992, p. 550). Both viewpoints have merit, and we suggest you experiment with each to find what works best for your students. One place for you to start is with the standards and benchmarks for your discipline, mining them for key terms that students must understand in order to grasp the content.

Students learn content-area vocabulary best through first-hand, purposeful interaction with the relevant concepts. Whenever possible, students should hear, read, and be exposed to the terms they are expected to learn and use. In addition, students should be exposed to new terms through contrived experiences such as demonstrations, field trips, and audiovisual examples. The most important thing a teacher can do is ensure direct instruction of academic terms and ample opportunities to use them. For students to gain a thorough understanding of technical concepts, teachers need to provide multiple opportunities for students to learn how the relevant vocabulary is conceptually related (Vacca & Vacca, 1993).

Marzano and Pickering propose the following six-step process for teaching content-specific vocabulary:

Step 1: Provide a description, explanation, or example of the new term.

Step 2: Ask students to restate the description, explanation, or example in their own terms.

Step 3: Ask students to construct a picture, symbol, or graphic representing the term.

Step 4: Engage students periodically in activities that help them add to their knowledge of the terms in their notebooks.

Step 5: Periodically ask students to discuss the terms with one another.

Step 6: Involve students periodically in games that allow them to play with terms. (2005, pp. 14–15)

Of course, you will not be able to teach every unfamiliar word students might encounter in their texts, so when you develop a unit and identify concepts on which you will focus, consider using an activity, such as the one that follows, that requires students to preview text and select their own words. Working in teams, students develop a list of unfamiliar terms they predict will be crucial for understanding the focus of the upcoming unit. They should be able to defend their lists and explain why they chose each term. The teacher then modifies the list by deleting terms deemed less important and adding terms students overlooked, clearly explaining his or her reasons for making these changes so students understand how to identify the most important terms. After vocabulary terms are agreed upon, content-area teachers need to determine which strategies will offer their students the best insights into concept meanings and the relationships among concepts.

During-Reading Strategies

To illustrate the benefits of teaching students to strategically tackle their texts, you might ask them to draw comparisons between textbook features and facial features. Just as a nose, eyes, or lips can distinguish one person from another, certain aspects of a page of text can differentiate it from others. Text features, literary devices, and word choice not only make printed pages unique but also significantly affect comprehension:

- Printed instructions for the assembly of a child's bicycle are much easier to comprehend if they are accompanied by detailed diagrams.

- Research articles in scientific and medical journals can be confusing to the average person because they contain specialized, technical terminology.

- A novel that jumps among settings and timeframes is harder to follow than one written chronologically.

Students need to recognize such features in their textbooks and understand that they vary from one content area to another. For example, mathematics textbooks require students to use math-specific reading skills, such as decoding symbols in an algebraic equation. The Common Core State Standards for Mathematics gives equal weight to the content standards—which include such concepts as number and quantity, algebra, and geometry—and the eight standards for mathematical practice, which describe what students must learn to do and whose aim it is to deepen students' understanding:

1. Make sense of problems and persevere in solving them.
2. Reason abstractly and quantitatively.
3. Construct viable arguments and critique the reasoning of others.
4. Model with mathematics.
5. Use appropriate tools strategically.
6. Attend to precision.
7. Look for and make use of structure.
8. Look for and express regularity in repeated reasoning. (Kendall, 2011, p. 24)

For students to learn mathematics and be able to express their understanding of mathematical concepts, they must know how to use the various reader aids throughout their textbooks—diagrams, examples, and sidebars—as tools for learning. To anticipate and be prepared to assist students with any problems they may have with these unique features of their textbooks, take a step back from your area of expertise and imagine you are a student with relatively limited knowledge of the material. By "thinking like a student," you might see various terms in chapter and section headings and realize that your students will need direct vocabulary instruction on these key words before reading. You might then select a categorization strategy such as Concept Circles (see Strategy 7) to help them make connections among the terms they will be learning. By looking at the mathematics textbook (which you probably know inside and out) with fresh eyes, you can better determine how to help students learn the reading skills they need to comprehend their assignments. You might even return to the Reflective Questions for Strategic Processing on pages 13–14 and try to answer those questions as your students might.

Figure 2.1 presents an example of a lesson that prepares students to better understand the features of a mathematics textbook, along with a sample list that students might create to post as a classroom reference.

Educators generally agree that once a student leaves high school, most of his or her reading will be informational reading, and much of it will be on complex or specialized topics. "Entry-level jobs today often have higher reading requirements than many of the more advanced positions in the same field" (Daggett, 2003, p.4). Work-related reading materials are diverse and include manuals, books, newspapers, journal articles, instructions and directions, and white papers, all of which are classified as expository (or informational) text. Preparing students to read and understand expository text seems like a reasonable expectation of our educational system. Nevertheless, the Carnegie Corporation points out that there still exist some very real reading challenges for middle and high school students, as seen in Figure 2.2 (Lee & Spratley, 2010).

FIGURE 2.1 ⇢   Sample Lesson for Understanding Reader Aids in
Mathematics Textbooks

Getting Ready to Read
Analyzing the Features of a Mathematics Textbook

A well-designed textbook has a variety of features, or reader aids, that help organize main ideas, illustrate
key concepts, highlight important details, and point to supporting information. Readers who understand how
to identify and use these tools spend less time trying to unlock the text and more time concentrating on the
content.

In this strategy, students go beyond previewing a textbook to analyzing and determining how its features
help them find and use information for learning. They can use the same strategy with magazines, e-zines,
newspapers, e-learning modules, and other reading materials.

Purpose(s)

- Familiarize students with the main features of their textbook so they can find and use information more
  efficiently.

- Identify patterns in longer texts.

- Create a sample template of reader aids to post in the classroom for reference.

Tips

- Text features (i.e., reader aids) may include headings, subheadings, table of contents, index, glossary,
  preface, paragraphs separated by spacing, bulleted lists, sidebars, footnotes, illustrations, pictures,
  diagrams, charts, graphs, captions, italicized or bolded words or passages, color, and symbols.

- Provide students with an advance organizer to guide them as they read (e.g., a series of prompts that ask
  students to preview particular features and note how they are related to the main body of the text).

- Teach students the SQ3R strategy (see Strategy 29).

- Model how students can use the features of computer software and Internet websites to help them
  navigate and read the program or site (e.g., URLs, pop-up menus, text boxes, buttons, symbols, arrows,
  links, color, navigation bar, home page, bookmarks, graphics, abbreviations, logos).

What Teachers Do	What Students Do
Introduce the activity:	
- Ask students to recall a magazine or informational book they recently read, or a website they recently viewed. Ask them to describe how the text looked and how they found information. Ask them what they remember about the content, and why they think they could locate and/or remember the information.	- Recall something recently read or viewed and identify features of that particular selection, making connections between what they remember and the features.

continued

What Teachers Do	What Students Do
Introduce the activity: • Provide copies of a text to every student. • Organize students into groups of 3 to 5, assign two different sequential chapters to each group, and ask students to scan the chapters, noting both similar and different features. • Groups record their findings on chart paper (e.g., point-form notes, Venn diagram, compare/contrast chart). • Ask each group to send an "ambassador" to the other groups to share one thing they discovered, trading it for one thing the other group discovered before returning to their original group.	• Quickly scan two chapters, and note similarities and differences of their text features. • Contribute to the group discussion and chart-paper note taking. • Share findings with other groups and their base groups.
During the activity: • Remind students that textbooks have many different elements or features to help them learn the material, and ask each group to report about the features of their text. • Create a textbook or chapter template on chart paper, indicating the common features and noting any unique features (see *Features of a Mathematics Textbook–Sample Class Template*).	• Share the group's findings. • Contribute to the class template.
Following the activity: • Assign a relevant reading task to small groups of students for practice using reader aids to locate information and help them understand and remember what they read. • Encourage students to use the template to make predictions about where they might find information. • Discuss how this strategy also helps navigate websites, e-zines, and online media.	• Use reader aids to complete the assigned reading task, noting those that help them locate, read, understand, and remember information. • Refer to the template for future reading tasks. • Recall how they have used features of electronic texts to find, read, and help understand information.

Features of a Mathematics Textbook
Sample Class Template

Textbook Title: *Doing Mathematics*

Table of Contents: A list of the topics and subtopics in each chapter.

Chapters: These group big, important mathematical ideas.

Chapter Introduction: A brief overview of the important mathematics in the chapter and the curriculum expectations. The Chapter Introduction also poses a problem that can be solved by applying the mathematical concepts in the chapter.

Skill Review: Provides review material for mathematical skills learned in earlier grades. Proficiency with these skills is an aid to doing the mathematics in this chapter.

Chapter Sections: Focus on a smaller part of the important mathematics in the chapter. They usually include a "Minds On" activity, information and examples about the key mathematics in the section, and a brief summary of the key ideas and practices questions. There are 3–15 sections in each chapter.

Chapter Review: A summary of the mathematics in the chapter, additional examples, and extra practice questions that connect the mathematics in each section of the chapter.

Chapter Review Test: A sample test that you can use to self-assess your understanding of the mathematics in the chapter.

Cumulative Review Test: A sample test that you can use to self-assess your understanding of the mathematics in several consecutive chapters.

Technology Appendix: This section has specific instructions for graphing calculators, CBRs, spreadsheets, Fathom, and The Geometer's Sketchpad. Technology icons throughout the chapter indicate this appendix contains more detailed instructions.

Icons: Technology, career, and math history icons that help quickly locate related text.

Answers: Answers to most practice questions, review, and review tests appear in the back of the textbook.

Glossary: An alphabetical listing of the new terms introduced throughout the textbook; italicized words in the text also appear in the glossary.

Index: A quick way to look up specific information or concepts using page references.

Source: From *Think Literacy: Cross Curricular Approaches, Grades 7–12.* Government of Ontario: Queen's Printer for Ontario. Copyright 2005 by Queen's Printer for Ontario. Adapted with permission.

Looking over the third column (Challenges to Comprehension), you may have been struck by how demanding reading really is for students, and for those students who are struggling, it can be daunting. The unspoken assumption among educators is that most students are proficient readers once they enter middle school, but it is evident that this is not the case (SEDL, n.d.; Shanahan & Shanahan, 2008). Unfortunately, few middle or high school students have the opportunity to sign up for a reading course. Miller (1997) notes that the science and social studies textbooks selected for a grade level are often above the reading level of many students in that grade. Similarly, an examination of mathematics textbooks reveals that even though the mathematical concepts may be grade-level appropriate, the reading level can be one, two, or even three years above grade level (Braselton & Decker, 1994; Lamb, 2010).

Who, then, could argue that teaching reading is solely the purview of English teachers? That belief has not served students well in the past, and it certainly won't serve them well in the future. Cross-curricular approaches to literacy, however, will.

Before asking your students to use any of the During-Reading strategies provided in Part II, you may want to intentionally introduce them to the concept of text structures—organizational patterns authors employ to express ideas.

In any discipline, a key concept for students to know and understand is that authors use expository text to organize information in several ways. One way effective readers construct meaning from a text is by identifying the most important information and organizing all of the ideas into a mental pattern or sequence that makes sense. Just as authors intentionally select a particular organizational pattern to best convey their ideas, readers can learn to look for one of these common organizational patterns: sequence, comparison/contrast, concept/definition, description, episode, generalization/principle, process/cause–effect (Marzano et al., 1997). Students who are familiar with these patterns are more likely to comprehend what they read because they use their knowledge of text structures to

- Locate information in the text.
- Differentiate between what is important and what is unimportant.
- Mentally sequence information in a logical order.
- Synthesize ideas that appear in different locations in the text or from a number of texts.
- Link new information to what is already known.
- Restructure and revise prior knowledge to account for new information.

The successful reader is familiar with different ways to organize information, able to recognize different organizational patterns, and able to impose patterns while reading. This is true of both informational and narrative text. A knowledge of organizational

FIGURE 2.2 →   Characteristics and Challenges of Content-Area Texts

Content Area	Text Types and Characteristics	Challenges to Comprehension
Science	abstracts, section headings, figures, tables, diagrams, maps, drawings, photographs, reference lists, endnotes, complex technical terms	Requires • visual literacy, mathematical literacy, or an ability to understand mathematical tables and figures • extensive knowledge of meanings of technical terms
History	political and legal documents, newspaper articles, letters, diaries, primary and secondary sources, published proceedings, cartoons, photographs, density of ideas, ambiguous references	Requires • the ability to logically connect ideas and infer relationships • the ability to understand motivations for actions and reactions • the ability to connect causes, events, and consequences
Literature	fiction, science fiction, biography, autobiography, short story, novel, poetry, drama, allegory, fable, myth, mystery	Requires • knowledge of rhetorical tools (e.g., symbolism, irony, satire, point of view) and genres • the ability to compare and contrast among texts and understand character types
Mathematics	mathematical notation, stipulated definitions, examples of theorems and proofs, technical language, syntax, logic	Requires • mathematical modeling, repeated practice, and real-world examples

patterns can exist both "inside the head" as a conceptual framework and "outside the head" in printed text. Text type and purpose often determine organizational structure. Content-area teachers can help students improve their reading comprehension by teaching the organizational patterns typically used in each, how to recognize those patterns, and the kinds of questions each pattern is intended to help answer.

The early work of Anderson and Armbruster (1984) suggests that textbook organization is either considerate or inconsiderate, and a more recent look at this idea also emphasizes the need for coherent text structures in classroom texts (Richardson, Morgan, & Fleener, 2009). Considerate text is easier to read because it is well organized and clearly written. Signal words cue readers to the author's organizational plan, and ideas appear in a logical sequence. By contrast, inconsiderate text is difficult to read because it is poorly organized and poorly written. The organization of ideas does not match the author's purpose, the sentence structure is complicated, and the vocabulary often is too difficult for the intended audience. When text is inconsiderate, students can rely on their knowledge of organizational structures to help them grasp the content.

Students benefit from being able to recognize a text's organizational pattern because they are able to read the information with specific questions in mind. That is, each organizational pattern suggests a series of questions that are answered within the text. Answering these questions helps students comprehend the intended message. Skilled authors incorporate certain signal words, linking expressions, or transitions that connect ideas. In order to identify different text patterns, students need to be able to recognize these signal words and transitions as clues.

Typically, expository text is written to inform or persuade, and the ideas expressed are usually organized in one of the following seven organizational patterns (see also Strategy 12) (Marzano et al., 1997).

1. **Sequence:** Organizes events in a logical sequence, usually chronological. **Signal words:** *after, afterward, as soon as, before, during, finally, first, following, immediately, initially, later, meanwhile, next, not long after, now, on (date), preceding, second, soon, then, third, today, until, when*

2. **Comparison/contrast:** Organizes information about two or more topics according to their similarities and differences. **Signal words:** *although, as well as, as opposed to, both, but, compared with, different from, either, even though, however, instead of, in common, on the other hand, otherwise, similarly, still, yet*

3. **Concept/definition:** Organizes information about a word or phrase that represents a generalized idea of a class of people, places, things, or events (e.g., dictatorship, economics, culture, mass production). Concept/definition text defines a concept by presenting its characteristics or attributes. **Signal words:** *for instance, in other words, is characterized by, put another way, refers to, that is, thus, usually*

4. **Description:** Organizes facts that describe the characteristics of specific people, places, things, or events. These characteristics can appear in any order. **Signal words:** *above, across, along, appears to be, as in, behind, below, beside, between, down, in back of, in front of, looks like, near, on top of, onto, outside, over, such as, to the right/ left, under*

5. **Episode:** Organizes a large body of information about specific events, including time and place, people, duration, sequence, and causes and effects of particular

events. **Signal words:** *a few days/months later, around this time, as it is often called, as a result of, because of, began, when, consequently, first, for this reason, lasted for, led to, shortly thereafter, since, then, subsequently, this led to, when*

6. **Generalization/principle:** Organizes information into general statements with supporting examples. **Signal words:** *additionally, always, because of, clearly, conclusively, first, for instance, for example, furthermore, generally, however, if . . . then, in fact, it could be argued, that, moreover, most convincing, never, not only . . . but also, often, second, therefore, third, truly, typically*

7. **Process/cause–effect:** Organizes information into a series of steps leading to a specific product. Organizes information in a causal sequence that leads to a specific outcome. **Signal words:** *accordingly, as a result of, because, begins with, consequently, effects of, finally, first, for this reason, how to, how if . . . then, in order to, is caused by, leads/led to, may be due to, next, so that, steps involved, therefore, thus, when . . . then*

Expert readers not only recognize these patterns but also use them to impose meaning on text. For example, a reader might recognize text written in a descriptive pattern yet select a comparison/contrast pattern to frame the selection, thereby "making meaning" by connecting the new information to something familiar. Another advantage of text structure knowledge is that when textbooks are not well organized (and some of them are not), skilled readers are able to impose a structure of their own to organize the information into something that makes sense to them. Thus, organizational patterns can exist both on paper and in the mind of the reader (Jones et al., 1987).

One way to teach students about organizational patterns is to tackle them one at a time, through a series of minilessons. Here are some possibilities:

- Activate students' prior knowledge of text structure and organization by posing a problem for them to solve. Examples include: How would you explain to your grandparent how to set the alarm on his or her cell phone? How would you teach your little brother or sister to dribble a basketball? How would you convince your parents to give you a credit card? After they share their responses, students should be able to explain how they organized their ideas and why they chose that particular approach.

- Introduce one of the organizational patterns used in expository text; explain its characteristics; and identify when and why writers use that pattern, related signal words, and any questions the pattern typically answers. Provide an example of the pattern in the textbook or another familiar book. Trade books offer in-depth information on a variety of content-area topics and often organize information more logically and coherently than content-area textbooks (Moss, 1991, 2004).

Model how to tell whether the example meets the criteria for the identified organizational pattern.

- Provide a graphic organizer for mapping out the information in the organizational pattern and demonstrate how to fill it in. Explain that a visual representation of a text's organizational pattern often aids comprehension and retention. Ask students to locate another example of this pattern in the textbook, a newspaper, a magazine, an online article, or a trade book. Students can then use a graphic organizer to organize the information in their selected example.

- To reinforce understanding, have students write paragraphs using the appropriate pattern. When readers write and edit different types of expository text, they improve their reading comprehension of content-area textbooks (Denti & Guerin, 2008; Raphael et al., 1988). Using a graphic organizer as a visual map, students can write rough drafts and add signal words where appropriate. Students can then edit one another's paragraphs, revise their drafts, and write a final copy.

After-Reading Strategies

Have you ever been asked to speak on a topic that you sort of—but don't really—know much about? Like most of us, you probably know a great many things (facts, anecdotes) on a superficial level, which is certainly adequate for friendly conversation, but not at an in-depth level where you could easily teach it to others and anticipate listener's questions. If you haven't said "I don't really know something until I teach it" at least once in your teaching career, we bet you know someone who has. The idea, of course, is that to thoroughly understand something, you have to use what you have learned about it, and to use it, you have to process that knowledge at deep levels. In turn, you must give yourself time to reflect on it, perhaps write about it, and try to apply it to various new situations. When you think of the role of reflection this way, it's easy to see why it is important for students to reflect on their reading.

Effective readers are rarely finished reading once they've closed their textbooks. They reflect on what they've read, and they

- Analyze how the material aligns with their prior knowledge and experience, measuring it against what they believe, what they know, and what they have experienced.

- Make inferences and draw conclusions about what they read.

- Revise their schema as needed, incorporating new learning into their knowledge base.

- Extend and refine what they have learned, deepening their understanding of the material.

Reflection activities you might ask students to do, such as writing in a journal or in response to a question you wrote on the board prior to reading, are ways for students to process what they've read. Although you may only invest a few minutes of class time on reflection activities, the reward—that students become aware of their new learning—is worth it. Reflection doesn't always have to be shared, though it can be affirming for students to discover that they are not alone in their perceptions or that classmates find merit in their thinking, but it should have a future outlet, perhaps in a later discussion when you call on students to think back to the assignment and recall their reflections. We suggest that you plan to include reflection activities in the majority of your lesson plans. For students to effectively use strategies, you must provide opportunities for them to exercise choice, execute deliberately, and reflect on their learning (Alexander, Graham, & Harris, 1998).

Reflective conversation

At one point or another, we've all found ourselves a bit embarrassed when someone has caught us talking to ourselves while thinking through a problem or issue. Reflective thought is not unlike having a conversation with oneself; it is an integral part of all learning. Successful readers reflect on what they read, which helps deepen their understanding of the text as a whole. Reflection also helps readers synthesize what they have read and integrate new learning into their existing schema. The intent of reflective conversation is to help students become ideal readers, but having reflective conversations in classrooms is less common than you might think. Similar to metacognition and metacomprehension, a reflective conversation can occur anytime during the reading process—before, during, or after.

When you first pick up a nonfiction book, all the information you really have is a title and an author's name, yet that often is enough to prompt reflection. Have you read this author before? If so, how do you feel about reading something else he or she has written? Are you dreading the task because the language is so dry, the vocabulary so academic, and the organization so confusing, or are you anticipating reading a fast-paced, fact-based story that reads like a novel because the author so skillfully reconstructs historical events and logically ties them all together? By reflecting on your own experiences, you can understand how students feel when assigned a mathematics or science text to read. Some of them might dread the idea of reading it because of their previous experiences with content-area reading, whereas others might have had positive experiences in the past and enjoy reading at many levels. Of course, most students will be somewhere between those two extremes.

We suggest allowing students to share their previous reading experiences with one another in small groups and in whole-group settings. Early in the year, for example, you might create a reading habits survey, asking questions about past experiences. Where do they like to read? What was the last book they read? What reading materials do they keep around? Alternatively, you might simply ask students to rate themselves as readers on a scale of 1–5 (with 5 being a diehard reader!) and then share the results with the entire class.

While reading, students stop to reflect on their progress, thought processes, and perceptions of their own behavior (e.g., what they had to reread, what they skimmed). They also might indicate where they are in their reading and set goals for pages read by a designated day, describe their thinking up to that point and reflect on whether it is changing, and define alternative reading strategies they intend to pursue to complete an assignment while fully understanding the material. These practices increase students' awareness of their behavior and allow them to adjust accordingly. After reading, students can evaluate how well they read and understood the selection, how productive the strategies were, and whether alternative strategies would be more helpful in the future.

Of course, learning—for both student and teacher— is the overall goal of a reflective conversation. Reflective conversation requires teachers to use nonjudgmental verbal behaviors such as silence, acceptance, and clarification. When you take on the role of a reflective coach, you should wait silently after asking a question, providing students with ample wait time to respond. Teachers often wait only one or two seconds after asking a question before asking another one or giving the answer. By waiting, you communicate respect for the student's reflection and processing time.

Science teachers Jennifer Smith and Cynthia Martin emphasize the importance of a teacher's use of wait time for questioning to be effective: "Wait time 1 (a 3+ second pause provided after a question is asked) provides students time to contemplate the question and develop an answer. Wait time 2 (an additional pause provided following a student response) encourages more student responses and elaboration of previously offered ideas. The initial discomfort felt by students and teachers during wait time is often necessary to draw out student responses and ideas, and is essential to the discussion process" (2007, p. 18).

When you do respond to students, it should be in the form of a nonjudgmental acceptance. You might paraphrase by repeating, rephrasing, translating, or summarizing what students say. For example, "You're saying the selection is about. . ." Maintaining the intent and accurate meaning of what students say is important. The paraphrase is possibly the most powerful of all nonjudgmental verbal behaviors because it communicates the idea that "I'm attempting to understand you," which, in turn, says "I value you" (Costa & Garmston, 1994). Willingly listening until a student has finished speaking and using open-ended questions communicate that you are a sensitive and attentive listener.

Another option is to clarify a student's response. Clarifying indicates that you do not understand what the student is saying and you need more information. For example, "Please expand on what you mean by 'gas-permeable.' I'm not sure I understand." The intent of asking clarifying questions is to better understand the student's ideas, feelings, and thought processes. Clarifying contributes to trust because it sends the message that students' ideas are worthy of exploration and consideration (Costa & Garmston, 1994).

Once students learn about and practice how to "listen to hear," to paraphrase what's been said, and to ask nonjudgmental questions, they can effectively combine these strategies and conduct a reflective conversation. It is then that they will have learned how to learn.

A Final Thought on the Strategies Gear

Effective readers are amazing strategists. They attack the material by consciously making a plan before they begin, they monitor what they read during the process, and they evaluate how well they understood the selection once they finish. On one level, they are actively engaged with the content, making mental notes about important concepts, revising predictions, answering questions, and noting main and subordinate ideas. On another level, they are observing and assessing their attitude toward the task and their reading style and whether each is helping accomplish the purpose. They adjust their attitude and style as needed to improve comprehension—perhaps slowing their pace, restraining any impulsive desire to stop reading, redirecting their focus, or selecting fix-up strategies (e.g., rereading confusing selections and examining the context of unfamiliar words to ascertain meaning). They summarize the text's main ideas, and if needed, they reread or review certain selections. They appraise their learning in terms of their original purpose, and they strategize how they might demonstrate their understanding if asked to do so. We think that's pretty awesome!

Just as awesome is a teacher who is purposeful and thoughtful about planning instruction. Unfortunately, studies reveal that teachers devote most of their time to presenting new content, which does little to prepare students to read text assignments or internalize what they read (Meltzer, 2001; Wood & Muth, 1991). Instead, teachers should teach students how to prepare for learning through prereading activities, ensure comprehension through the use of metacognitive strategies during reading, and extend and refine the new knowledge they acquire.

Teaching strategically means analyzing how every aspect of a lesson contributes to the instructional goal or objective. It means selecting teaching and learning strategies that enhance student learning, and it means helping students acquire the skills they need in order to be self-directed, independent learners. Content-area teachers can accomplish this by sharing a variety of strategies with students, by explaining their value, and by repeatedly modeling and having students practice these behaviors. In this way, students learn the content they need to master and how to read effectively. Ultimately, though, they come to value reading. (With this in mind, Appendix B presents a 10-point checklist to assist in your strategic planning.)

03

The Goals & Dispositions Gear

"The secret to high performance isn't rewards and punishments, but that unseen intrinsic drive. The drive to do things for their own sake. The drive to do things 'cause they matter."

—Daniel Pink, *Drive: The Surprising Truth about What Motivates Us*

Daniel Pink, a career analyst, studied the science of human motivation before writing and speaking about the gulf that exists between "what science knows" and "what business does" about motivating workers. Specifically, he credits social science with revealing the truth about using contingent motivators (i.e., telling someone "if you do this, then you will get that") for 21st century tasks: not only do they not work, they often cause harm (Pink, 2009a). Pink argues that the best approach revolves around three elements: autonomy, or the urge to direct our lives; mastery, or the desire to get better and better at something; and purpose, or the longing to do something that relates to a greater purpose. He proposes these as the building blocks of 21st century business. It then follows that they should also be the building blocks for 21st century education.

To understand what is unique about 21st century education, we should begin with a look at the "then" and "now" of educators' views on reading and learning. Figure 3.1 provides a convenient look at just a few of the ways that education has changed.

Developing Goal-Directed, Motivated Learners

Throughout the past couple of decades, as offices transformed into cubicles and conference rooms became collaboration rooms, schools began to reflect the larger cultural influences

FIGURE 3.1 ⟶   Our Changing Views of Reading

Reading is . . .	A Fixed Ability (traditional view)	A Dynamic Relationship (new definition)
Research base:	• Behaviorism	• Cognitive science
Goals:	• Focus on mastery of isolated facts and discrete skills. • Meet stated achievement goals. • Study and learn information.	• Focus on self-awareness and regulation. • Move toward deeper understandings. • Make meaning within a discipline.
Classroom expectations:	• Rote memorization. • A single instructional approach. • Teachers ask questions with predetermined answers. • Broad content coverage.	• Reading as an interaction among the reader, text, and context. • Students experiment with multiple problem-solving approaches. • Students grapple together with ideas. • Students use reading and writing to access complex disciplinary content.
Learner experience:	• Passive process. • Knowledge relies on external sources. • Students work alone answering superficial questions. • Discussion is based on teacher prompts. • Students drill on subskills of reading.	• Active and social process. • Students know and use strategies; make connections across lessons, classes, and grades; and apply vocabulary, comprehension, and study skills. • Students regularly engage in discussion and conversations. • Discussion is a learning tool for stimulating thinking and helping students extend and refine their understanding of the content. • Support is differentiated to meet individual student needs.

continued

FIGURE 3.1 ⇢   Our Changing Views of Reading (*continued*)

Reading is . . .	A Fixed Ability (traditional view)	A Dynamic Relationship (new definition)
Assessment:	• Test preparation is set apart from regular class time. • Students regurgitate facts from text. • Teachers check to see if students have learned what they "should have" learned.	• Test preparation is integrated into class time as part of ongoing learning goals. • Activities clarify, reinforce, and extend knowledge.

and changes in the workplace. Once a passive and solitary experience for students, learning has become social, collaborative, and, at times, customized to reflect societal changes and what cognitive science has revealed about how we learn.

Today's business environment isn't a place for graduates who are good at only one thing. Of course we want students to be good mathematicians, scientists, linguists, and historians. Nevertheless, they also need to be strong communicators who can think critically about problems and issues, express ideas fluently in writing and speech, and adapt to a variety of work environments. "In today's knowledge-based society, our students need to be expert readers, writers, and thinkers to compete and succeed in the global economy" (Kamil, 2003, p. 30).

As we've discussed, readers read for different purposes—sometimes for pleasure and sometimes for information. Wherever students find information—be it online or in a textbook—their goal remains constant: *learning*. Teaching reading in the content areas means more than learning the content relevant to each discipline; it also means helping students think as if they were members of the discipline's community of experts and learners. This is one reason why it is so important to communicate explicitly what students should learn by verbally stating learning objectives, displaying them in writing, and calling attention to them throughout a unit or lesson. In 2010, McREL completed a study that demonstrated the positive impacts that setting objectives and providing feedback can have on student achievement (Dean et al., 2012).

Two sets of goals are better than one

Fundamental to goal setting is the process of establishing direction and purpose. Research on cognition (the mental process of acquiring knowledge) and on metacognition (the act of thinking about and controlling one's thinking process) reveals that learners have two goals: to understand the meaning of learning tasks (often referred to as constructing meaning) and to regulate their own learning (Center for Development and Learning, 1997; Jones et al., 1987).

For students, goal setting is a way to focus on what's important to learn, and as we've mentioned before, taking charge of their learning is a new idea for many students. To increase their comfort level with this process, help students understand that you regularly set instructional goals while planning units of instruction by modeling your own process. Similarly, students will learn to write personal learning goals related to those instructional goals. Since instructional goals are relatively narrow, take care not to set goals that are too specific, otherwise students may ignore information that is not directly related to the goal and thereby limit their learning (Dean, Doty, & Quackenboss, 2005). When you develop instructional goals, keep in mind that you will be asking students to write their learning goals based on the instructional goals you identify. Therefore, you want your instructional goals to be specific enough to guide students yet still flexible enough for them to set their own learning objectives, as illustrated in Figure 3.2.

FIGURE 3.2 ⇢   Levels of Specificity in Learning Objectives

Too Broad	Too Specific	Appropriately Specific
Students will read about and understand the cultural contributions of various regions of the United States and how they help to form the national heritage.	After reading, students will be able to list three differences between games from the Colonial era and from today.	Students will read to learn the differences between games that children played during the Colonial era and games played today.
Students will read about and understand the concept of checks and balances.	After reading, students will be able to create a detailed comparison matrix of the tasks handled by each branch of the government.	Students will read to learn about the roles and responsibilities of the legislative and executive branches.
ELLs will learn vocabulary related to weather.	After five practice sessions, ELLs will be able to connect 10 pictures with the matching vocabulary terms with 80 percent accuracy.	ELLs will be able to predict meanings of weather-related vocabulary while reading and demonstrate their understanding by drawing a representative picture of each term.

In addition, it is good practice for teachers to form contracts with their students in order to develop appropriately specific learning objectives or goals (Dean et al., 2005). Opportunities to personalize teacher-created learning objectives can increase students' motivation to learn by giving them a greater sense of control over the process (Dean et al., 2012). To help students write personal learning goals that are attainable, provide sentence starters such as "I want to know. . ." or "I wonder. . .," which can help establish their individual interests related to the topic. When content is new and challenging, students can skim through the textbook chapter or preview other relevant resources before they write their goals. The act of previewing serves as an advance organizer—a well-known and widely used technique for organizing and interpreting new information that is especially effective when students have limited or no prior knowledge of the material (Mayer, 2003).

Encourage students to write concrete and measurable goals. For example, if a student writes "I want to be a good artist," then encourage revision to something along the lines of "I want to learn how to use perspective in my drawings." Likewise, "I want to learn what the chapter says about the causes of the Civil War" is a better goal than "I want to read the whole chapter in one sitting." When teachers set clear learning goals and students have opportunities to personalize them, students are more likely to be able to explain what they are learning and be more interested in learning in general (Dean et al., 2005).

Motivation makes a difference

We have established that reading comprehension improves when teachers foster the development of vocabulary, comprehension skills, and related writing activities, but what about motivation? Motivation alone does not help students acquire these abilities, but an unmotivated student isn't going to develop them at all. Many reading researchers have noted that student motivation is an important concept that continually surfaces in adolescent literacy, and some view it as one of the primary determiners of adolescent literacy (Collins, 1997; Kamil, 2003; Moore, Alvermann, & Hinchman, 2000; Schunk & Zimmerman, 1997). It thus appears that motivation is an essential aspect of reading comprehension—one that teachers must consider when planning for instruction.

Guthrie and Humenick (2004) examined a variety of frequently used classroom practices (e.g., reading aloud, posing questions, modeling curiosity) that are likely to foster student motivation for reading, and they identified experimental evidence to support the effectiveness of at least four strategies:

1. Using learning goals to guide and support reading instruction.
2. Providing a range of choices in reading activities.
3. Providing students with interesting texts for reading instruction.
4. Ensuring collaboration among students in the classroom.

Naturally, it is possible (and advisable) to combine or merge these strategies, such as offering choices among interesting texts. Guthrie and Humenick also found that when students set personalized learning goals, they are more intrinsically motivated. For example, when introducing a lesson on the ecology of wetlands, teachers might ask students to develop their own questions about the topic that are both personally interesting and related to something they are doing in class (e.g., an upcoming field trip or a book they are reading). Once students have written their questions, they can be posted on a class chart. Therefore, as individual questions are answered, all students learn.

The motivating power of choice

Another way to increase student motivation toward literacy is to provide a variety of reading material options and allow students to self-select the texts they read. Providing a range of reading choices is easy to do if you already incorporate independent reading time in your classroom or maintain a classroom library. Greenleaf and colleagues (2001) found that students were more motivated to read when they were allowed to choose among a variety of genres that offered multiple perspectives—particularly if those options included electronic and visual media.

Allowing for self-selection, whenever possible, provides opportunities for students to make valuable connections between texts and their daily lives. Therefore, it is important for students to be provided with research topics or writing assignments they find interesting and personally relevant. When teachers make an effort to learn about their students' interests and tailor assignments with those interests in mind, they are more likely to engage their students in reading about those topics, thereby motivating them to learn. "Self-regulation is only developed when students are given choices and the instructional support and aids needed to succeed at their chosen tasks" (Biancarosa & Snow, 2006, p.16).

Disciplinary literacy scholar Elizabeth Birr Moje (2008) advocates a more profound change: shifting textbooks to the back burner and replacing them with tools that historians, English professors, mathematicians, and scientists actually use, including new media, fan fiction, and mathematical and scientific models. She contends that by using primary, authentic texts more and textbooks less, literacy moves to the forefront of learning. According to Moje, simply using the same reading strategies in different content areas is too limiting, yet she acknowledges that her suggested approach places new demands on teachers—from identifying user-friendly materials to scaffolding instruction in order to teach primary source texts appropriately. Moje calls for more professional development to prepare teachers to model how to look back to texts and draw from them to make arguments and draw conclusions.

If your students quickly lose interest in the textbook you've assigned, consider relying less on the text and more on alternative sources: magazines, newspaper articles, and trade books that deal with the same subject. When selecting additional books and reading materials for your classroom, keep struggling readers in mind. In addition to high-interest topics and issues, look for the following supports that will encourage students, especially those who are struggling readers, to keep reading:

- A compelling storyline and credible characters (plausible plot and teenage protagonists).

- Supportive formatting that includes illustrations and appropriate text placement on the page (hyphenation is a problem for struggling readers, line spacing is more important than type size, and some type faces are more easily readable than others).

- Careful introduction and reinforcement of difficult vocabulary and concepts (difficult words should be used more than once, and every difficult word should be presented in such a way as to make its meaning clear).

- Straightforward plot development (flashbacks, time shifts, and confusing changes in point of view are not used).

- Simple sentence structure (the subject and predicate must be physically close to each other, subordinate clauses should follow the main clause or be clearly set off by commas, semicolons are avoided). (Rog & Kropp, 2001, n.p.)

Positive mental dispositions

When most people recall their experiences reading *Romeo and Juliet* in high school, for example, they remember not only the plot of the play but also how much they enjoyed or hated the experience itself. This is because the human brain stores memories in many different ways, but everything we learn has an emotional connection (McBrien & Brandt, 1997; Vacca, 2006). A student's mental disposition, then, refers to his or her affective response toward reading—toward the emotions and values involved—rather than just toward the facts and ideas presented. It includes the student's motivation to do what is required, confidence in his or her ability to succeed, and interest in actively pursuing meaning while reading. It also includes how much new learning the reader wants to integrate into his or her current schema and, of course, how he or she feels about the content (Frager, 1993; Giancarlo, Blohm, & Urdan, 2004).

In addition, students need to see value in what they are asked to do. Although content-area teachers are fascinated by their own subjects, their students may not immediately share that excitement. Enthusiasm can be contagious, but explanations about what students will gain by learning content material can also help motivate students. Explaining the role of statistical models in determining the winner of the Cy Young award or using the law of physics to explain why a head-first slide is faster than going for the bag feet first will peak many students' interests.

The power of "I can" beliefs

Our mental habits influence everything we do. For example, if a student has a negative attitude toward reading because of a self-perception that he or she is a poor reader who can't understand unfamiliar text, chances are that this attitude will become a self-fulfilling prophecy. "Whether or not a reader feels confident that he or she has the skills to handle a given reading situation makes a difference in that reader's approach" (Vacca, 2006, p. 56). If a student has a defeatist attitude, that student will approach difficult text reluctantly, give up easily when encountering obstacles, and ultimately not understand the content covered in the reading assignment. An "I can" belief, or a belief that you can accomplish what you want to accomplish, is an important factor in successfully executing certain tasks or reaching certain goals.

Psychologist Carol Dweck and her colleagues at Stanford University conducted research in which they identified two mind-sets, or ways of viewing intelligence and learning—fixed and growth—and the effect each has on school behaviors. Students who subscribe to a growth mind-set, however, believe they can develop their intelligence over time, and they see challenging work as an opportunity to learn. By contrast, students who view intelligence as fixed (an inborn trait) place an inordinate value on "looking smart" and are reluctant to exert effort beyond their comfort zone. They avoid activities that could possibly lead to failure, and they are more easily discouraged when they encounter the same obstacles that students with a growth mind-set find engaging. "Within a classroom culture that supports a growth mind-set, teachers can design meaningful learning tasks and present them in a way that fosters students' resilience and long-term achievement" (Dweck, 2010, p. 18). To reach all students, teachers should present challenges as fun and exciting, give students a clear sense of progress toward mastery, and grade on actual growth (e.g., use a grade of "not yet").

"I can" beliefs are particularly important in science and mathematics, where students who struggle or experience failure tend to adopt a permanent attitude of "I'm just not good at that, and I never will be." A belief that you either have a gift for learning science and mathematics or you don't can be quite harmful. Stephen Pellathy, a science curriculum specialist and physicist says, "The reality of science is you're basically always failing. . . . So if you don't have that mindset that your failures are setting you up for your subsequent success, you won't keep going" (Roth, 2011).

Of course, anyone can experience problems reading and understanding text in any discipline if they haven't developed effective mental habits. Indeed, you can probably recall a time when you easily breezed through a novel yet had difficulty trying to understand the instruction manual that came with a new computer. Technical material typically includes specialized vocabulary and requires some background knowledge. Motivated by the need to get your computer up and running, you most likely persevered through the material, acting out what you thought it was instructing you to do. In essence, you applied the mental habits of maintaining an open mind, pushing the limits of your knowledge and abilities, applying familiar strategies, and sticking to it. Over time, you probably got better at reading and comprehending technical instructions, and as your ability increased, so too did your confidence.

These mental habits are referred to as "intelligent behaviors" or "habits of mind" (Costa, 1991; Marzano et al., 1997; Paul, 1990; Perkins, 1993), and they help learners both in school and throughout their lives. Productive mental dispositions look like this:

- Be open-minded and flexible about ideas and solutions.
- Be aware of your own thinking, behaviors, and feelings.
- Be accurate and seek accuracy.
- Be clear and seek clarity.
- Monitor and control your behavior, learning, and work.
- Plan appropriately.
- Respond appropriately to feedback.
- Identify and use necessary resources.
- Restrain impulsivity.

How can teachers help students acquire positive habits of mind? First, they must explain that certain behaviors can enhance learning and what those behaviors look like in the classroom. This might sound obvious, but lower-achieving students often fail to realize that their attitude, mental habits, and frame of mind affect their learning. They also do not understand that they have the power to regulate these feelings, attitudes, and behaviors. Similarly, ELLs, who may become easily discouraged because they are at various levels of English acquisition, will benefit when their teachers make visible the thinking tools that experienced readers and writers use to construct meaning (Olson & Land, 2007).

Second, teachers must provide clear examples for students. They need to model productive habits of mind, discuss real-world examples that appear in the news or other popular media, and reinforce their use in class. Self-efficacy, text comprehension, and motivation work together to create a collective "I can" belief among students (Vacca, 2006). Students who practice these behaviors regularly become self-directed learners who are aware of their mental disposition, monitor it, and modify it as needed. Likewise, effective readers know that comprehension is not something that just happens; they take an active role in the reading process to ensure comprehension.

One teacher's steps to success

Educator and author Cindi Rigsbee (2011) describes what she has learned about motivating students while working to increase their engagement and learning in her English classroom. Here are three steps she offers from personal experience:

1. *Establish an environment that celebrates success.* Be careful not to "overpraise." Be sure to notice small victories for every student, but guard against effusive praise that may become meaningless.

2. *Establish an environment that supports struggling students, enriches the high flyers, and pushes those in the middle by offering* activities that are appropriate for every student in the class. In addition, try not to demand a "performance" in front of peers unless students have had adequate time to prepare and know what is expected of them. Providing students with choice in assignments and projects also is an optimal way to differentiate for all students while increasing buy-in and engagement.

3. *Establish an environment that says "we're a community of learners in here."* Make sure each student feels safe and can learn in an atmosphere that is nonthreatening. Activities that allow for social interaction ensure that students feel more comfortable sharing what they do (or don't) know and understand. Have clear expectations for how students treat one another, and model the respect you want them to display.

This type of classroom culture "can only be attained when the teacher makes an effort to really *know* the students—their strengths, weaknesses, likes, dislikes, fears, and dreams" (Rigsbee, 2011, p. 2). A few ways teachers can get to know their students better are informal conversations, scheduled conferences, or by reading their opinions on assigned journal topics (e.g., free writing on a daily topic from current events at the beginning of class).

Sharing the Responsibility for Learning with Students

There is considerable research evidence to support the teaching of strategies that are geared toward developing students' sense of personal responsibility. Results of a meta-analysis on classroom management showed a decrease in disruptive behavior when students were taught two kinds of strategies: (1) self-monitoring and control strategies, and (2) cognitively based strategies. Both strategies involve teaching students to observe and monitor their behavior, but the first one also emphasizes keeping a record of behavior, establishing a criterion level of behavior, and receiving rewards when the student achieves the criterion (Marzano, 2003).

Regardless of the evidence, teaching responsibility strategies is not a common practice among K–12 educators. Why is this so? Many teachers consider this "above and beyond" their role as educators, and, indeed, responsibility instruction can be a demanding task that often involves dealing with complex, longstanding problems. Nonetheless, teachers should be encouraged to recognize the value of such instruction and "rise to the occasion," when needed. For instance, sharing the Reading Troubleshooting Chart (Figure 3.3) with students is one way to help them understand they have the ability to help themselves and have the power to respond to whatever reading challenges they encounter.

Aside from the sheer value of hard work, it is also important for students to learn how to analyze problems and figure out solutions—not just accumulate facts. Teachers can

FIGURE 3.3 ⟶   Reading Troubleshooting Chart

The Challenge	The Reading Lifeline
You almost "get" it but not quite.	Reread.
You "get" the overall idea, but the details escape you.	Discuss what you are reading with someone else, clarifying points that support the "big picture."
You don't understand much of what you are reading or viewing.	• Ask someone who understands the content to explain it to you and then reread. • Look up the topic online to build background knowledge.
You can recite facts from the text, but you really don't understand what the author is trying to communicate.	• Go back and/or read ahead, looking at nonprint features of the text (graphs, charts, illustrations, chapter titles, words in bold). • Try to identify important parts of the text and skim through those passages again. • Read through the table of contents, the introduction, or the text on the back of the book. • Think of questions you would like to ask the author and continue reading to see if your questions have been answered.
You are having trouble understanding because you don't know enough about the subject to "put it all together."	Build your background knowledge by finding information from another text on the same topic, such as an online resource, a book, a magazine, or a video, or by talking to someone who is knowledgeable about the subject.
You feel as if you are reading a foreign language.	Determine key vocabulary you don't know and find the meaning by using context clues, asking someone for meanings, or using a dictionary or glossary.
You find yourself distracted or bored when you read and are unable to concentrate.	• Read more quickly or slow down, forcing yourself to pay attention by stopping at intervals to think (or talk about) what you have read. • Take mental or physical breaks from the text. • Try to visualize what is happening, placing yourself within the text rather than reading as an observer. • Set a purpose for reading, even a small one to keep you focused.

FIGURE 3.3 → Reading Troubleshooting Chart (*continued*)

The Challenge	The Reading Lifeline
You understand what you are reading up to a certain point and then you seem to lose it.	• Summarize what you have read so far, either by talking to someone, reviewing it out loud, or writing about it. • Try to predict what might come next. Read to find out if your predictions are correct. • Try to pinpoint when the confusion started and go back and reread a few paragraphs before that point.
You have difficulty because you disagree with the author or have strong feelings about the text.	• Write to explore your feelings about the text and gain understanding of the author's viewpoint. • Return to the text and mentally engage the author in a conversation or debate about the issues. Think about what you would say to the author to change his or her mind. • Remember that you have the right to your opinion about a text. Allow yourself time to stop and think through what is bothering you.
You've reread but you still don't get it.	• Read the text orally or ask someone to read it to you. • Try to pinpoint what is confusing and ask your teacher or someone else to help you clarify.
You are having trouble knowing what is important in the text.	• Set a purpose for reading. Tell yourself that you will read a part of the text for a specific reason (such as to find out why something happened) and concentrate only on that purpose. • Use a double-column note-taking approach, "What's Important" on one side and "Why?" or "What's Interesting?" on the other. • If you are reading a textbook, look at chapter headings, words in bold, and captions for illustrations or charts.

Source: From *Literacy for Real: Reading, Thinking, and Learning in the Content Areas* (pp. 68–69), by R. C. Lent, 2009, New York: Teachers College Press. Copyright 2009 by Teachers College Press. Reprinted with permission.

provide direct and explicit instruction on the appropriate strategies, but it is up to students to focus their attention on the reading or learning tasks at hand. Here are some things teachers can do to help students make personal connections with the reading materials and read with a clearly defined purpose:

- Express confidence in every student's ability to access prior knowledge.

- Fill in any gaps in students' background knowledge before assigning reading.

- Demonstrate how to "chunk" assigned work into manageable pieces.

- Acknowledge small successes in addition to large ones.

- Encourage risk taking when students answer questions about what they have read.

- Validate responses and give credit for specific aspects of a response that are correct.

Give students the metacomprehension edge

Thus far, we have focused on ways to help students plan for reading, such as activating their prior knowledge, previewing the selection for reader aids, identifying unfamiliar vocabulary, setting purpose, and practicing productive habits of mind. However, monitoring the effectiveness of one's reading behaviors on comprehension means something more. It involves the abilities to observe and assess those behaviors and to select alternative behaviors and strategies, as needed, to improve comprehension.

Think about a particular activity in which you engaged recently—teaching a specific class, playing a game of tennis or golf, working out, preparing a meal, or even playing a video game. Create a mental visual of what you did, what you thought, and how you behaved as you engaged in this activity. Assuming that you wanted to successfully accomplish the task, you may remember how you thought about and evaluated your actions as you were doing them. Just as you are doing now, you stepped outside yourself to observe or monitor the effectiveness of your actions and attitudes at different points during the activity. As necessary, you adjusted your behavior so you would be more likely to achieve your goal. Ultimately, you were strategic and reflective as you performed the activity. Various researchers use the term *metacomprehension* to refer to this strategic and reflective approach to reading comprehension (e.g., Caverly et al., 1995; Gavelek & Raphael, 1985; Osman & Hannafin, 1992).

Some reading researchers distinguish among the terms *metacognition*, *metacomprehension*, *self-explanation*, and *self-regulation*, but the concepts expressed by each overlap significantly. "Metacognition as it relates to reading involves the reader being aware of the reading process and knowing what to do when the reader's level of comprehension is not sufficient, or does not satisfy the reader's goals and desires" (McNamara & Magliano, 2009, p. 61). Metacomprehension, on the other hand, refers to the ability to monitor one's own understanding of information, to recognize failures to comprehend, and to employ appropriate repair strategies. Self-explanation is the process of explaining text to oneself, either orally or in writing, and self-regulation refers to one's ability to make adjustments to the learning process in response to feedback.

Strategic and reflective learners are aware of their learning style and able to select and regulate their use of learning skills and strategies. For example, students are being strategic (and using metacognition) when they keep track of the steps in a multistep problem and know which ones they've completed and which to do next; when they realize they have lost track of events in a text and turn back a few pages to reread; or when they recognize that using context clues to determine the meaning of an unfamiliar word isn't working, so they persevere and become motivated to find a strategy that will work.

Few teachers would argue with the importance of metacognition and metacomprehension skills, but acquiring these skills does require instruction and practice. An easy, effective tool for teachers in any discipline is the following metacognition checklist, which is composed of five simple questions students should ask themselves. As they answer each question, students begin to understand that they have the ability not only to understand how they learn best but also to improve in some areas. For example, if a student answers "no, I can't recall the details" to the first question, then you (and your student) have a place to begin improving. To help build memory skills, your student may need to look for key words from a list you provided, and read with a pencil and sticky notes nearby. With each key word encountered, the student can write out and place a sticky note on the page. In this way, students can recognize their unique learning needs and practice ways to effectively learn new knowledge.

After introducing students to the concept of metacognition, assign a reading/writing task. Afterwards, instead of grading it, ask students to answer some, or all, of the following questions:

- Can I recall the details from the reading assignment?
- Does my answer to the question make sense?
- Did I understand any new words?
- Did I read and follow directions?
- Did I give the number of required examples?

The importance of questions before, during, and after reading

Noted educator John Dewey is credited with saying that we learn by doing if we reflect on what we have done. Certainly, ideal readers reflect on content while they read, weighing it in light of what they already know, think, and believe. Guided, active reading requires teachers to pose questions at strategic points—questions that demand a certain amount of introspection and reflection from students while they are reading. Research on the role of questioning as it relates to reading and learning reveals the following (Graesser, Ozuru, & Sullins, 2010):

- Most students don't ask very many questions while in learning settings.
- Most student- and teacher-posed questions tend to be shallow, including those written by textbook writers.

- When teachers invest time in teaching students how to ask deeper questions, they are facilitating comprehension and learning.

- There are several psychological models that specify how to stimulate more and deeper questioning (e.g., teachers modeling deep questions; teachers presenting challenges that place students in cognitive disequilibrium, such as presenting obstacles to goals, contradictions, conflict, and anomalies).

Since questioning helps readers think about what they read, it is helpful to have a framework for developing and asking questions. You may want to share the table in Figure 3.4 with students and let them select and adapt questions they think will be the most helpful as they read.

A Final Thought on the Goals and Dispositions Gear

We know that students are more likely to learn when they feel capable of succeeding and when they recognize a purpose of the learning activities. Teachers can boost students' competence by helping them see relevance in what they are learning, pressing them to achieve at high levels, and providing adequate support. The results of a study by the Southern Region Education Board (SREB), an organization that has spent more than 20 years examining the high school experiences of students nationwide, provide insight into the power of high expectations that are coupled with the right supports (SREB, 2004).

Researchers at SREB studied 13 Georgia high schools where both test scores and student graduation rates were rising. Looking for the common factor among the schools, the researchers concluded, "These most-improved schools were not just about rigor; they were about students seeing a purpose in what they were being asked to learn" (Goodwin, 2010, p. 23). It is almost assured that the students in these Georgia schools are experiencing success because teachers deliver challenging instruction and set the bar high.

FIGURE 3.4 ⇢   Questions for Reading Strategically

Prereading Questions

- What do I think the reading selection will be about? What predictions can I make?

- What are some things I already know about the topic?

- What are my reading goals? What concepts do I want to learn from reading this selection?

- What is my purpose for reading? What will I need to do with the information I learn? (Take a quiz or a multiple-choice test? Complete a performance activity? Write an evaluative essay?) How will this affect the way I read the selection?

- What strategies can I use as I read to understand the selection? What will I do if I encounter difficulty?

- How will I know I understood the author's intended message?

During-Reading Questions

- What do I think the main ideas are so far? Why?

- What kind of graphic organizer can I use to begin organizing these ideas?

- What can I picture in my mind about these ideas?

- Is the information in this selection similar to anything I have learned before? How?

- What questions do I have at this point in my reading? (Write them down.)

- What is my attitude toward reading the selection at this point? Do I need to modify any of my behaviors, attitudes, or resources to reach my goal?

After-Reading Questions

- Were my predictions about the main ideas accurate?

- What other information do I want to remember? How will I remember it?

- Did I accomplish my reading goal?

- Which reading and learning strategies did I find most helpful? Why?

- Which parts of the selection interested me most? Which ideas made me think?

- How has my thinking changed as a result of reading this selection? What have I learned about myself?

- What should I do differently next time I read a similar selection?

04
Creating Literacy-Rich Environments

"Outstanding reading education programs are grounded by content, powered by teaching, energized by apprenticeships, enriched by diversity, evaluated by assessment, and sustained by vision and good governance."

—Susan Pimentel, *Teaching Reading Well*

Characteristics of Literacy-Rich Content-Area Classrooms

What does today's classroom look like when teachers intentionally plan lessons that support adolescent literacy development? Research provides an answer: "School and classroom cultures that successfully promote the development of adolescent literacy skills are characterized by connections, interaction, and responsiveness, which lead to student engagement and reflection" (Meltzer, 2001). Though socioeconomic status, class size, and teacher credentials certainly are important, research indicates that collective efficacy—a shared belief among teachers that they can help students succeed—has the greatest impact on student achievement (Goodwin, 2010). The following examples present glimpses of literacy-rich classroom environments in three content areas where motivation, literacy strategies, and reading across the curriculum effectively come together (Meltzer, 2001).

In literacy-rich mathematics classrooms, language processes support students while they are learning new content and help them demonstrate what they have learned.

- The teacher models problem-solving techniques such as think alouds, and students talk and write about how they solve problems.
- Students actively develop concepts with their teacher.
- The teacher helps students make connections to real-life applications.

- Students actively construct mathematics-specific vocabulary and explicitly use reader aids to enhance their understanding of mathematics texts.
- Students work in varied, flexible groupings to present mathematical solutions to problematic scenarios.

In literacy-rich science classrooms, reading, writing, and discussion are a daily occurrence.

- Students use a variety of texts, including academic journal articles, scientific websites, science fiction, and essays.
- Students have access to electronic media, film, visuals, and lab experiences, which further support reading comprehension.
- Students actively construct science-specific vocabulary and explicitly use reader aids to enhance their understanding of science texts.
- Students frequently discuss, present, and write about possible hypotheses, predictions, analyses, findings, and ideas.
- Students include elements of the writing process in their lab reports, solutions to problem sets, and research findings.

In litercy-rich social studies classrooms, students' interests are taken into account, and students work in various groupings on different kinds of assignments.

- Students use various resources, including reproductions of primary sources such as diary entries, maps, film, historical fiction, and newspaper accounts.
- Students explicitly call out reader aids, use specialized vocabulary in spoken and written communications, and investigate the thinking and approaches of anthropologists, archaeologists, economists, sociologists, and social historians.
- Students actively explore essential questions and make frequent connections between and among eras, people, and events from the past and present.
- Students use research skills and examine how languages develop and how various cultures use them.

We don't mean to imply that content-area teachers should become reading and writing teachers. Rather, they should emphasize the reading and writing practices that are specific to their disciplines. All teachers should use the tools (e.g., graphic organizers, outlines, guided discussions) that research shows support all students—those who are experiencing success and those who are struggling. In addition, the idea of a reading apprenticeship has been proposed as a model for direct, explicit comprehension instruction (Biancarosa & Snow, 2006). In it, students act as apprentices to their teachers, who are the content-area experts, and learn how to read and write in a particular discipline. Reading apprenticeship classrooms focus less on strategy implementation and more on creating an environment in which students become active and effective readers and learners. To accomplish this, teachers need to plan along four dimensions—social, personal, cognitive, and knowledge building—and encourage metacognitive conversations in their classrooms (Jordan, Jensen, & Greenleaf, 2001).

- The social dimension focuses on establishing and maintaining a safe and supportive environment in which all members' processes, resources, and difficulties are shared and collaboration is valued. One simple and effective way to do this is to use the "turn to your neighbor" technique.

- The personal dimension focuses on improving students' identities, their attitudes as readers, and their interest in reading. It also promotes self-awareness, self-assessment, metacognition, and ownership. Teachers should gradually release the responsibility for learning to students.

- The cognitive dimension is where students are given the reading tools and strategies they need to read like experts in the discipline. Students need to practice these skills and receive feedback. Ultimately, students must learn to transfer their skills to new learning situations.

- The knowledge-building dimension focuses on building content, topic knowledge, and knowledge of a discipline's typical text structures and styles.

Establishing Safe and Productive Learning Environments

Picture the following scenario: you are on a plane home after attending a conference on teaching innovations for the 21st century, and you have a binder full of conference material you want to read. In addition, you have a meeting scheduled with your superintendent an hour after your plane lands in order to share key ideas from the conference and a summary of the materials. It was raining when the plane took off, and the captain announces that the turbulence you feel will be getting worse. Everyone should remain seated for the duration of the flight, and seatbelts should remain tightly fastened. The young mother sitting next to you is trying desperately to soothe her 10-month-old baby, who is squalling and pulling at his ear. The woman apologizes for the noise, explaining that the baby has an ear infection. How well do you think you would be able to focus on your reading?

Truly, the environment in which reading occurs influences comprehension. When you ask young people about a good place to read, they respond with everything from "in bed" to "at the park," "in the car," or "by the pool." Although teachers have little control over the environment in which students read outside of school, they are able to create an environment in their classrooms that enhances learning. For example, research suggests students learn best in a pleasant, friendly climate where they

- Feel accepted by their teachers and peers.

- Feel a sense of safety and order because academic expectations, instructions, and purpose for assignments are clear.

- Feel confident in their ability to complete tasks successfully.

- See value in the learning activities. (Marzano et al., 1997; McCombs & Barton, 1998)

Ensuring acceptance, safety, and order

"In the classrooms of [the most successful teachers], also referred to as warm demanders, students actively participated in class discussions and were willing to work hard for their teachers, with whom they had developed a positive and mutually respectful rapport" (Goodwin, 2010, p. 10). Teachers can create a climate of acceptance in several ways. Even a simple, sincere gesture can help students feel connected to their teachers and to the school. Students report feeling accepted when their teachers listen to them and respect their opinions. Calling students by their preferred names, making eye contact, planning varied activities that address different learning styles and that capitalize on individual differences, encouraging even unassertive students to participate in class discussion—all of these help students feel as if they matter and their opinions count.

Many teachers find that standing at the classroom door at the beginning and end of each class is beneficial. As students enter or leave the room, teachers have a moment to gauge their attitudes, greet them with a warm smile, or praise contributions made that day in class. In addition, teachers communicate acceptance when they ask students about their performance in extracurricular activities such as sports, drama, or scouting.

Naturally, individuals need to feel safe from physical harm in order to be receptive to learning. Across the nation, teachers, administrators, and parents are working together to introduce and enforce schoolwide procedures aimed at violence prevention. Students also need to feel a sense of emotional safety—that is, that they are safe from emotional abuse. Within their individual classrooms, teachers can create a healthy climate by making it clear that any and all forms of put-down or abusive behavior will not be tolerated.

It should come as no surprise to hear that students are more receptive to learning if they feel accepted by their classmates and teachers. Successful language instruction is composed of social aspects that augment explicit teaching of syntax, grammar, vocabulary, pronunciation, and norms of social usage (Goldenberg, 2008). Collaborative learning activities require teamwork and therefore can be an excellent means for all students, whether native English speakers or ELLs, to learn about one another's strengths, aptitudes, and personalities. It follows that having ample opportunities to use language in meaningful and motivating situations is essential for all students.

Sometimes, students feel open to ridicule by their classmates when they are called upon to answer questions about classwork they don't understand. There are strategies that can help alleviate this problem, though. For example, a middle school mathematics teacher in Colorado reserves a large table in the classroom for students who need extra help during class. At the beginning of the school year, she explains to her classes that this table is "sacred"; it is a place where anyone can join her and receive help without worrying about what other students might say. Students quickly learn to regard this space with respect, knowing that there will be times when they need to use it. The teacher reports that, at times, there may be several students with her at the table; whereas at other times, there may only be one or two. However, all of her students treat those classmates who elect to be there with respect.

A sense of order is enhanced when teachers clearly articulate classroom rules and the purpose of each reading assignment. Students should be told ahead of time what they will be doing with the information they read (e.g., writing a summary, collaborating with others on an extended performance activity, participating in a discussion of the material). As we mentioned earlier, ineffective readers do not differentiate among reading assignments. They read all textbooks in the same fashion. Therefore, it is important for students to learn that a reader's purpose determines which strategies to employ, the pace at which to read, the type of mental questions to ask and answer while reading, and how to monitor comprehension.

Understanding the importance of a classroom library

"I believe a classroom library is the heartbeat of a teacher's environment. It is the window into an educator's own personality, and it reflects the importance of literacy in the classroom. I believe every teacher—no matter what subject he or she teaches—should have one" (Wolpert-Gawron, 2009, para. 1). Indeed, classroom libraries are as relevant today as they have ever been. In fact, they may be more important than ever before. Teachers would be well advised to weave libraries and the resources to which they provide access into their lessons, find creative ways to hold students accountable for reading (e.g., create book covers to decorate the classroom, design ads to persuade classmates to read a particular book, write and display reviews), and think of classroom libraries as interactive areas that students will use extensively. The following practical tips are invaluable (Ibid.):

- Require students to check out books by tracking titles on slips of paper that are filed in the library. When students return the books they borrow to the library, they file them on the correct shelves and then, with permission, tear up the appropriate checkout slips.

- Label every book in the library with genre-specific stickers to help categorize and organize the collection. As a class activity, students can decide which stickers to place on new books that are added to the library.

- Identify some high-interest books as noncirculating and for classroom reading only. Allow other to be checked out for seven-day periods.

- Perform classroom-library scavenger hunts with questions such as the following:
  — Which book has a map on the inside front cover?
  — Which author has written books in each of the genres in our library?
  — Which book series is a television show of the same name?
  — What is the title of the biography about the founder of Microsoft?

There are many types of readers in any given classroom—from reluctant readers to those who excitedly seek out favorite authors or genres—and it is the responsibility of all teachers to provide a safe and comfortable place where students can find appropriate reading materials. In addition, classroom libraries introduce students to the concept of short, teacher-monitored, and silent reading periods. Twenty minutes of silent reading is best followed by a five-minute open-ended discussion (Block & Parris, 2008).

Maximizing classroom discussions

Reading is a social act, which makes it ideally suited for adolescents who naturally want to be connected to others their age with similar interests. Discussion helps students clarify their understanding of what they read, refine their thinking, share their ideas, and explore related issues. In this way, reading (and writing) can become the driving force behind activism. Two forms of discussion—guided and reflective—can help students interact with the content, one another, and the topics about which they are passionate.

In guided discussion, the teacher uses questioning techniques and study guide materials to direct student thinking. Ultimately, the teacher's role is to encourage student questions about the content and provide additional information and clarification when needed (Vacca & Vacca, 1993).

When using guided discussion, teachers should take care not to let the discussion become a lecture. If the teacher is both asking and answering questions, then students quickly realize that it is unnecessary for them to speak up and share their thoughts. Another common pitfall in guided discussion is the tendency of teachers to allow a few bright, verbal students to monopolize class discussion. When this happens, other students feel self-conscious about participating, so they withdraw and don't feel comfortable sharing their ideas. Teachers should instead pose questions that require students to interpret the text, explore what the text means to them, and share these interpretations with one another. This independent construction of meaning requires students to interact with one another (Brophy, 1992). Discussion allows students the chance to think through and paraphrase the content of any discipline and then "make it their own" by exploring the relationships between that content and their prior knowledge. Teachers can ensure more active participation if they clearly explain the purpose of the discussion, give explicit directions, and model the discussion skills of active listening, paraphrasing, and clarifying.

Mortimer and Scott (2003) explored classroom talk as it relates to the particular academic discipline of science by asking two research questions: Does it matter whether students are talking when they are directly engaged in science learning? Does it matter if a teacher's style is limited to the presentation style? Their findings support the importance of classroom dialogue in secondary science classrooms: "It is through talk that the scientific view is introduced to the classroom. Talk enables the teacher to support students in making sense of the view. Talk enables the students to engage consciously in the dialogic process of meaning making, providing the tools for them to think through the scientific view for themselves" (Ibid., p. 3). They go on to identify four steps for teachers to follow when using their district's science curriculum to plan discourse in their classrooms:

1. Identify the unique language that scientists use in the particular area of science you plan to teach.

2. Consider how students' everyday social language reflects the concepts of this specific area of science.

3. Identify the learning demand by appraising the nature of any differences between steps one and two.

4. Develop a teaching sequence to address each aspect of this learning demand, identifying: (a) the teaching purposes for each phase of the sequence; (b) how those purposes might be addressed through an appropriate communicative approach; and (c) how this approach might be put into action through appropriate teaching activities, patterns of discourse, and teacher interventions.

By contrast, the purpose of reflective discussion is to help students extend and refine their knowledge by making judgments, defending their opinions, and thinking critically and creatively. Teachers guide students into being more independent learners by modeling productive ways of responding, reacting to diverse viewpoints and sensitive issues, and demonstrating how to think critically about difficult concepts (Alvermann, Dillon, & O'Brien, 1988; Phan, 2009). When students have a good grasp of the concepts they are studying, teachers should encourage reflective discussion and shift their role from leader/authority to participant. Here are a few general guidelines for creating a classroom environment that supports reflective discussion:

1. Arrange desks so students can see one another or easily break into smaller discussion groups.

2. Teach, model, and encourage active listening.

3. Clearly articulate the topic under discussion and the goal of the discussion.

4. Ensure that students stick to the topic of the discussion and don't go off on tangents.

5. Draw out students who are naturally quiet, shy, or reluctant to participate.

6. Avoid behavior that might stifle discussion (e.g., facial expressions or posture that betrays a personal judgment about students' opinions).

Prior to introducing a reflective discussion, the teacher should develop a main question to ask students and probable follow-up questions that students are apt to ask one another. A question to ask in a social studies classroom, for example, might be something such as this: Because the United States has a powerful and influential international status, should it be the world's "policeman"? Students should then spend time answering the question together, challenging one another's comments, and asking for clarification. As facilitator, it is important that the teacher refrain from dominating the discussion. Instead, the teacher should encourage students to explore as many aspects of the topic as time allows and to point out contradictions in one another's logic. In this way, the teacher shares the control and direction of the lesson with students, which further fosters students' interactions. For the conclusion, the teacher reasks the main question and lets students respond by stating either "Yes, the United States should police other nations because. . ." or "No, the United States should not police other nations because. . ." Finally, students might write a summary of the information they obtained from the discussion, what was learned, and why the discussion was useful. (Teaching Techniques, n.d.)

The two approaches are equally beneficial; guided discussion is particularly useful in encouraging students to be active participants in their learning, and reflective discussion is especially appropriate when a topic calls for making a decision, such as whether purchasing stocks in a particular company is a good investment or whether global warming is an imminent threat.

Creating a Culturally Responsive Classroom

Ladson-Billings (2010) calls attention to the ways that some teachers in urban schools are positively affecting the literacy performance of African American children. Three major themes that emerge are immersion in text-rich environments, exposure to meaningful texts through both reading and writing, and meaningful links between literacy and real-life experiences. She asserts that teachers who link literacy activities to students' cultures and wider social contexts ensure that those students acquire the skills and understandings necessary to read and write well.

Culturally responsive teachers focus on academic achievement while maintaining and celebrating their students' cultural identities and heritages. When teaching literature, they select stories that reflect multiple ethnic perspectives and literary genres. When teaching mathematics, they incorporate the economics, employment statistics, and consumer habits of various ethnic groups. Culturally responsive teaching, then, incorporates students' cultural knowledge, prior experiences, and performance styles to make learning more appropriate and effective by teaching to and through students' strengths (Gay, 2000). Specifically, culturally responsive teaching can be identified by the following characteristics:

- It acknowledges the legitimacy of various cultural heritages, both as legacies that affect students' dispositions, attitudes, and approaches to learning and as content worthy to be taught in the formal curriculum.

- It builds meaningful connections between home and school experiences and between academic abstractions and sociocultural realities.

- It uses a wide variety of instructional strategies that are connected to different learning styles.

- It teaches students to recognize, understand, and respect the variety of cultural heritages represented in their classroom.

- It incorporates multicultural information, resources, and material in all of the content areas.

Culturally responsive teaching has also been described as comprehensive, multidimensional, empowering, and transformative (Ladson-Billings, 2010). It is comprehensive when students see themselves as part of a collective effort to achieve academic and cultural excellence. When teachers are intentional about exhibiting the successful interpersonal relationships they expect from their students, students learn to be accountable to the larger group while also feeling supported and encouraged by it. It is multidimensional when teachers from various disciplines (e.g., language arts, science, social studies, music) collaborate and teach a single cultural concept. It is empowering when students believe they can succeed in learning tasks and have the motivation to persevere and when teachers demonstrate ambitious and appropriate expectations while supporting their efforts. Ultimately, it is transformative because it helps "students to develop the knowledge, skills, and values needed to become social critics who can make reflective decisions and implement their decisions in effective personal, social, political, and economic action" (Banks, 2001, p. 131).

Using Writing as the Ultimate Reading Strategy

Author and educator Mike Schmoker describes a research study conducted by the Leadership and Learning Center that reveals approximately 25 percent of students scored proficient or higher on state assessments in schools where writing and note taking were rare in science classes. By contrast, in schools where science teachers required writing and note taking, 79 percent of students scored at the proficient level. In his words, "writing matters—hugely" (Schmoker, 2011, p. 192).

After giving a writing assignment, many teachers have heard questions such as these: Are you grading this? How long does it have to be? Does spelling count? Students ask these kinds of questions when they don't connect writing to learning; rather, they think of writing as a separate assignment—one disconnected from usual learning activities. Students sometimes view writing in this light because teachers traditionally use it only as a product—an essay test, theme, or lab report to be completed at the end of a lesson or unit. However, the very act of writing requires deep thought and active engagement with the content. As students write, they construct meaning around the content, make connections, and discover what they do and do not know. Writing is a tool for learning; it is fundamental to acquiring, thinking about, and communicating knowledge in all disciplines (Bazerman, 2009; Fulwiler, 1987). Because of its value as formative assessment, writing should never be used solely as summative assessment. Rather, writing is a powerful vehicle for teachers to provide students with feedback and encouragement to further explore a topic and revisit their ideas.

When teachers do use writing as a culminating activity, it is usually to sum up a lesson or unit and to determine whether students have learned what was intended. Examples of lesson plans that include after-reading writing activities abound on the Internet, and first-person summary narratives are particularly popular. In a summary narrative, students retell events or a process from an imagined personal perspective. For example, following a social studies unit about the Texas Revolution, students write dramatic narratives based on historical facts pertinent to the Battle of the Alamo. Likewise, a science teacher might assign a narrative entitled "A Day in My Life as a Volcano," or a health or physical education teacher might assign a narrative about the effects of exercise written from the perspective of a heart or pair of lungs. The summary narrative is a versatile and motivational tool because it requires students to process and make sense of expository text. Nevertheless, to emphasize the ways in which writing helps students learn, and to help students think of writing as a useful learning activity, teachers need to regularly assign writing-to-learn activities.

Writing-to-learn activities are informal writing tasks that help students think through key concepts or ideas that were presented in class. They differ from essays, reports, and themes in that they are exploratory. Although grammar and mechanics are still important, the purpose of writing-to-learn activities is to reflect on what's been learned, develop some parameters around it, and make meaningful, personal connections between it and students' life experiences.

Writing-to-learn activities work equally well as both in-class and homework assignments. Here are some basic tips for developing writing-to-learn topics in content-area classrooms:

- Keep assignments short (e.g., Give students "think time," but ask them to write for only five minutes).

- Expect creative thinking and exploration of the content, and share expectations with students (e.g., Ask students to write about what the topic means to them).

- Identify the intended audience (other than you, the teacher) ahead of time.

- Display student writing—representative of all levels of quality—in the classroom. (Students will write more carefully if they think someone other than the teacher will be reading it.)

- Vary the types and formats of writing required (e.g., learning log entry, analogy, poem, editorial, letter to the textbook publisher or a friend, respond to reading).

- Encourage students to interact with their reading assignments by summarizing key points, clarifying confusing material, asking questions about material, recording observations over time, and defining key terms.

Some teachers are hesitant to incorporate writing-to-learn activities because they are wary of the additional work and paper load they might create. Assessing student writing means evaluating it in light of the depth of thought displayed, and there are many creative ways to keep it simple:

- Don't grade every single assignment.

- Use a rubric that has been previously shared with students.

- Use feedback forms with familiar sentence starters, such as:
  - I like what you said about . . .
  - When I read what you wrote, it reminded me of . . .
  - Have you thought about . . . ?
  - I'd like to read more about your personal experience with . . .

- Teach students to read and comment on one another's writing constructively.

Characterizing Literacy-Rich Schools and Districts

Biancarosa and Snow (2006) identify 15 key elements of effective adolescent literacy programs, which they divide into two categories—instructional improvements and infrastructure improvements. The three school-level structures we discuss next—(1) teacher teams, (2) teacher leadership, and (3) a comprehensive and coordinated literacy program—are identified as essential infrastructure improvements, along with extended time for literacy, professional development, and ongoing summative assessment of students and programs.

Teacher teams

Interdisciplinary teacher teams are supportive school structures because they ensure coordinated instruction and planning for all grade levels and content areas. When such teams are in place, teachers meet regularly to discuss the learning needs of students they have in common and to align instruction across content areas. The teams provide opportunities for language arts teachers to better support content-area teachers, and they create more consistent instruction by reinforcing reading and writing skills, such as note taking and comprehension strategies, in all content areas.

This is especially important in middle and high school because students in these grades have several teachers during discrete blocks of time devoted to different subjects. Too often in today's schools, one teacher has no idea what another is teaching; this is particularly true in high schools. Teacher teams can prevent a loss of consistency in literacy instruction or reestablish coordinated instruction once it is lost. In addition, teacher teams promote collegiality, which enhances communication and information sharing about areas in which students might need additional support and heightens the likelihood that no child will slip through the cracks.

Teacher leadership

Teacher leadership is a supportive structure because teacher leadership teams are responsible for clarifying the decision-making process and communicating decisions and actions to the rest of the staff. Teachers play a critical role in ensuring the success of curricular reform, and their involvement is all the more crucial if a principal or other administrator has not assumed the instructional leadership role. Of course, for any curricular or instructional reform to succeed, it needs a principal's clear commitment and enthusiasm. When teacher leadership teams are in place within a school, principals are less removed from classroom instructional concerns. By regularly participating in scheduled meetings of their teacher leadership teams, principals hear input that team members have solicited from the rest of the staff. Therefore they are more likely to know how students' needs differ and to understand how some struggle with reading and writing. In addition, a principal who is a true instructional leader attends professional development sessions along with teachers in order to obtain the same knowledge and skills and to understand how best to organize and coordinate changes in the school's literacy program. Such training provides principals with the proper foundation to make decisions that alter structural elements, such as class schedules and teacher planning periods, and to ensure opportunities for collaborative data analysis, collaborative examination of student work, action research, or similar programs that support literacy efforts and student learning.

A comprehensive and coordinated literacy program

A well-designed literacy program goes beyond teacher teams and includes other school personnel—such as librarians, reading specialists, literacy coaches, and resource room teachers—in truly comprehensive teams. An effective literacy program recognizes that creating fluent and proficient readers and writers is a very complex task and requires consistent and coordinated implementation of several unique elements—from direct, explicit comprehension instruction to intensive writing to ongoing summative assessment of students and programs in all classrooms. Because the literacy needs of adolescents are so diverse, the intensity and nature of instruction in a comprehensive and coordinated literacy program—as well as one in which teachers are involved—varies substantially.

Biancarosa and Snow (2006) call for funders, researchers, policymakers, administrators, teachers, parents, and students to join forces as common stakeholders in the improvement of adolescent literacy. In addition, they call on secondary schools to recognize adolescents' varying needs and develop schoolwide comprehensive programs that will successfully address those needs. Whereas some students need their content-area teachers to make only modest accommodations or adjustments, other students need learning strategies, explicit strategy instruction, or even instruction in basic literacy skills embedded within content-area material. Alternatively, entire schools may need to follow in the footsteps of San Diego's Hoover High School and implement a content-area Sustained Silent Reading (SSR) program.

One of the lowest-performing high schools in the state in 1999, Hoover embraced SSR as part of a larger schoolwide improvement effort that included professional development with literacy strategies; a focus on standards; block scheduling; administrative accountability; and a variety of writing classes, including a required class for freshman. Hoover's approach to SSR meant all students and most staff members stopped to read at designated times, a strategy that required buy-in from the entire staff and a ready supply of books (Strickland & Alvermann, 2004). After five years, reading achievement increased by an average of 2.4 years, and the school demonstrated the city's most significant gain on the state accountability test (Lent, 2009).

Many factors influence a school's decisions about literacy instruction. One thing teachers can do to better understand their school's approach to literacy development is to meet with other teachers to analyze and discuss the school's literacy environment. This might mean collecting and sharing writing rubrics and writing samples and then examining them in light of what the school defines as "good writing." It could also simply be asking, reflecting on, and actively discussing questions such as the following:

- What is working about our literacy program?
- Do others agree with us?

- What can we improve?
- What do we need to learn more about?

A comprehensive and coordinated literacy program must include initiating and augmenting collaborations with external organizations and the local community to provide broad-based interactions and greater support for all students. These collaborations further secure student motivation by providing them with a sense of consistency between what they experience in and out of school (Biancarosa & Snow, 2006).

Going Beyond Professional Development

Brozo and Fisher (2010) write that research allows us to know, with certainty, that teachers must participate in comprehensive staff development to significantly improve adolescents' literacy skills (e.g., Sturtevant et al., 2006). Nevertheless, many middle and high school teachers have not been adequately trained in the current theories of content literacy, and they are unable to make disciplinary knowledge accessible to all of their students because they lack the skills to do so. The following five principles should guide district-level leaders' decisions about professional development aimed at nurturing adolescents' content-area reading skills.

1. **Offer teachers a manageable number of new strategies.** Having a relatively small set of strategies allows teachers to build their expertise. When a district focuses its professional development efforts on ensuring teachers can effectively implement a few strong strategies, teachers and students alike are more likely to experience success, which, in turn, motivates them to want to do and learn more. Who isn't encouraged by "quick wins"?

2. **Move from workshop to classroom.** Team teaching and in-class modeling build teacher comfort and confidence. In addition to quick wins, districts should keep an eye on more distant goals, which requires an investment in sustained, job-embedded, and ongoing professional development.

3. **Establish forums for teacher empowerment.** Teacher focus groups or committees also are forums for brainstorming new ideas and approaches. Districts should encourage school-level teacher forums as a source for innovation and a way to better address the needs of students within a particular district's surrounding community.

4. **Vary the formats used in staff development.** Flexibility in formats, whether one-on-one or mini-coaching clinics, provides teachers with options and opportunities to share. For example, districts might explore purposeful learning communities, online learning groups, or regional consortia as ways to provide choice and more flexible professional development opportunities.

5. **Start with those teachers who are most eager, and then spread the learning.** Enthusiasm is contagious, and those teachers who are early adopters of literacy reform efforts deserve recognition. Districts would be wise to recognize, support, and tap the excitement of those educators who build on successes.

Although providing high-quality professional development is a significant responsibility for districts, district leaders also play a considerable role in raising literacy expectations across grades and curricula by taking steps to help all educators understand real-world demands and the importance of promoting literacy rooted in academic disciplines.

For example, in Tennessee's Hamilton County Public Schools, the district superintendent led an effort to raise curricular requirements. The Public Education Fund (PEF) in Chattanooga and the Chattanooga Area Chamber of Commerce strongly supported the initiative. To make the case for more rigorous standards, district leaders, the PEF, and the Chattanooga Area Chamber of Commerce conducted surveys of local employment requirements. The surveys revealed a shrinking pool of local jobs that required only a high school diploma and substantiated the need to increase student achievement (National Governors Association Center for Best Practices, 2005).

Districts can also develop their own literacy plans, which can be extensions of schoolwide improvement plans that include an explicit focus on literacy. Alternatively, schools and districts can use the same literacy plan template, and school and district leaders can attend the same training on how to develop a literacy plan. It is imperative that there is agreement on how to provide all students with reading comprehension instruction and embed literacy instruction in content-area classes. District-level plans should also

- Address ways to support students in meeting state standards.

- Be based on real-time school data.

- Draw on research-based teachers' practices and methods for teaching adolescents.

- Differentiate between instructional approaches (e.g., curricula, pedagogy, materials) and structural approaches (e.g., time, facilities, teachers' assignments).

- Detail ways to reach and support students who struggle with reading and writing.

- Identify training and other technical assistance resources that can help teachers, principals, and district administrators analyze performance data and use data to inform planning, practice, and professional development (National Governors Association Center for Best Practices, 2005).

A Final Thought On Creating Literacy-Rich Environments

Today, adolescent literacy is considered a hot topic in education, and there is a growing body of research to guide decisions at the classroom, school, and district levels. Even so, it is hard to shake the feeling that something has long been awry and that change is long overdue. Some even call it a case of neglect (Heller, n.d.). Perhaps it has just been too easy to assume that children are learning to read in the early grades, but we now know that reading achievement is not finite—children don't attain proficiency and "hold" at an "acceptable" reading level for a lifetime; there is no ceiling for reading proficiency. Instead, children use language in various ways, as needed, throughout their lives and throughout their K–12 schooling. In truth, we should be aiming to create more than literacy-rich learning environments; we should be creating a literacy-rich world.

PART

II

Reading Strategies

Let's Get Started

Welcome to the strategies section of *Teaching Reading in the Content Areas*. Here in the 3rd edition, we have combined many tried and true strategies from previous editions with those from the mathematics, science, and social studies supplements. In addition, we've added some favorite strategies that emphasize rich discourse, writing, and collaboration—all of which are hallmarks of effective teaching and learning.

As is evident in this section, we think it is critically important for teachers to model every new strategy they introduce in the classroom. Regardless of your content area, we encourage you to use think alouds (Strategy 35). It's been our experience that many teachers and coaches view this particular strategy as the single most important one they use. Moreover, when we are in the field working with teachers and professional staff developers, we see over and over again that without explicit teacher modeling, students too often do not understand the essence of a particular reading or learning strategy.

We also want to remind you that new strategies are examples of procedural knowledge, which helps build automaticity and allows students to retrieve and use the facts, generalizations, and principles they have learned (Marzano & Brown, 2009). Research tells us that when building procedural knowledge, students must practice the relevant skills about 20–24 times before they really "get it." Therefore, don't give up if your students fail to understand or recognize the value of a strategy the first time it is used. Of course, many of these strategies enhance vocabulary development, and we encourage you to use the direct instruction five-step approach for the critical concept words and content you are teaching.

Direct Instruction Six-Step Approach for Vocabulary Development

Step 1: Provide a description, explanation, or example of the new term.

Step 2: Ask students to restate the description, explanation, or example in their own terms.

Step 3: Ask students to construct a picture, symbol, or graphic representing the term.

Step 4: Engage students periodically in activities that help them add to their knowledge of the terms in their notebooks.

Step 5: Periodically ask students to discuss the terms with one another.

Step 6: Involve students periodically in games that allow them to play with terms.

As You Begin

Neuroscience research has revealed that learning literally changes the brain by repeatedly organizing and reorganizing neurons, which actually changes the physical structure of the brain (Keil, Schmidt, Löwel, & Kaschube, 2010; Medina, 2008). We also know that different parts of the brain may be ready to learn at different times and that during the learning process, nerve cells in the brain become more powerful and efficient (Wang, Conner, Rickert, & Tuszynski, 2011). These and similar findings suggest that the brain is a dynamic organ, shaped to a great extent by experience and by what a living being does (Bransford et al., 2004). Thus, we encourage you to use the strategies in this section with an understanding of what is happening in your students' brains.

The new knowledge we have gleaned from neuroscience, cognitive science, and developmental science applies to all learners, including teachers. Throughout this book, we ask you to intentionally integrate literacy into all of your instruction. We know that for this to happen successfully, you (and your brain) need to have your questions answered; be able to decide for yourself when, how, and why to integrate literacy with your content; be able to try new strategies and receive feedback; and be part of an actively supportive learning community. These four aspects of professional development—learner-centered, knowledge-centered, assessment-centered, and community-centered—will help produce the best teaching possible (Bransford et al., 2004).

We also have emphasized that teaching and learning vary from discipline to discipline. In other words, the evidence that supports a historical claim is different from evidence that proves a mathematical theorem or scientific theory. As an expert in your field, you are the person who best knows the structures of your discipline. Together with your pedagogical knowledge, you also know the best ways to use—and teach students to use—the strategies in this section. Recent research demonstrates that instruction is trending toward teaching fewer strategies and that students benefit from learning to combine those strategies (Block & Parris, 2008; Shanahan & Shanahan, 2008).

The following is a list of nine strategies that have been studied since 2000 and are deemed to be highly successful by the National Reading Panel. Students should be taught to

1. Predict by examining the features, or reader aids, present throughout the text.

2. Monitor through the use of metacomprehension.

3. Question when meaning is unclear.

4. Construct images and mental pictures while reading.

5. Use look-backs, rereads, and fix-it strategies.

6. Infer quickly, connecting ideas to known information and previous experiences.

7. Find main ideas, summarize, and draw conclusions.

8. Evaluate by noting aspects of story grammar and structure.

9. Synthesize all noticeable aspects of a text, from reader aids to conclusions. (Block & Parris, 2008)

For ease of use, we've arranged the strategies in this section alphabetically. At the beginning of each strategy is a description box , like the one below, that indicates the strategy's many uses.

```
____ Narrative Text
____ Informational
     Text
____ Prereading
____ During Reading
____ After Reading
____ Writing to Learn
____ Reflection
____ Discussion
____ Vocabulary
     Development
```

Types of Text

- Narrative Text: stories, fiction books, poems, biographies, historical narratives

- Informational Text: nonfiction books, newspaper articles, Internet research articles, editorials, textbooks, advertisements

Potential Uses

- Prereading: The strategy may be used to activate prior knowledge before students begin reading and to provide an incentive to read.

- During Reading: The strategy may be used as students are reading to assist them in monitoring their comprehension.

- After Reading: The strategy may be used after students have completed the reading to assist them in summarizing their comprehension.

- Writing to Learn: The strategy may be used to introduce writing tasks (assigned after reading without explicit instruction in writing skills) and help students enhance their learning of content material.

- Reflection: The strategy may be used during and after reading to help students think about their learning, experience, and skills—and areas that need improvement.

- Discussion: The strategy may be used to help students reflect upon their newly acquired knowledge, process what they are learning by talking with and actively listening to their peers, and develop a common understanding about what they have read.

- Vocabulary Development: The strategy may be used to increase students' academic vocabulary before, during, and after reading to increase comprehension.

1. Academic Conversation

X Narrative Text
X Informational Text
___ Prereading
___ During Reading
X After Reading
___ Writing to Learn
X Reflection
X Discussion
___ Vocabulary Development

What is it?

This strategy includes a set of conversational skills teachers can model and teach to help all students engage in extended meaningful conversation about narrative or informational texts (Zwiers & Crawford, 2009). Although these skills were designed specifically for ELLs who need scaffolding to use the skills effectively, they are pertinent to and necessary for all students. The skills include the following:

- Initiating a worthwhile topic
- Elaborating and clarifying
- Supporting one's ideas
- Building on or challenging another's ideas
- Applying ideas to life
- Paraphrasing/Summarizing

How do I use it?

1. Make a set of six visual reminder cue cards, so you can show students what they will make for themselves. Note cards work fine as cue cards. Then have students make a similar set.

   - On one side of each card, students should draw the symbol for one of the conversation features and label the feature.
   - On the other side of each card, have students write two headings: "Prompts for Using the Feature" and "Prompts for Responding."
   - Beneath each heading, write or have students write the prompts from the template.

2. Have students memorize one "Prompt for Using the Feature." For example, students can begin by memorizing "Why do you think the author wrote this?"

3. Teach the suggested hand motions for each feature. Model and use the hand motions consistently to reduce dependence on the cue cards.

4. Model how to use the cards and prompts repeatedly to increase fluency and familiarity with the strategy.

FIGURE S1.1 ⇢   Academic Conversation Features

Features of Conversations (with symbols and hand motions)	Prompts for Using the Feature	Prompts for Responding
1. Come up with a worthy topic (*put palm of hand up*)	• Why do you think the author wrote this? • What are some themes that emerged in. . . ?	• I think the author wrote it to teach us about. . . • One theme might be. . .
2. Elaborate and clarify (*pull hands apart*)	• Can you elaborate? • What do you mean by. . . ? • Can you tell me more about. . . ? • What makes you think that?	• I think it means that. . . • In other words. . .
3. Support ideas with examples (*put two palms up*)	• Can you give an example? • Can you show me where it says that? • Can you be more specific? • Are there any cases of that?	• For example. . . • In the text it said that. . . • One case showed that. . .
4. Build on the author's idea(s) or others' comments (*layer hands*)	• What do you think? • Can you add to this idea? • What might be other points of view?	• I would add that. . . • Then again, I think that. . . • I want to expand on your point about. . .
5. Apply/connect (*hook both hands together*)	• So how can we apply this idea to our lives? • What can we learn from this character/part/story? • If you were. . .	• In my life. . . • I think it can teach us. . . • If I were. . ., I would have. . .
6. Paraphrase and summarize (*cup both hands into a ball*)	• What have we discussed so far? • How should we summarize what we talked about?	• We can say that. . . • The main theme/point of the text seems to be. . .

Source: From "How to Start Academic Conversations," by J. Zwiers and M. Crawford, 2009, *Educational Leadership 66*(7), pp.70–73. Copyright 2009 by ASCD. Reprinted with permission.

FIGURE S1.2 ⟶   Modeling an Academic Conversation Example

---

1. Read a text selection, stopping from time to time to elicit students' comments and questions.

2. As students offer their responses, ask them to elaborate, using the appropriate hand motion.

3. Ask students to pair-share and tell their partners whether they agree or disagree with their ideas.

4. Model by saying, "I agree with [Juan's] interpretation because. . ."

5. Lead a short whole-class discussion to brainstorm possible themes for the text selection.

6. Have students choose the themes they think are most relevant to the text selection and then identify examples from the text that support those themes.

7. Conduct a minilesson in which you carry on a conversation with the whole class, using the cue cards as necessary.
   - a. Students: "Why do you think the author wrote this story?"
   - b. Teacher: "Perhaps she wrote it because. . ." (*pause*) "Now what might you ask me?"
   - c. Students: "Can you elaborate?"
   - d. Teacher elaborates with more details from the text.

8. Remind students of the prompts on their cards.

9. Pair students for a conversation.

10. Have partners take out their cards and quiz each other on the symbols and prompts before beginning.

11. Tell students to use their notes and discuss possible themes of the text selection.

12. Go around the room and monitor the conversations.

13. Have each pair write an "exit ticket" synopsis of the conversation they had and then present that synopsis to the class.

14. Reflect on the process and have students self-assess with a kid-friendly rubric, such as the following:

---

continued

FIGURE S1.2 →   Modeling an Academic Conversation Example (*continued*)

Conversation Skill	3: *I am practicing all of the skills.*	2: *I am getting better at some of the skills.*	1. *I need to practice the skills.*
Stay on topic	• I suggested a logical theme. • I stayed on topic the whole conversation. • I listened and built on the author's ideas and others' comments.	• I stayed on topic. • I tried building on others' comments.	• I came up with ideas that were not in the text. • I had a hard time staying on topic. • I have not tried building on others' comments yet.
Support ideas by explaining and showing examples from the text	• I prompted others to explain or give examples. • I gave explanations for my thinking and showed examples and details from the text.	• I gave explanations for my thinking. • I showed one example from the text.	• I had a difficult time explaining my thinking.
Make connections	• I could explain how this text connects to things in my life. • I could talk about what I learned from this text.	• I could explain how this text connects to things in my life.	• I could not explain how this text connects to things in my life.
Use appropriate conversation behaviors	• I actively listened to others. • I took turns speaking. • I paraphrased what others said.	• I took turns speaking. • I listened to others. • I don't know how to paraphrase yet.	• I think I talked too much. • I don't know how to paraphrase yet.

2. Anticipation Guide

X Narrative Text
X Informational Text
X Prereading
___ During Reading
X After Reading
___ Writing to Learn
___ Reflection
X Discussion
___ Vocabulary Development

What is it?

Anticipation guides are advance organizers that can be used to activate and assess students' prior knowledge, focus reading, and motivate reluctant readers by stimulating their interest in the topic (Dean, Hubbell, Pitler, & Stone, 2012). Because anticipation guides revolve around a text's most important concepts, students are prepared to focus on and pay attention to this information while reading. Students are motivated to read closely in order to search for evidence that supports their answers and predictions. Consequently, anticipation guides promote active reading and critical thinking and are especially useful in identifying any misperceptions students might have. This allows the teacher to correct these errors prior to reading.

How do I use it?

1. Identify the major concepts that you want students to learn from reading. Determine ways these concepts might support or challenge students' beliefs.

2. Create four to six statements that support or challenge the students' beliefs and experiences about the topic under study. The statements can address important points, major concepts, controversial ideas, or misconceptions.

3. Ask students to react to and formulate a response to each statement and be prepared to defend their opinions. Students can work in groups if the subject matter is fairly complex, or you can ask students to fill in their answers on their own.

4. Discuss each statement with students before they read the material. Ask one student from each side of the issue (for/against, agree/disagree) to explain and justify his or her response.

5. Have students read the selection with the purpose of finding evidence that supports or refutes their responses on the guide.

6. After students finish reading the selection, have them confirm their original responses, revise them, or decide what additional information is needed. Encourage students to rewrite any statement that was not true in a way that makes it true.

7. Lead a discussion about what students learned from the reading. Two discussion formats you might want to try are Chapter Discussion Protocol (Strategy 3) and Discussion Web (Strategy 10).

FIGURE S2.1 → Anticipation Guide for Science

Directions: In the *Me* column, place a check next to any statement with which you agree. As you read, place a check in the *Text* column next to statements that the text states are true. After reading, compare your original opinions with information contained in the text.

Me	Text	
_____	_____	1. Matter is made up of elements.
_____	_____	2. An element is made up of many different atoms.
_____	_____	3. An element is the same thing as a compound.
_____	_____	4. Most compounds are made of molecules.
_____	_____	5. Elements are represented by chemical symbols.
_____	_____	6. Molecules are represented by chemical formulas.

Source: From *Teaching Reading in Science: A Supplement to Teaching Reading in the Content Areas Teacher's Manual* (2nd ed.) (p. 73), by M. L. Barton and D. L. Jordan, 2001, Aurora, CO: McREL. Copyright 2001 by McREL. Reprinted with permission.

FIGURE S2.2 ⇢   Anticipation Guide for Social Studies

Directions: Respond to each statement twice—once before reading and once again after reading. Write *A* if you agree with a statement or *D* if you disagree with a statement.

Response Before Reading	Topic: Cold War	Response After Reading
	Stalin believed communism and capitalism could not exist peacefully.	
	Churchill called the division between Western Europe and communist Eastern Europe the "Iron Curtain."	
	The U.S. policy of blocking communist expansion was called containment.	
	The Berlin Airlift was the response by the United States and Great Britain to the Soviet blockade of West Berlin.	
	The Warsaw Pact was a worldwide alliance of communist nations.	
	Chinese intervention in the Korean War kept North Korea from being defeated by UN troops.	
	The policy of containment was successful in stopping the spread of communism.	
	The so-called domino theory proved to be false.	
	The Cuban Missile Crisis was an exercise in brinkmanship.	
	The failure of U.S. policy in Vietnam led to a change of policy called détente.	
	The Cold War ended when communism collapsed in Eastern Europe.	
	The Cold War was only between the United States and the Soviet Union.	
	The Cold War did not impact domestic affairs in the United States.	

Source: From *Teaching Reading In Social Studies: A Supplement To Teaching Reading in the Content Areas Teacher's Manual* (2nd ed.) (p. 114), by J. K. Doty, G. N. Cameron, and M. L. Barton, 2003, Aurora, CO: McREL. Copyright 2003 by McREL. Adapted with permission.

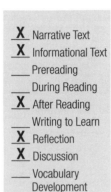

X Narrative Text
X Informational Text
___ Prereading
___ During Reading
X After Reading
___ Writing to Learn
X Reflection
X Discussion
___ Vocabulary Development

3. Chapter Discussion Protocol

What is it?

Using a protocol to discuss the books, chapters, or articles being studied helps ensure that students tap into the power of discussing their own and listening to other's ideas. Discussion protocols build students' discourse skills. The protocol helps students identify what is significant to themselves, to the group, and to the class as a whole. It also requires students to explore ways in which the reading has influenced their thinking about the topic and how the reading might guide the group's actions related to the topic.

How do I use it?

Day One

1. Before students try this strategy on their own with a new text, demonstrate the protocol with a familiar text they have already read. Use a volunteer demonstration group in a "fish bowl" set-up.

2. As the class observes, guide a group of five students through the protocol, as outlined in Figure S3.1.

3. After this "fish bowl" activity, have the class debrief the protocol and discuss how it worked.

4. Have students read the new text either in class or as homework. Assign specific text-coding symbols (Strategy 35) to use as they read.

Day Two

1. Organize the class into discussion groups of five students each.

2. Assign a facilitator and timekeeper for each group to guide discussion.

3. Review all of the steps from the chapter discussion protocol before students begin the activity.

4. Circulate around the room as students discuss and work on the protocol. Monitor the discussions and provide feedback as necessary.

5. Finally, debrief the protocol with the entire class.

FIGURE S3.1 ⇢   Chapter Discussion Protocol

1. Have students read the following questions and record their thoughts (*five minutes*):

   a. In your opinion, which ideas in the text (chapter/article/book) are most significant?
   b. What, if anything, in the text makes you reconsider ideas about the topic? Why?
   c. What, if anything, in the text reinforces your ideas about the topic? Why?

2. Have students use the following format to discuss the above questions in small groups:

   a. Conduct a "whip around" discussion, in which each person has one minute to answer the first question. (The timekeeper needs to keep everyone on track.)
   b. After everyone has had an opportunity to respond, the group spends two minutes in open discussion of the question. (*With a five-person group, the entire round should take seven minutes.*)
   c. Move to the next question and repeat the process.

3. Have students record the general consensus about one of the following questions (*five minutes*):

   a. What influenced the group's thinking about the topic in the text?
   b. What actions might the group want to take as a result of the information in the text?

4. Have each group present its thoughts to the class (*five to ten minutes*).

Source: From *Chapter Protocol. Success in Sight: Module 3.2* (p. 20), by C. Dean and D. Parsley, 2008, Denver, CO: McREL. Copyright 2008 by McREL. Adapted with permission.

X Narrative Text
X Informational Text
___ Prereading
___ During Reading
X After Reading
X Writing to Learn
___ Reflection
X Discussion
___ Vocabulary Development

4. Character/Historical Figure Comparison Organizer

What is it?

The Character/Historical Figure Comparison Organizer is a strategy for students to identify similarities and differences among characters in narrative text or among individuals who have made significant contributions to mathematics, science, music, art, technology, and history in informational text. Graphic representation of similarities and differences enhances students' understanding of content (Dean et al., 2012). For many students, the process of comparing is not easy or intuitive; therefore, teachers should introduce the process by modeling and thinking aloud.

How do I use it?

1. Determine which characteristics students will be comparing about the characters or historical figures. For example, if Albert Einstein and Isaac Newton are to be compared, some characteristics might be when they lived and their countries of origin, fields of expertise, and impact on science. In narrative texts, two characters in one text or between two texts might be compared with regard to their personalities, problems, appearances, and impact on the primary conflict in the story or book.

2. Model how to use the organizer by using a think aloud (Strategy 35).

3. Identify two characters or historical figures from texts the class is currently reading, and ask students to complete the comparison organizer, either individually or in pairs.

4. Have students share their completed comparison organizers in small groups. Encourage students to add to their organizers as a result of the group discussion.

FIGURE S4.1 → Character/Historical Figure Comparison Organizer

Character/Historical Figure 1:	Character/Historical Figure 2:
Text:	*Text:*
Characteristic #1	
Similarities:	*Differences:*
Characteristic #2	
Similarities:	*Differences:*
Characteristic #3	
Similarities:	*Differences:*
Characteristic #4	
Similarities:	*Differences:*

FIGURE S4.2 → Character Comparison Organizer Example for Narrative Text

Character 1: Charles Bingley	Character 2: Fitzwilliam Darcy
Book/Story: *Pride and Prejudice*	**Book/Story:** *Pride and Prejudice*
Where they live	
Similarities: Both live on grand estates in England—Darcy lives at Pemberley, and Bingley lives at Netherfield.	*Differences:* Bingley has just come into money and is renting Netherfield while he decides where he wants his estate to be. Darcy is from "old" money and inherited his estate.
Their personalities	
Similarities: They like each other very much and are best friends. Both men are young, single, and wealthy. Both men are honest and trustworthy. Both men are considered to be gentlemen.	*Differences:* Bingley is an extrovert—lively and friendly. He is trusting and easily persuaded by Darcy. He is not as concerned with class differences as Darcy is. He is indecisive. Darcy is proud and concerned with class differences. He feels superior to the local people. He is quick to judge people. He is decisive. He is not swayed by Bingley.
Their main problems	
Similarities: Neither man can determine if Jane Bennet really loves Bingley or is out to get a wealthy husband. Both men love a Bennet daughter, and the Bennets are not in the same social class.	*Differences:* Bingley loves Jane and sees her as she really is, but he is persuaded by Darcy to believe that she does not love him. At first, Darcy misjudges Elizabeth's character and treats her with disdain, leading Elizabeth to dislike him. He must come to see her accurately and then prove himself worthy of her love.
What they must do to solve their problems	
Similarities: Both men come to realize that Jane and Elizabeth are truly good people they love.	*Differences:* Bingley learns to believe in his initial judgment about Jane. Darcy has to overcome his mistaken judgment of both women.

5. Claim/Support Outline

What is it?

In the Common Core State Standards, there is new emphasis on students' ability to analyze and support a proposition or claim. Claim/support outlines help students learn to be critical readers and recognize different viewpoints, theories, hypotheses, facts, opinions, and debatable assertions made by authors (Buehl, 1995). In addition, such outlines provide a framework for analyzing the different types of evidence authors present to support their propositions. A claim/support outline can also be a guide for students' independent research. It provides students with a framework for examining expository texts and reference material for relevant information and arguments.

___	Narrative Text
X	Informational Text
___	Prereading
X	During Reading
X	After Reading
___	Writing to Learn
___	Reflection
X	Discussion
___	Vocabulary Development

How do I use it?

1. Discuss the difference between facts and opinions by helping students brainstorm definitions and examples for each. For example, "The Colorado Rockies' home park is named Coors Field" is a factual statement, whereas "The Colorado Rockies is a great baseball team" is an opinion that may or may not be supported by facts.

2. Introduce and define the word *claim*, which is a statement about the subject of an argument. Claims (or propositions) can be argued. Provide students with possible claims, such as "today's movies are too violent"; "the school playground needs new playground equipment"; or "gun control prevents crime." Divide students into collaborative groups and have each group generate a list of arguments that might be used to support one of these claims.

3. Help the class categorize types of arguments that could be used to support various claims. Introduce a blank claim/support outline, and model how support for a claim could be classified as any of the following: facts, statistics, examples, expert authority, logic, or reasoning.

4. Assign a text passage that follows a claim/support structure, and have students complete a claim/support outline as they analyze the author's arguments. Have students work in pairs to identify the claim and point out the text clues that helped them identify that claim.

5. In collaborative groups, have students use their outlines to categorize the arguments that support the claim. Then have groups share their organizers with the rest of the class.

6. As students become confident with this strategy, ask them to use claim/support outlines with a variety of texts that could include support for opposing claims (e.g., controversial topics and current events).

FIGURE S5.1 ⟶ Claim/Support Outline

Reading assignment:
Topic:
Claim:

Support
Facts
Statistics
Examples
Expert Authority
Logic and Reasoning

Source: From *Classroom Strategies for Interactive Learning* (2nd ed.), by D. Buehl, 2001, Newark, DE: International Reading Association. Copyright 2001 by the International Reading Association. Adapted with permission.

FIGURE S5.2 ⟶ Claim/Support Outline Example

Reading assignment: "Facts about Global Warming"
Topic: Global warming
Claim: Global warming is real and not a hoax.

Support

Facts

- The average global temperature is rising rapidly.
- Plants and oceans absorb carbon dioxide.
- Oceans are not absorbing as much carbon dioxide as they used to.
- Rain forests, which supply breathable air, are being destroyed.
- Industrialization, deforestation, and pollution have increased greenhouse gases that trap heat near Earth's surface.

Statistics

- Average temperatures have increased 1.4 degrees Fahrenheit since 1880.
- Carbon dioxide emissions have increased by 40 percent during the past few decades.

Examples

- Arctic ice is rapidly disappearing.
- Montana's Glacier National Park has 27 glaciers today, versus 150 glaciers in 1910.
- Much of the world's population is located in coastal cities vulnerable to rising sea levels. In the United States, Louisiana and Florida are especially at risk.

Expert Authority

- The United Nations' Intergovernmental Panel on Climate Change (IPCC) reports that 11 of the past 12 years were among the dozen warmest since 1850.
- In 2007, the Intergovernmental Panel on Climate Change warned that global warming could lead to large-scale food and water shortages and have catastrophic effects on wildlife.

Logic and Reasoning

- Humans have caused global warming.
- There is data to support the claim that global warming is real and not a hoax.
- Global warming will have devastating effects on animals, plants, and humans—the atmosphere will become noxious, the oceans will rise and destroy coastal cities, deforestation will cause droughts.

_____ Narrative Text
X Informational Text
_____ Prereading
_____ During Reading
X After Reading
X Writing to Learn
_____ Reflection
_____ Discussion
X Vocabulary Development

6. Comparison Matrix

What is it?

The Comparison Matrix is a graphic organizer used for teaching students how to compare two or more concepts or events after reading a text for the first time. As noted in Strategy 5, using graphic organizers to assist in determining similarities and differences enhances student understanding of text. The Comparison Matrix is a more detailed approach to comparisons than the commonly used Venn Diagram (see Figure S12.2). This approach to comparison involves students in finding the concepts or events to be compared and also in developing which characteristics they will compare. Then they describe the similarities and differences between or among concepts/events for each characteristic.

How do I use it?

1. Before students use this strategy on their own, model how to use it. Identify two concepts or events to be compared and, with students following along, write them into the appropriate boxes on the graphic organizer.

2. Brainstorm and list possible characteristics for comparison. Have students add those characteristics to their graphic organizers.

3. Using a think aloud approach (Strategy 35), identify similarities and differences for the first characteristic, and include them on the matrix. Have students follow along and continue to fill out their graphic organizers.

4. Repeat the process for the second characteristic on the matrix.

5. Have students work independently or in small groups to identify similarities and differences for the remaining characteristics.

6. As students become comfortable comparing two items, have them set up their matrices to compare three concepts or events as they reread a text.

FIGURE S6.1 → Comparison Matrix Example for Two Events

Characteristics	Items to be Compared		Comparisons
	Lewis and Clark Expedition	*Pike's 1806 Arkansas River Expedition*	
1. Who commissioned the expedition?	Thomas Jefferson	General James Wilkinson	*Similarities:* As president, Jefferson had an interest in the findings of both expeditions.
			Differences: The expeditions were commissioned by different people in different roles.
2. Purpose of the expedition	To find a northwest passage; to report on western geography, climate, and plants.	To explore the Arkansas and Red Rivers; to obtain information about Spanish territory; and to improve relations with American Indians.	*Similarities:* Both expeditions helped to establish claim to U.S. territories, provided geographic information, and established relations with American Indians.
			Differences: (At this point, have students begin to take over and fill in the matrix on their own or with partners.)
3. Areas explored			*Similarities:*
			Differences:
4. Outcomes of the expedition			*Similarities:*
			Differences:

Source: From *A Participant's Manual for Classroom Instruction That Works (Research into Practice Series)* (p. 214), by C. B. Dean, S. Quackenboss, and J. K. Doty, 2005, Denver, CO: McREL. Copyright 2005 by McREL. Adapted with permission.

FIGURE S6.2 → Comparison Matrix Template for Three Concepts or Events

Characteristics	Items to be Compared			Comparisons
	#1	#2	#3	
1.				*Similarities:*
				Differences:
2.				*Similarities:*
				Differences:
3.				*Similarities:*
				Differences:
4.				*Similarities:*
				Differences:

Source: From *Classroom Instruction That Works: Research-Based Strategies for Increasing Student Achievement* (p. 19), R. J. Marzano, D. J. Pickering, & J. E. Pollock, 2001, Alexandria, VA: ASCD. Copyright 2001 by McREL. Adapted with permission.

7. Concept Circles

What is it?

Concept Circles is a versatile categorization strategy for students to study words or concepts critically and relate them conceptually to one another (Vacca & Vacca, 1999). With a concept circle, students identify common attributes that exist among several terms. Use this as a prereading activity to introduce new vocabulary concepts or as an activity intended to reinforce and extend knowledge of a concept after reading.

___	Narrative Text
X	Informational Text
X	Prereading
___	During Reading
X	After Reading
___	Writing to Learn
___	Reflection
___	Discussion
X	Vocabulary Development

How do I use it?

1. Choose common attributes or relationships among several terms.

2. Draw a circle divided into three to six equal sections, and write a term (word or phrase) into each section.

3. Have students identify the common attributes or name the relationship that exists among the terms in all sections of the circle.

Modification #1: Leave a section of the circle blank, and direct students to identify the concept shared by all of the given terms and then fill in the blank section with an appropriate term.

Modification #2: Choose a term for one section of the circle that does not fit—in other words, it is not an example of the concept exemplified by all of the other terms. Challenge students to identify the term that does not belong and identify the concept that relates the other terms.

FIGURE S7.1 → Concept Circle Template

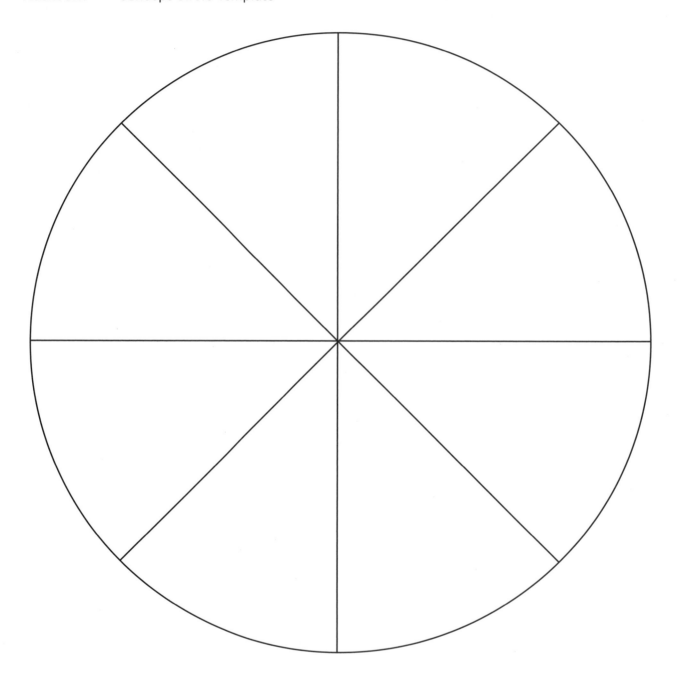

FIGURE S7.2 → Concept Circle Example for Conic Sections

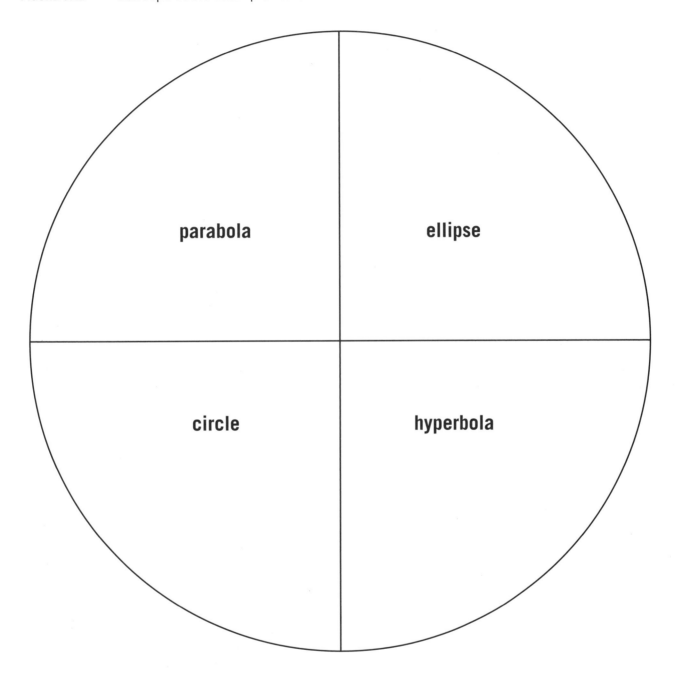

FIGURE S7.3 →   Concept Circle Example for Linear Equations

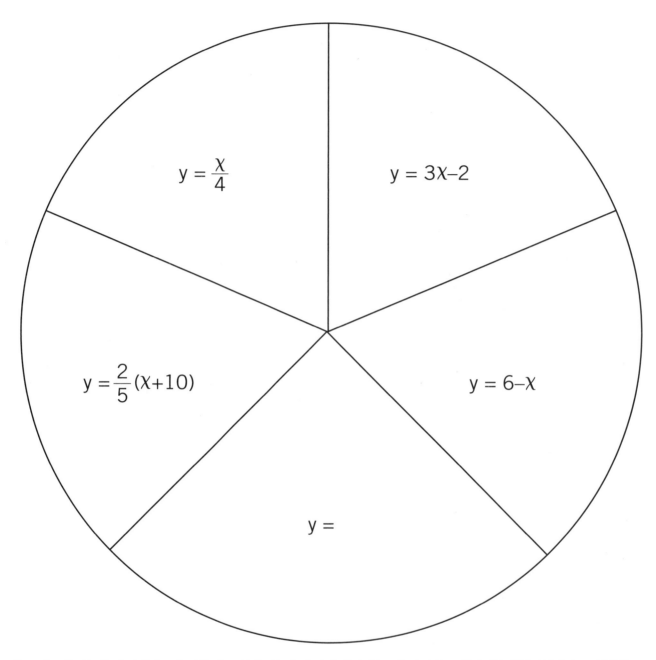

8. Concept Definition Map

X Narrative Text
X Informational Text
X Prereading
X During Reading
X After Reading
___ Writing to Learn
___ Reflection
___ Discussion
X Vocabulary Development

What is it?

Concept definition mapping is a strategy for teaching students the meaning of key concepts in their readings (Schwartz, 1988). Concept definition maps are graphic organizers that help students understand the essential attributes, qualities, and characteristics of a concept or word's meaning. This strategy can be used before, during, and after reading to enhance students' comprehension of the text. Students must describe the concept and cite examples of it; examples may come from the text. Teachers can encourage students to find pictures or create nonlinguistic representations for their maps. Nonlinguistic representations provide students with images to help them store information in memory (Dean et al., 2012). Looking up a concept's definition in the dictionary, for example, is not nearly as effective as this process, which gives students a more thorough understanding of what the concept means, includes, and implies. The mapping process also aids recall in that it helps students organize information into a conceptual framework in their brains (Ibid.).

How do I use it?

1. Display an example of a concept definition map.

2. Discuss the following questions that an adequate definition should answer:

   • What is it? What broader category or classification of things does it fit into?

   • What is it like? What are its essential characteristics? What qualities does it possess that make it different from other things in the same category?

   • What are some examples of it?

3. Model how to use the map by selecting a familiar vocabulary term or concept from a previous unit of study and mapping its features. Using pictures to match characteristics and examples is also helpful.

4. Select another familiar term and ask students to volunteer information for a map.

5. Have students work in pairs to complete a map for a concept in the current unit of study. Allow students to use their text, but encourage them to focus on their own experience and background knowledge as well.

6. After students complete their maps, have them use the information to write a complete definition or summary of the concept.

7. Encourage students to refine and add to their maps during the unit of study as they read and learn more information, additional characteristics, and further examples.

FIGURE S8.1 → Concept Definition Map

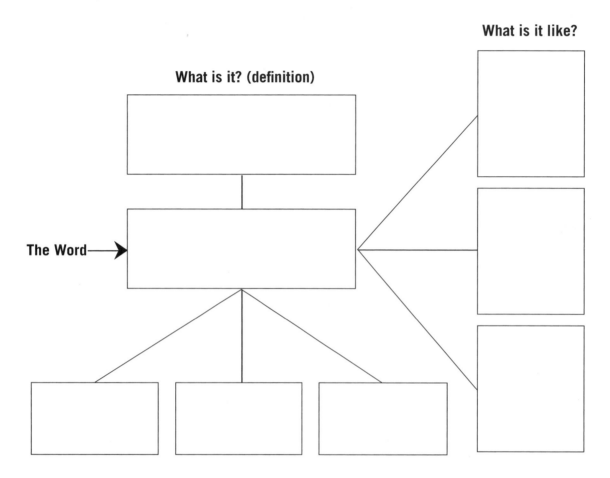

What is it? (definition)

What is it like?

The Word →

What are some examples?

FIGURE S8.2 →   Concept Definition Map Example

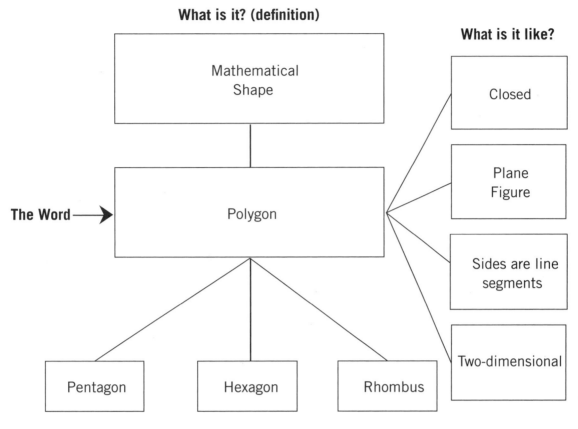

What is it? (definition)

Mathematical Shape

What is it like?

Closed

Plane Figure

Sides are line segments

Two-dimensional

The Word ———▶   Polygon

Pentagon

Hexagon

Rhombus

What are some examples?

Narrative Text
X Informational Text
X Prereading
During Reading
X After Reading
X Writing to Learn
X Reflection
Discussion
Vocabulary Development

9. Directed Reading/Thinking Activity

What is it?

The Directed Reading/Thinking Activity (DR/TA) is similar to the commonly used KWL graphic organizer in both concept and versatility (Stauffer, 1969). As you introduce a new reading, "there is no need to be subtle or ambiguous with students about what you want them to learn" (Dean et al., 2012. p. 62). The DR/TA strategy directs students to be active readers by providing questions that activate their prior knowledge. In addition, the strategy directs students to make predictions and check the accuracy of their predictions. When students complete the DR/TA organizer, they will discuss with one another their predictions and what they learned as a result of the process.

How do I use it?

1. Have students preview the text selection, noting the title and any subheadings, pictures, or graphic aids. From this preview, students will focus on the topic.

2. Ask students to complete the first two sections of the DR/TA form. They should write down what they know and what they think they know about the subject of the selection.

3. Have students discuss what they wrote with partners or in small groups. Discussing the first two sections can help reveal misperceptions students might have about the topic.

4. Ask students to formulate predictions or questions about what they think they will learn from reading the text. They should write these ideas in the third section of the organizer. This process sets the purpose for reading.

5. After students read the text selection, have them revisit each of their predictions or questions. They should then confirm, revise, or reject those ideas, based on what they read.

6. Have students complete the organizer by writing the takeaway knowledge they gleaned from the text in the fourth section. They can also include material they thought the text would address but didn't. Discussing this material with classmates helps reinforce understanding of the material.

FIGURE S9.1 ⟶   Directed Reading/Thinking Activity

Topic
What I know I know:
What I think I know:
What I think I'll learn:
What I know I learned:

FIGURE S9.2 →   Directed Reading/Thinking Activity Example

<table>
<tr><td colspan="3">Flowering Plants and Reproduction</td></tr>
<tr><td colspan="3">

What I know I know:

Flowers have these parts:

sepals	ovary	filament
petals	stigma	pistil
anther		

</td></tr>
<tr><td colspan="3">

What I think I know:

Flower structure and functions:

       sepal—base of flower

       petals—attract insects

       anther & filament—male reproductive part

       ovary & stigma—female reproductive part

       pollen grains—male reproductive cell

       ovule—female reproductive cell

</td></tr>
<tr><td colspan="3">

What I think I'll learn:

What is involved in the germination process?

What kinds of plants reproduce without seeds?

Why are some people allergic to pollen?

What makes a plant grow?

What is the role of plant hormones?

What is the difference between annual, biennial, and perennial?

</td></tr>
<tr><td colspan="3">

What I know I learned:

Germination: Inside a seed is an embryo, which is an immature plant that has all the parts of an adult plant. The first sign of germination from a seed is the absorption of water by the embryo. Water absorption activates an enzyme, respiration increases, and plant cells are duplicated. When the embryo becomes too large, the seed coat opens and the growing plant begins to emerge. The root emerges first, and it will anchor the seed. The root allows the embryo to absorb water and nutrients from the soil so it can grow.

</td></tr>
</table>

Source: From *Teaching Reading in Science: A Supplement to Teaching Reading in the Content Areas Teacher's Manual* (2nd ed.) (p. 79), by M. L. Barton and D. L. Jordan, 2001, Aurora, CO: McREL. Copyright 2001 by McREL. Adapted with permission.

10. Discussion Web

___	Narrative Text
X	Informational Text
X	Prereading
X	After Reading
___	During Reading
X	Writing to Learn
X	Reflection
X	Discussion
___	Vocabulary Development

What is it?

The Discussion Web strategy gives all students—not just verbally talented students—an opportunity to assume responsibility and share their ideas in discussion after reading a common text (Alvermann, 1991). Using the discussion web, students think about and write down the items from the text they want to share in the discussion and then share their ideas with discussion partners. This private "think time" promotes total class involvement in that everyone has time to write and think before the discussion, and it honors the wait time necessary to develop insightful thoughts. Student accountability is also included by having students share their thinking and writing with their partners before the discussion. Discussion webs incorporate all four areas of language arts—listening, speaking, reading, and writing—which science, history, and technical subject area teachers can easily adapt for their content areas.

How do I use it?

1. Select a text that can generate opposing viewpoints about a topic (e.g., global warming, tax increases).

2. Prepare students for reading by introducing new vocabulary words and activating their background knowledge with an anticipation guide (see Strategy 2).

3. Introduce the discussion web with the relevant discussion question in the central section.

4. Model how to construct support for both viewpoints by citing specific reasons and including them in the appropriate columns of the graphic organizer.

5. Have students read the text and think about and write their own contributions to each column, which they should then add to the graphic organizer.

6. Have partners share their ideas and continue to discuss and record reasons for each viewpoint.

7. Pair sets of partners, and ask each group of four students to compare the information in their graphic organizers. Once they have compared notes and added new ideas to their webs, they should form a conclusion to share with the class. This statement will be included at the bottom of the web.

8. Call on a designated spokesperson from each group to report out as part of the whole-class discussion. After each group has an opportunity to share its conclusion, encourage further discussion by the entire class. Monitor the conversation for effective discussion skills (see Strategy 1).

9. Have students use a learning log (Strategy 16) to reflect on the specific discussion skills they used throughout the activity and identify which areas might still need improvement.

FIGURE S10.1 → Discussion Web

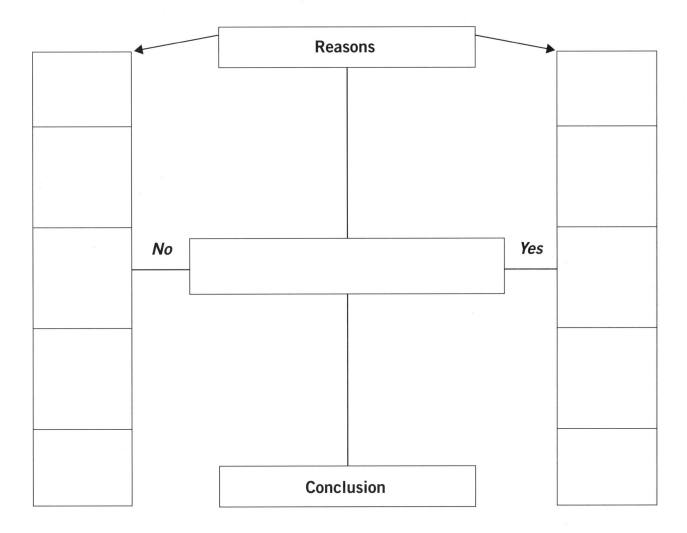

FIGURE S10.2 → Discussion Web Example

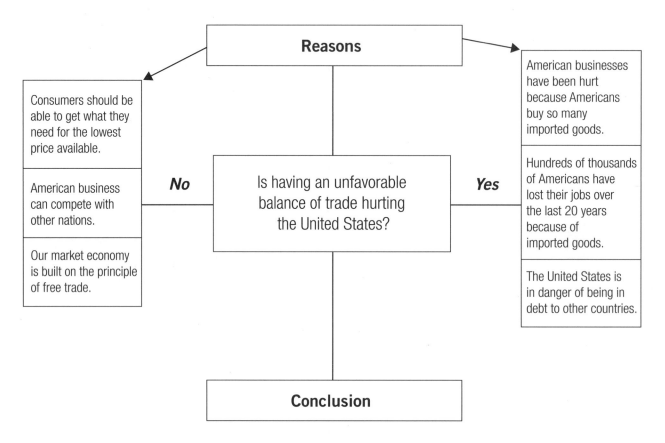

Yes, but the government should not intervene.

Free trade is important and American business has a history of adaptation and competition.

Source: From *Teaching Reading In Social Studies: A Supplement To Teaching Reading in the Content Areas Teacher's Manual* (2nd ed.) (p. 163), by J. K. Doty, G. N. Cameron, and M. L. Barton, 2003, Aurora, CO: McREL. Copyright 2003 by McREL. Reprinted with permission.

11. Frayer Model

What is it?

The Frayer Model is a word categorization activity (Frayer, Frederick, & Klausmeier, 1969). The strategy helps learners develop their understanding of concepts by studying those concepts in a relational manner. Using the Frayer Model, students analyze a concept's essential and nonessential characteristics and then refine their understanding of the concept by choosing relevant examples and nonexamples. In order to understand a concept completely, one must know what the concept both is and isn't. The Frayer Model layout can be adapted to ELLs and younger students by asking them to write a definition and associated characteristics instead of essential and nonessential characteristics. In addition, teachers can model the Frayer Model with pictures and drawings.

How do I use it?

1. Assign the concept or word from the text to be studied.

2. Explain all of the attributes of the Frayer Model to be completed.

3. Model for students using the Frayer Model with an easy word or concept from a familiar text.

4. Have students work in pairs and complete their model diagram using the assigned concept or word. Students may enjoy constructing their diagram with chart paper and markers or with a computer graphics software program.

5. Once the diagram is complete, have students share their work with other students.

FIGURE S11.1 ⟶ Frayer Model

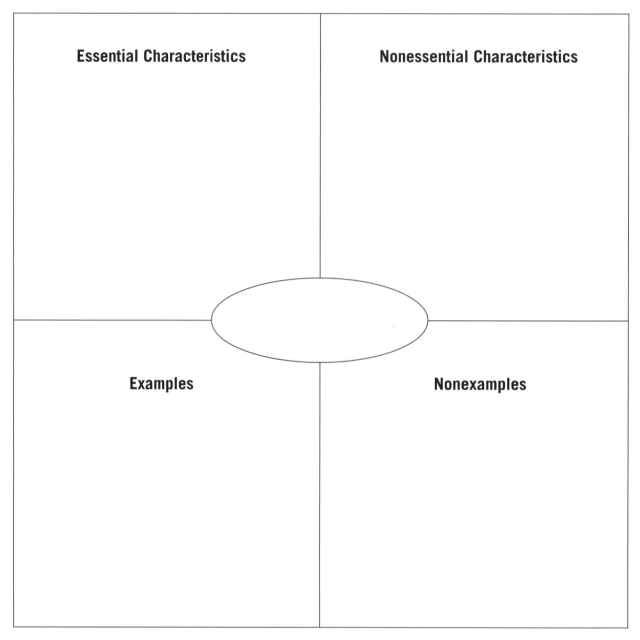

Source: From "A Schema for Testing the Level of Concept Mastery," by D. A. Frayer, W. C. Frederick, and H. G. Klausmeier, 1969, Technical Report No. 16. Copyright 1969 by the University of Wisconsin, Madison. Reprinted with permission.

FIGURE S11.2 ⟶ Frayer Model Alternative Layout

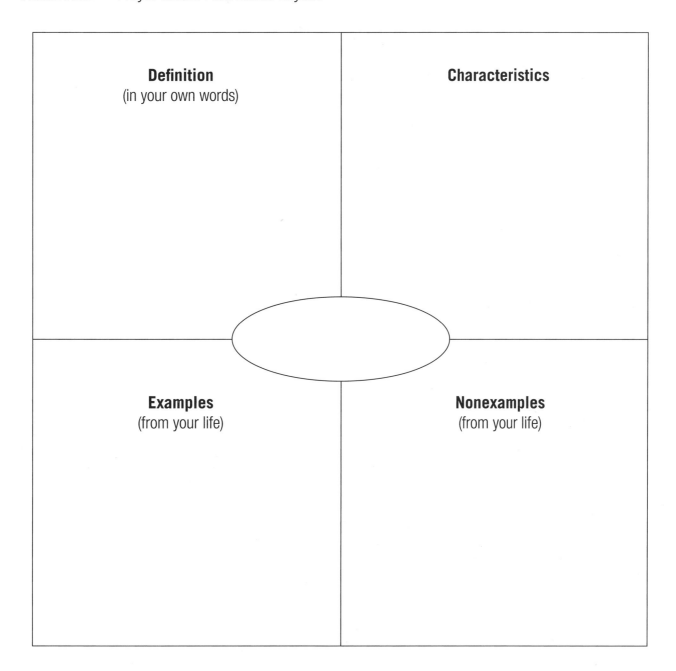

FIGURE S11.3 ⟶ Frayer Model Example

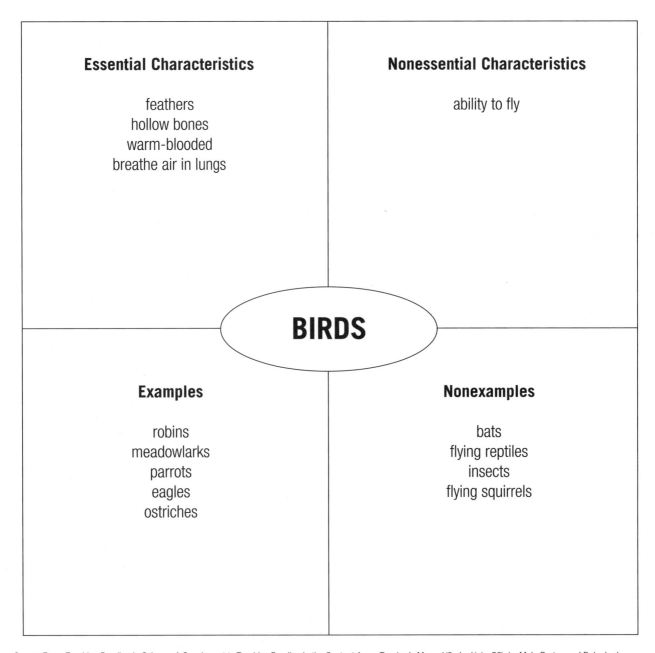

Source: From *Teaching Reading in Science: A Supplement to Teaching Reading in the Content Areas Teacher's Manual* (2nd ed.) (p. 56), by M. L. Barton and D. L. Jordan, 2001, Aurora, CO: McREL. Copyright 2001 by McREL. Reprinted with permission.

12. Graphic Organizers

X Narrative Text
X Informational Text
X Prereading
___ During Reading
X After Reading
X Writing to Learn
___ Reflection
___ Discussion
X Vocabulary Development

What is it?

In every content area, it is critical for students to know and understand that informational text can be organized in a variety of ways. Authors intentionally select a particular organizational pattern to best convey their ideas in a particular text. In order to answer questions and learn from the text, readers should learn to identify the following organizational patterns: chronological sequence, compare/contrast, concept/definition, description, episode, generalization/principle, and process/cause-effect. Graphic organizers provide visual representations of these organizational patterns. Students who are familiar with these patterns are more likely to comprehend what they read because they can use their knowledge of text structures to ask relevant questions and reflect on their understanding.

How do I use it?

1. Introduce an organizational pattern by explaining its characteristics, when and why writers use it, its related signal words, and any questions this pattern typically answers.

2. Provide students with an appropriate graphic organizer for mapping out the information in a familiar example text, and demonstrate how to complete it correctly.

3. To reinforce understanding, have students write paragraphs using the pattern.

FIGURE S12.1 → Chronological Order Graphic Organizer

(Organizes events according to when they occur)

Questions that guide the use of this graphic organizer:

1. What sequence is being described?
2. What are the major incidents that occur?
3. How is the pattern revealed in the text?

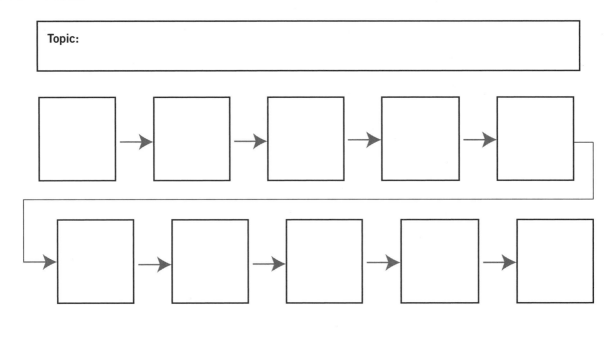

Topic:

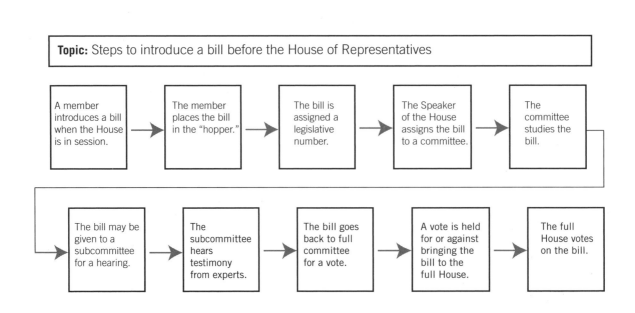

Topic: Steps to introduce a bill before the House of Representatives

A member introduces a bill when the House is in session. → The member places the bill in the "hopper." → The bill is assigned a legislative number. → The Speaker of the House assigns the bill to a committee. → The committee studies the bill.

The bill may be given to a subcommittee for a hearing. → The subcommittee hears testimony from experts. → The bill goes back to full committee for a vote. → A vote is held for or against bringing the bill to the full House. → The full House votes on the bill.

FIGURE S12.2 ⇢ Compare/Contrast Graphic Organizer: Venn Diagram

(Organizes information about two or more topics according to their similarities and differences)

Questions to guide the use of this graphic organizer:

1. What items are being compared?
2. What characteristics form the basis of the comparison?
3. What characteristics do the items have in common; how are they alike?
4. In what way(s) are these items different?
5. What conclusion does the author reach about the degree of similarity or difference between the items?
6. How did the author reveal this pattern?

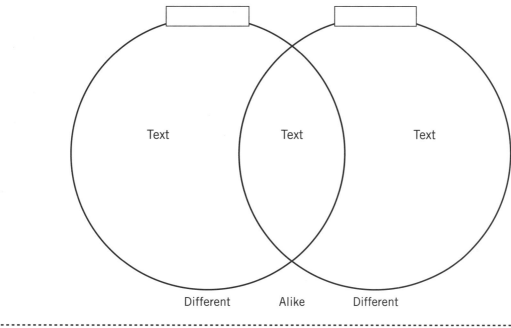

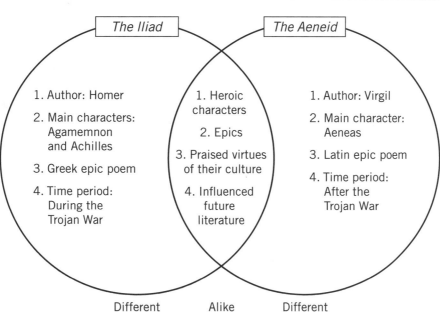

Source: From *Teaching Reading in Social Studies: A Supplement to Teaching Reading in the Content Areas Teacher's Manual* (2nd ed.) (p. 109), by J. K. Doty, G. N. Cameron, and M. L. Barton, 2003, Aurora, CO: McREL. Copyright 2003 by McREL. Adapted with permission.

FIGURE S12.3 ⇢ Concept/Definition Graphic Organizer

(Organizes information by presenting general characteristics and attributes of a concept.)

Questions that guide the use of this graphic organizer:

1. What concept is being defined?
2. What are its attributes or characteristics?
3. How does it work? What does it do?
4. What examples are given for each of the attributes or characteristics?
5. How is the pattern revealed in the text?

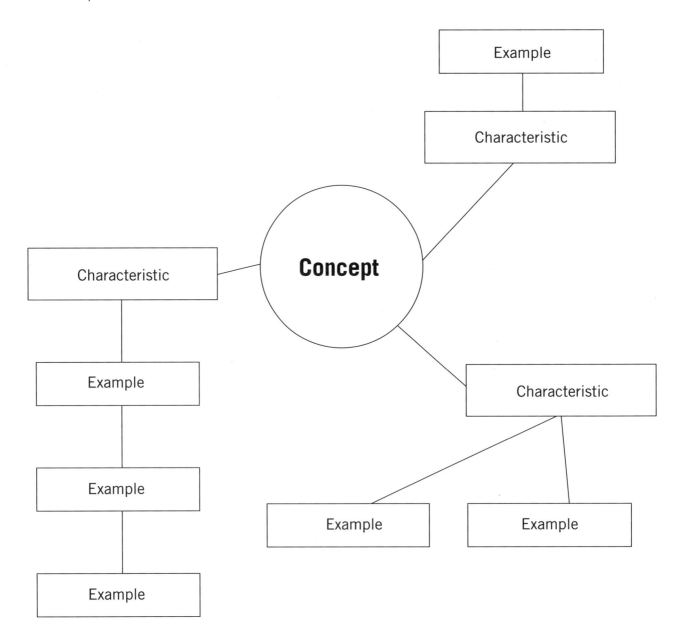

FIGURE S12.3 → Concept/Definition Graphic Organizer Example

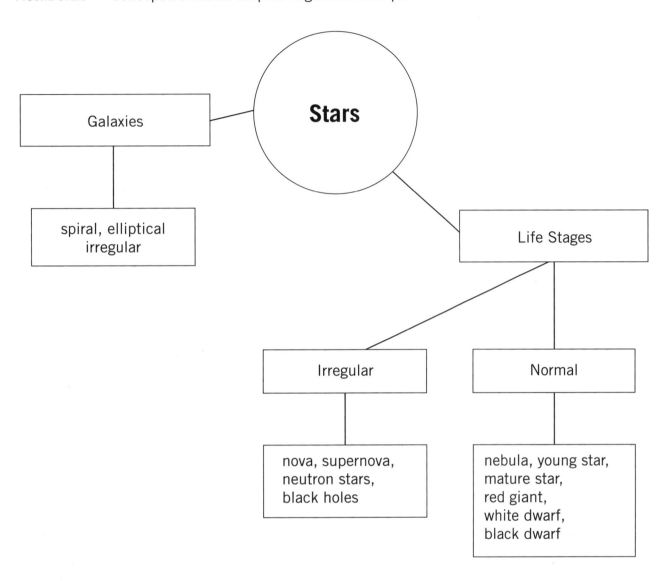

FIGURE S12.4 → Description Graphic Organizer

(Organizes information by presenting specific characteristics and attributes of a concept.)

Questions that guide the use of this organizer:
1. What specific person, place, thing, or event is being described?
2. What are the most important attributes or characteristics?
3. Why are these particular attributes important or significant?
4. Why is this description important?

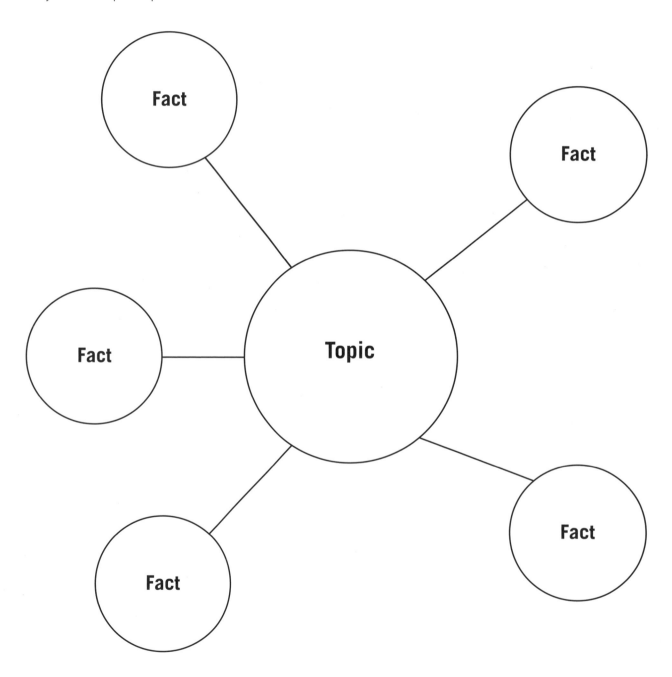

FIGURE S12.4 ⇢ Description Graphic Organizer Example

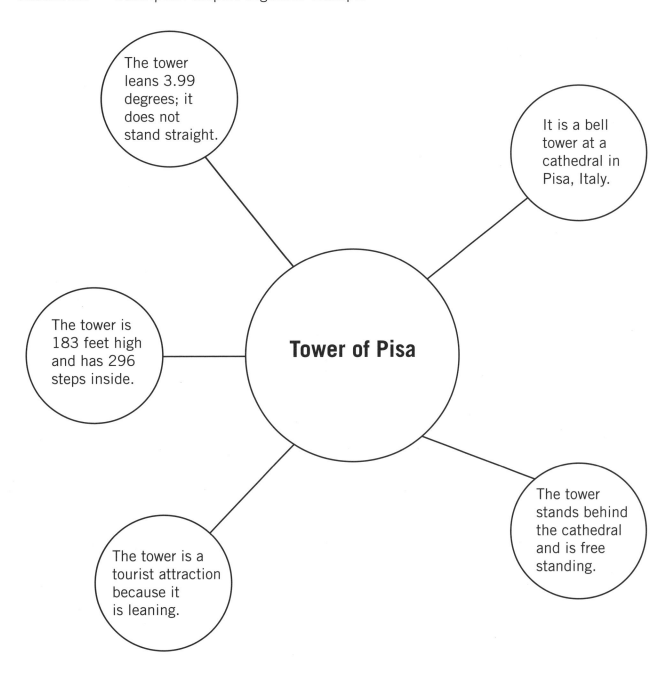

FIGURE S12.5 → Episode Graphic Organizer

(Organizes a large amount of diverse information about a specific event.)

Questions to guide the use of this graphic organizer:
1. What event is explained or described?
2. What is the setting where the event occurs?
3. When did this event occur?
4. Who are the major figures or characters that play a part in this event?
5. List, in the order they occur, the specific incidents involved with this event.
6. What caused this event?
7. What effects has this event had on the people involved?
8. What effects has this event had on society in general?

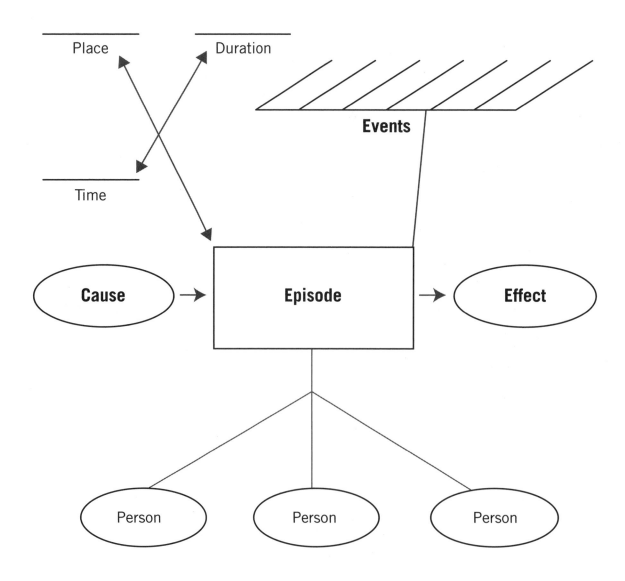

FIGURE S12.5 ⇢ Episode Graphic Organizer Example

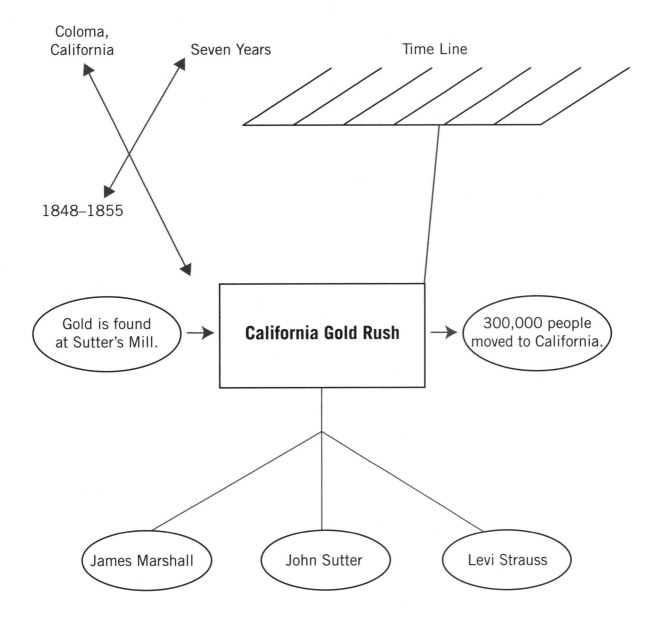

FIGURE S12.6 ⇢ Generalization/Principle Graphic Organizer

(Organizes information into general statements and supporting examples.)

Questions to guide the use of this graphic organizer:

1. What generalization is the author making? What principle is being explained?

2. What facts, examples, statistics, and expert opinions are given that support the generalization or explain the principle?

3. Are these details written in a logical order? Why or why not? (Provide examples.)

4. Are there enough facts, examples, statistics, and expert opinions included to clearly support or explain the generalization/principle? Explain why or why not.

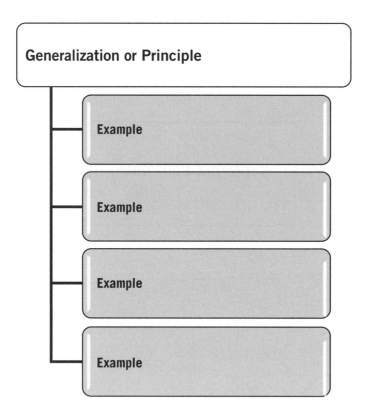

FIGURE S12.6 → Generalization/Principle Graphic Organizer Example

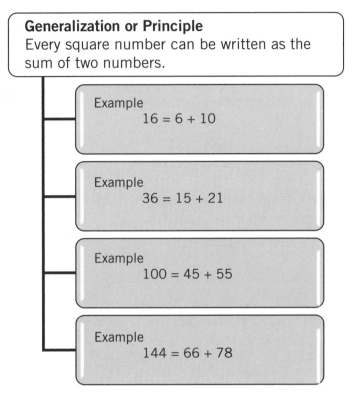

Generalization or Principle
Every square number can be written as the sum of two numbers.

Example
16 = 6 + 10

Example
36 = 15 + 21

Example
100 = 45 + 55

Example
144 = 66 + 78

Source: From *Teaching Reading in Mathematics: A Supplement to Teaching Reading in the Content Areas Teacher's Manual* (2nd ed.) (p. 103), by M. L. Barton and C. Heidema, 2002, Aurora, CO: McREL. Copyright 2002 by McREL. Reprinted with permission.

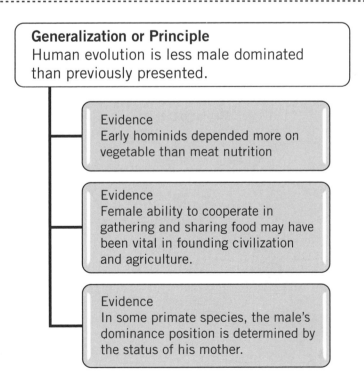

Generalization or Principle
Human evolution is less male dominated than previously presented.

Evidence
Early hominids depended more on vegetable than meat nutrition

Evidence
Female ability to cooperate in gathering and sharing food may have been vital in founding civilization and agriculture.

Evidence
In some primate species, the male's dominance position is determined by the status of his mother.

Source: From *Teaching Reading in Science: A Supplement to Teaching Reading in the Content Areas Teacher's Manual* (2nd ed.) (p. 86), by M. L. Barton and D. L. Jordan, 2001, Aurora, CO: McREL. Copyright 2001 by McREL. Reprinted with permission.

FIGURE S12.7 ⇢ Process/Cause-Effect Graphic Organizer

(Organizes information into a series of steps that lead to a specific product or outcome.)

Questions to guide the use of this graphic organizer:

1. What process or subject is explained?
2. What are the specific steps in the process? What specific causal events occur?
3. What is the product or end result of the process? What is the outcome of the causal events?

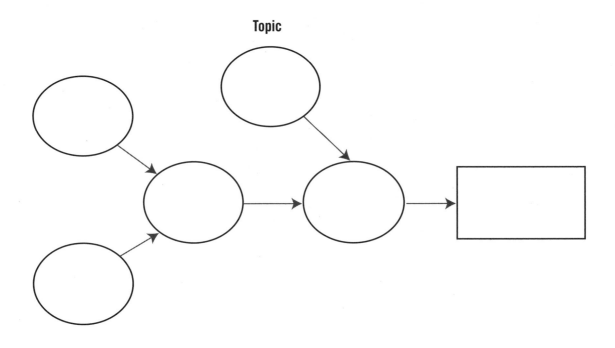

13. History Frames

What is it?

A history frame is an application of story maps to historical events (Jones, 2001). The history frame sets the purpose for reading. The basic components of a history frame are the title of the event, key people/players, major problem or goal, where and when the event occurred, key episodes of the event, resolution or outcome, and the theme or lessons learned. A story map is a visual representation of the story structure (Strategy 31). This strategy helps students know what to look for when they read. Students can then organize what they learn from the text to explain the who, what, where, how, and why of historical events.

How do I use it?

1. Use the history frame organizer and model how to use it with a familiar history text, for example, a chapter in a textbook.

2. Before students read a new selection, provide them with blank history frame graphic organizers to use while they read. As students read the selection, they will be reading with a purpose: to find relevant information in the text to write on the graphic organizer.

3. After students finish reading the selection, have them share their history frames with one another and discuss the information they comprehended from the text. Encourage them to fill in additional information, based on their classmates' responses.

FIGURE S13.1 ⇢ History Frame

TITLE OF EVENT:	PARTICIPANTS/KEY PLAYERS:

PROBLEM or GOAL:	WHERE: WHEN:

KEY EPISODES or EVENTS:

RESOLUTION or OUTCOME:

THEME/LESSONS:

Source: From "Story Mapping History Frame," by R. C. Jones, 2001. Retrieved from www.readingquest.org. Reprinted with permission.

FIGURE S13.2 ⇢ History Frame Example

TITLE OF EVENT:

Battle of Agincourt

PROBLEM or GOAL:

Henry V and his army of 6,000 troops were trying to reach Calais in order to sail to England. A French army of over 20,000 troops, led by heavily armored nobles, gathered to defeat the English.

PARTICIPANTS/KEY PLAYERS:

King Henry V (England)
6,000 English troops (including archers)

French nobles
20,000+ French troops (including heavily armored knights)

| **WHERE:** | Between the villages of Agincourt and Tramecourt, France |
| **WHEN:** | October 25, 1415 |

RESOLUTION or OUTCOME:
• The English routed the French.

• The English lost a few hundred men.

• The French lost several thousand men, including many nobles.

• Henry V and his army made it to Calais and then to England.

KEY EPISODES or EVENTS:

• Henry V ordered longbowmen to fire on the French from a long range.
• French charged with cavalry over muddy terrain.
• The charge was stopped by English archers.
• The French continued the charge on foot.
• The heavily armored French were slow, exhausted, and easy targets for English longbowmen.

THEME/LESSONS:

The success of the longbow ended the Age of Chivalry. Medieval knights in heavy armor were no longer a nation's most valuable military asset. This is an example of changing technology having a significant impact on military history.

Source: From *Teaching Reading In Social Studies: A Supplement To Teaching Reading in the Content Areas Teacher's Manual* (2nd ed.) (p. 107), by J. K. Doty, G. N. Cameron, and M. L. Barton, 2003, Aurora, CO: McREL. Copyright 2003 by McREL. Reprinted with permission.

14. Knowledge Rating Scale and Vocabulary Definition Card

What is it?

Teachers can access students' prior knowledge by using tools and strategies such as the knowledge rating scale or vocabulary definition cards before a new lesson or unit (Davis & Gerber, 1994). Knowledge rating of new words and concepts is a good idea for teachers and students in all content areas and at all levels of language development. This strategy allows students to activate prior knowledge by previewing a topic before reading or before instruction from the teacher. Teachers can then use the information that students provide to adapt their instruction during the lesson or unit. Along with writing and drawing to demonstrate understanding, vocabulary definition cards are another way to have students rate themselves. Teachers can ask students to rate their knowledge of new words before, during, and after reading a text or a unit of study.

How do I use it?

Knowledge Rating Card

1. Present students with a list of the major concepts to be learned from a reading in the unit or lesson.

2. Ask students to rate how familiar they are with the words or concepts.

3. Adapt instruction based on this formative information from students.

Vocabulary Definition Card

1. Present students with a brief explanation or description of the new term, concept, or phrase, and have them write it on the card.

2. Present students with a nonlinguistic representation of the new term or phrase.

3. Ask students to generate their own explanations or descriptions of the term or phrase on the card.

4. Ask students to create their own nonlinguistic representations of the term or phrase on the card.

5. Ask students to rate their knowledge of the term or concept and write an explanation of the score they gave themselves in the space provided on the card.

FIGURE S14.1 ⇢ Knowledge Rating Scale

Rate the following terms as follows:

1. I've never heard the term before.

2. I've heard the term, but I don't know what it means.

3. I understand the meaning of this term.

4. I can apply the meaning of this term to _____.

	1 2 3 4		1 2 3 4
	1 2 3 4		1 2 3 4
	1 2 3 4		1 2 3 4
	1 2 3 4		1 2 3 4
	1 2 3 4		1 2 3 4
	1 2 3 4		1 2 3 4

Source: From "Open to Suggestion: Content Area Strategies in Secondary Mathematics Classrooms," by S. J. Davis and R. Gerber, 1994, *Journal of Reading, 38*(1), 55–57. Copyright 1994 by the International Reading Association. Reprinted with permission.

FIGURE S14.2 → Knowledge Rating Scale Example

Rate the following terms as follows:

1. I've never heard the term before.

2. I've heard the term, but I don't know what it means.

3. I understand the meaning of this term.

4. I can apply the meaning of this term to a mathematics problem.

mean	1 2 3 4	range	1 2 3 4
median	1 2 3 4	flat distribution	1 2 3 4
mode	1 2 3 4	skewed distribution	1 2 3 4
weighted average	1 2 3 4	bimodal distribution	1 2 3 4
line of best fit	1 2 3 4	normal distribution	1 2 3 4
correlation	1 2 3 4		1 2 3 4

Source: From "Open to Suggestion: Content Area Strategies in Secondary Mathematics Classrooms," by S. J. Davis and R. Gerber, 1994, *Journal of Reading, 38*(1), 55–57. Copyright 1994 by the International Reading Association. Reprinted with permission.

FIGURE S14.3 ⇢ Vocabulary Definition Card

Vocabulary Word/Concept	My Understanding
	1. I have never heard this word before.
	2. I have heard or seen this word before.
Explanation/Description	3. I understand this word.
	4. I understand this word and can use it in a sentence.
Nonlinguistic Representation/Drawing	**Why I scored my understanding the way I did:**

FIGURE S14.4 ⇢ Vocabulary Definition Card Example

Vocabulary Word/Concept	My Understanding
food chain	1. I have never heard this word before.
	(2. I have heard or seen this word before.)
	3. I understand this word.
Explanation/Description	4. I understand this word and can use it in a sentence.
Bigger and faster things eat smaller things. Those smaller things eat even smaller things. And so on.	
Nonlinguistic Representation/Drawing	**Why I scored my understanding the way I did:**
	I have heard this concept before and I think I understand it, but I have never used "food chain" in any of my writing or speaking.

Source: From *Building Academic Vocabulary: Teacher's Manual* (p. 27), by R. J. Marzano and D. Pickering, 2005, Alexandria, VA: ASCD. Copyright 2005 by ASCD. Adapted with permission.

___ Narrative Text
X Informational Text
X Prereading
___ During Reading
___ After Reading
X Writing to Learn
___ Reflection
X Discussion
___ Vocabulary Development

15. KNFS

What is it?

In this strategy, students use a graphic organizer to analyze and solve word problems in mathematics or science. This strategy helps students read and comprehend the problem; they answer what facts they *know,* what information is *not* relevant, what the problem asks them to *find*, and what *strategy* they can use to solve the problem.

How do I use it?

1. Introduce students to the four-column KNFS graphic organizer.

2. Present students with a word problem, and model how to include appropriate information in each of the columns. Model the process with a think aloud (Strategy 35) and explain how you knew what information should be included in each column. It is important both to show "how" and to explain "how you know."

3. Ask students to work in groups and complete KNFS organizers as they read other word problems.

4. Have group members discuss how they decided which information should be included in each column, and have them then write short explanations at the bottom of their organizers.

5. Make sure students continue to use this strategy and have ongoing independent practice reading and comprehending what word problems are asking them to do.

FIGURE S15.1 ⟶ KNFS Chart

K	N	F	S
What facts do I KNOW from the information in the problem?	*Which information do I NOT need?*	*What does the problem ask me to FIND?*	*What STRATEGY, operation, or tools will I use to solve the problem?*

Write an explanation of your reasoning process:

FIGURE S15.2 → KNFS Chart Example

Problem: The ends of a rope are tied to two trees 500 feet apart. Every 10 feet, an 8-foot post is set 2 feet into the ground to support the rope. How many support posts are needed?

K	N	F	S
What facts do I KNOW from the information in the problem?	*Which information do I NOT need?*	*What does the problem ask me to FIND?*	*What STRATEGY, operation, or tools will I use to solve the problem?*
Trees are 500 feet apart. Posts are placed at 10-foot intervals between the trees.	The posts are 8 feet tall. The posts are set 2 feet into the ground.	How many support posts are needed?	I could draw a model to understand how to place posts. Maybe I could use division. There are 50 (500 ÷ 10) 10-foot intervals between the trees.

Write an explanation of your reasoning process:

I sketched this out first because I think in pictures a lot. Then in my group, we discussed making this a division problem. I could see from my sketch how division would work.

Source: From *Teaching Reading in Mathematics: A Supplement to Teaching Reading in the Content Areas Teacher's Manual* (2nd ed.) (p. 113), by M. L. Barton and C. Heidema, 2002, Aurora, CO: McREL. Copyright 2002 by McREL. Adapted with permission.

16. Learning Log

X Narrative Text
X Informational Text
___ Prereading
X During Reading
X After Reading
X Writing to Learn
X Reflection
___ Discussion
___ Vocabulary Development

What is it?

One of the most effective means of writing to learn is keeping a learning log. Learning logs foster reflection on content and on students' own reading and learning processes. They differ from journals in that they focus on content covered in class, not on students' personal and private feelings. Students may reflect on how they feel, but it is always in relation to the academic content studied in class. Students should be encouraged to express their thoughts both verbally and visually.

How do I use it?

1. Select a concept or process students have already read about for this writing-to-learn strategy.

2. A learning log entry can be assigned at any time during class, depending upon the topic and your purpose. For example, the following topic could be assigned in the middle of a reading assignment: Based on what you have read thus far, explain whether your initial predictions about the story/passage were correct. Prereading Predictions (Strategy 20) or Probable Passages (Strategy 21) are two possible strategies you could use at the beginning of class.

3. Assign the topic and give students one to three minutes of think time to consider their responses. Then have them write for five minutes in their learning logs.

4. At the end of the reading or the lesson, have students reread their learning logs and reflect on how their ideas either stayed the same or changed.

FIGURE S16.1 → Sample Learning Log Prompts

1. Which story or text passage from this unit have you found the most interesting? Explain your answer.

2. Write about the importance of _____ (an idea or concept students have read about) to the world in general and to you in particular.

3. Summarize the text material we read in class today. Explain how it relates to or reminds you of information or skills you have learned elsewhere.

4. Write about an upcoming test or quiz. List the questions that you think might be asked, and then develop answers for each.

5. One topic we have studied during this unit is _____. Why do you think this topic was included as part of this course?

6. Write about an idea or concept in the text that confuses you. What is it you find particularly difficult to understand? What could you do to gain a better understanding of this idea or concept?

7. Write a letter to the editor of the school newspaper in which you argue for or against a controversial issue we are studying or have studied this year.

17. Metaphor and Analogy

X Narrative Text
X Informational Text
X Prereading
___ During Reading
X After Reading
___ Writing to Learn
___ Reflection
___ Discussion
X Vocabulary Development

What is it?

"Students benefit from explicit instruction in the use of processes associated with identifying similarities and differences" (Dean et al., 2012, p. 121). Using metaphors and analogies to compare and understand vocabulary words or key concepts helps students identify similarities and differences in abstract ways. It has been demonstrated that analogies are the most complex format for identifying similarities and differences because they constitute relationships within relationships. Therefore, students can use metaphors and analogies to extend and refine their learning.

How do I use it?

Metaphor Pattern: A:B (*A is B*)

1. Introduce the organizational pattern for creating a metaphor.

2. Model the process of choosing a concept/word, identifying its literal meaning, taking the literal meaning into the abstract, and identifying another concept/word that connects to the first.

3. Have students identify the meaning, structures, or processes of the concept/word.

4. Demonstrate how to restate the meaning, structure, or process in an abstract or nonliteral way.

5. Have students brainstorm and identify another concept/word they can connect to the first concept/word in an abstract way.

6. Have students write and share metaphors in which the original concept/word is equated to the second concept/word.

Analogy Pattern: A:B::C:D (*A is to B as C is to D*)

1. Present students with a simple analogy and explain the relationship between the two sets of words.

2. Present students with another, similar analogy and have students determine the relationship between those words.

3. Provide students with several word pairs and have them identify a relationship between each (A:B). Then have them work with partners to identify appropriate complementary pairs that could complete the analogy (C:D).

4. Once students become proficient with teacher-directed analogies, have them collaborate to create original analogies that use words and ideas relevant to the current lesson or unit.

FIGURE S17.1 ⟶ Metaphor Organization Chart

Concept/Word	Literal Meaning or Pattern	Abstract Relationship	Literal Meaning or Pattern	Concept/Word
Metaphor:				

FIGURE S17.2 ⟶ Metaphor Organization Chart Example

Concept/Word	Literal Meaning or Pattern	Abstract Relationship	Literal Meaning or Pattern	Concept/Word
cell	a very small unit of protoplasm	a part of the whole system	a very small unit of a fleet of aircraft carriers	USS *Nimitz*
nucleus	the central, spherical mass of protoplasm in a cell, which directs the growth of the cell	the part that runs the system	the central hub of a ship, which directs the course of the ship	the bridge

Metaphor:

The <u>bridge</u> is the <u>nucleus</u> of an aircraft carrier.

FIGURE S17.3 ⇢ Template for Creating Analogies

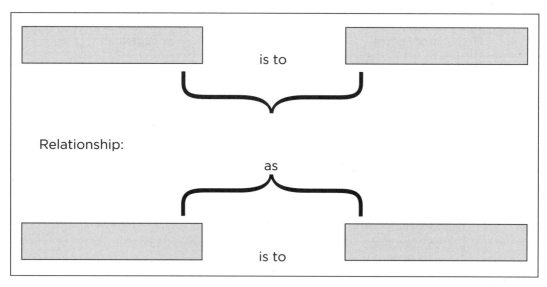

FIGURE S17.4 ⇢ Analogy Example

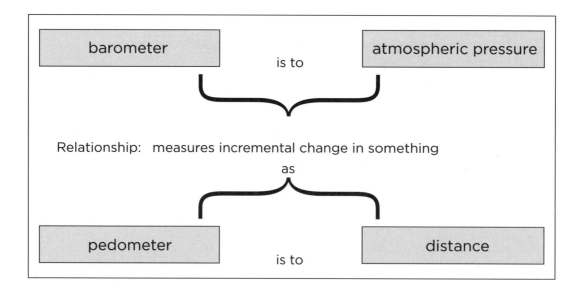

18. Pairs Reading and Summarizing

X	Narrative Text
X	Informational Text
___	Prereading
X	During Reading
X	After Reading
X	Writing to Learn
___	Reflection
X	Discussion
___	Vocabulary Development

What is it?

Pairs Reading is a strategy that requires cooperative learning as students read and digest text. Students work together in pairs toward a common goal—comprehension of text. Students help one another increase their knowledge and understanding; the success of one student is not at the expense of another (Dean et al., 2012.) While one student reads aloud, his or her partner listens and then summarizes the main idea. The shared learning gives students an opportunity to engage in discussion, take responsibility for their own learning, and thus become critical thinkers (Totten, Sills, Digby, & Russ, 1991).

How do I use it?

1. Select a passage for students to read, and organize students into pairs.

2. Partner A reads the first paragraph of the selected passage aloud to Partner B.

3. Partner B orally summarizes the main idea of the paragraph and discusses any supporting details necessary for understanding. Both students should ask questions to help clarify the reading.

4. The students then reverse roles and repeat steps 2 and 3.

5. Have students continue to alternate roles so they each have multiple opportunities to read and summarize the passage.

6. Finally, have students cooperatively summarize the main idea of the entire passage and discuss the supporting details.

FIGURE S18.1 ⇢ Summarizing Template

A reads aloud	[Paragraph]	B summarizes

Both students ask each other questions to help clarify the reading.

B reads aloud	[Paragraph]	A summarizes

Both students ask each other questions to help clarify the reading.

A reads aloud	[Paragraph]	B summarizes

Both students ask each other questions to help clarify the reading.

B reads aloud	[Paragraph]	A summarizes

Both students ask each other questions to help clarify the reading.

Cooperative Summary Statement

FIGURE S18.2 ⇢ Summarizing Example

	Common Sense **by Thomas Paine**	
A reads aloud	I have never met with a man, either in England or America, who hath not confessed his opinion, that a separation between the countries would take place one time or other: And there is no instance in which we have shown less judgment, than in endeavoring to describe, what we call, the ripeness or fitness of the continent for independence.	*B summarizes* People always thought that America would separate from England someday.
Both students ask each other questions to help clarify the reading.		
B reads aloud	As all men allow the measure, and vary only in their opinion of the time, let us, in order to remove mistakes, take a general survey of things, and endeavor if possible to find out the very time. But I need not go far, the inquiry ceases at once, for the time hath found us. The general concurrence, the glorious union of all things, proves the fact.	*A summarizes* People haven't always agreed on when the two powers would separate, but the time for the separation is now.
Both students ask each other questions to help clarify the reading.		
A reads aloud	'Tis not in numbers but in unity that our great strength lies: yet our present numbers are sufficient to repel the force of all the world. The Continent hath at this time the largest body of armed and disciplined men of any power under Heaven: and is just arrived at that pitch of strength, in which no single colony is able to support itself, and the whole, when united, is able to do any thing. Our land force is more than sufficient, and as to Naval affairs, we cannot be insensible that Britain would never suffer an American man of war to be built, while the Continent remained in her hands. Wherefore, we should be no forwarder an hundred years hence in that branch than we are now; but the truth is, we should be less so, because the timber of the Country is every day diminishing, and that which will remain at last, will be far off or difficult to procure.	*B summarizes* We have the ability to separate from England if we are united, because united we have greater numbers than England, and when we are united we can do anything.
Both students ask each other questions to help clarify the reading.		
B reads aloud	Were the Continent crowded with inhabitants, her sufferings under the present circumstances would be intolerable. The more seaport-towns we had, the more should we have both to defend and to lose. Our present numbers are so happily proportioned to our wants, that no man need be idle. The diminution of trade affords an army, and the necessities of an army create a new trade.	*A summarizes* Our population is just the right size for every person to find work even with England suppressing our trade; the work now is building an army that will increase our trade.

continued

FIGURE S18.2 ⇢ Summarizing Example (*continued*)

Both students ask each other questions to help clarify the reading.

Cooperative Summary Statement

Thomas Paine is saying that the time for America to separate from England is now. He believes Americans can do this if the colonies are united against England in this endeavor.

Source: Text excerpts from *Common Sense*, by T. Paine. Available: www.ushistory.org/paine/commonsense/sense5.htm

19. PLAN

___	Narrative Text
X	Informational Text
X	Prereading
X	During Reading
X	After Reading
X	Writing to Learn
___	Reflection
X	Discussion
___	Vocabulary Development

What is it?

Predict-Locate-Add-Note (PLAN) is a reading strategy for informational text that helps students read strategically (Caverly, Mandeville, & Nicholson, 1995). PLAN includes four distinct steps that students are taught to use before, during, and after reading. Texts in all content areas continually introduce new concepts and ideas that are related to previously discussed content. This strategy provides students with a way to illustrate the relationships between and among ideas and episodes in the text and to create a visual organizer they can use to take notes while reading. Using graphic organizers helps students recognize connections as they construct their understanding of concepts. The PLAN strategy encourages students to self-assess what they know about a topic, and it provides students with an opportunity to organize and summarize what they already know or have learned through their reading.

How do I use it?

1. Model the four steps of the PLAN process (Predict, Locate, Add, Note) with a chapter in a familiar text from the current or a previous unit.

2. Predict: Before you read, predict the content and structure of the text by creating a map or graphic organizer that includes information gleaned from the title, subtitles, highlighted words, and graphics and reader aids.

3. Locate: Locate known and unknown information on the organizer by placing check marks next to familiar concepts and question marks next to unfamiliar concepts. This causes students to activate and assess their prior knowledge about the topic.

4. Add: As you read, add words or short phrases to explain unfamiliar concepts or to confirm and extend familiar concepts.

5. Note: After you finish reading, note new understanding by using this new knowledge to fulfill a task. Tasks such as the following reinforce learning and ensure that the purpose for reading has been fulfilled:

   • Reproduce the organizer from memory.

   • Share the final organizer with another student and discuss what has been learned.

   • Write a summary of the content in the PLAN.

6. Have students follow the PLAN strategy and create an organizer with a new text.

FIGURE S19.1 ⟶ PLAN Organizer

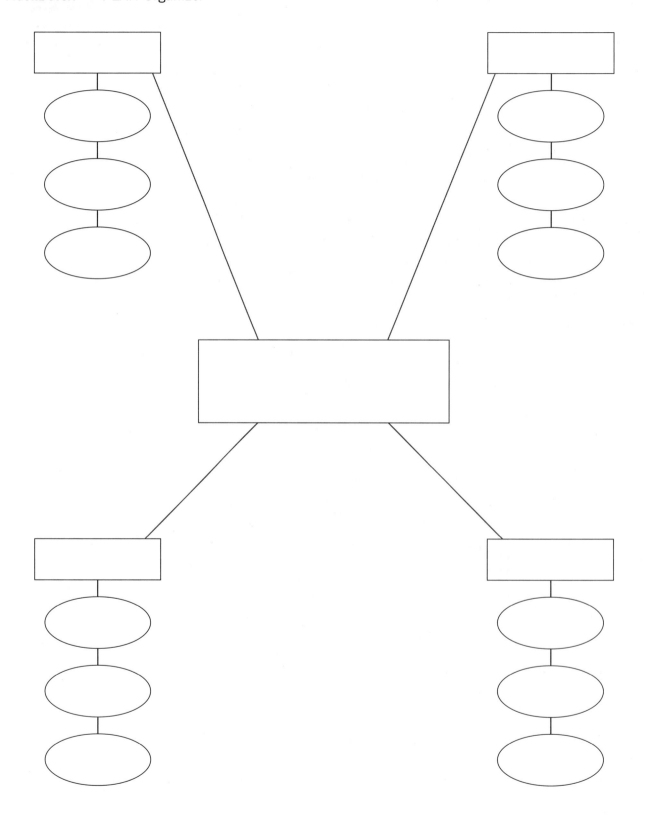

FIGURE S19.2 ⟶ PLAN Organizer: Predict

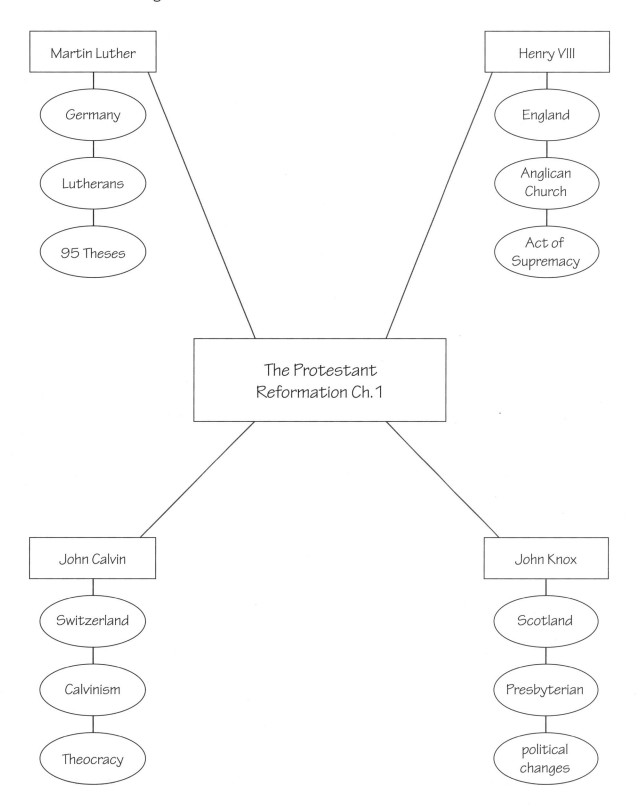

FIGURE S19.3 ⟶ PLAN Organizer: Locate

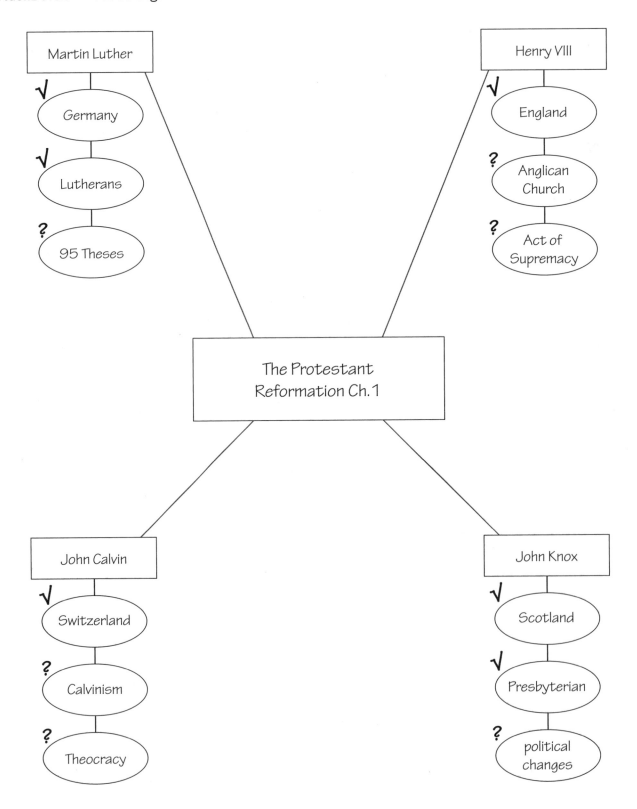

FIGURE S19.4 ⟶ PLAN Organizer: Add

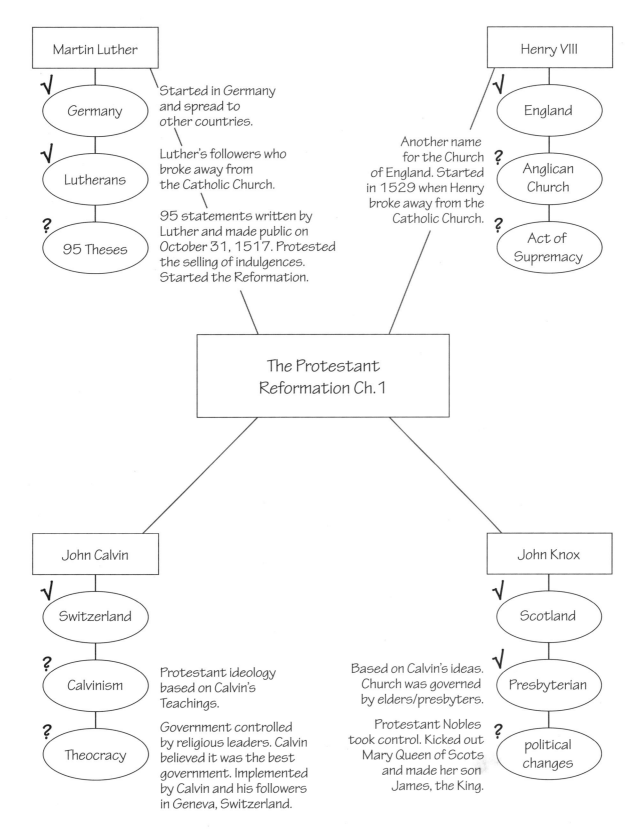

Source: From "PLAN: A Study-Reading Strategy for Informational Text," by D. C. Caverly, T. F. Mandeville, and S. A. Nicholson, 1995, *Journal of Adolescent and Adult Literacy,* *39*(3), pp. 190-199. Copyright 1995 by the International Reading Association. Adapted with permission.

FIGURE S19.5 → PLAN Organizer: Note

I had heard the term Reformation before, but I didn't know it was started as a movement to reform the Catholic Church. I never realized that the Reformation from long ago affects me today, in that many of the churches we have today sprouted from the Reformation. Studying the Reformation has helped me begin to see the differences among the four doctrines/churches we studied—Lutheranism, Calvinism, Anglicanism, and Presbyterianism.

20. Prereading Predictions

What is it?

The Prereading Predictions strategy is useful for helping students activate prior knowledge and make predictions about a text's content. Students use vocabulary to predict the content of a reading selection. This strategy also assists students in identifying parts of speech and the structure of sentences. Once students complete the graphic organizer, they make predictions about the content of the text orally or in writing. Specific vocabulary instruction on new words is effective for all students.

How do I use it?

1. Before students read a text, identify 15–30 colorful, unusual, and/or unfamiliar vocabulary words that the author uses.

2. Use a chart to organize these words in columns, according to part of speech. In other words, all of the nouns should be listed in one column, all of the verbs in another, and so on.

3. Have students examine this list of words and then work in small groups both to review the meanings of familiar terms and to guess about the meanings of unfamiliar words.

4. Model a few ways that words in different columns might be combined to form simple sentences. Ask students to explain which combinations "make sense," which do not, and why.

5. Have students write a few simple sentences and share these with one another.

6. Have students predict, in writing or orally in small groups, what the text might be about.

7. After students read the text, have them discuss or write about whether their predictions were correct or needed revision.

8. Finally, have students revisit their word lists and identify how the author actually uses each word.

FIGURE S20.1 → Prereading Predictions Organizer

Nouns	Verbs	Adjectives	Adverbs

FIGURE S20.2 ⇢ Prereading Predictions Organizer Example

"Thank You M'am" by Langston Hughes			
Nouns	**Verbs**	**Adjectives**	**Adverbs**
half-nelson	slung	frail	barely
kitchenette	rattled	presentable	firmly
supper	permit	devilish	simply
pocketbook	snatch	barren	already

Model:

A man tried to snatch a woman's pocketbook.

He thought the woman was frail.

The woman was simply cooking supper in the kitchenette.

Predict:

Student A: I predict the story is about someone snatching a frail woman's pocketbook while she was cooking supper in the kitchen.

Student B: No, I don't think her pocketbook was snatched in the kitchen—that doesn't make sense. She was outside, I bet.

Student C: I predict the story is about a wrestler that lives in an apartment with a kitchenette, because it says half-nelson, and that is a wrestling word.

Discuss:

Our predictions were partially correct. The woman's name is Mrs. Luella Bates Washington Jones, and she did not allow the boy to snatch her pocketbook. Instead, she locked him in a half-nelson and took him home. The woman wasn't frail at all. She was strong. She held the boy firmly in her half-nelson! She asked him why he wanted her pocketbook. He wanted to buy shoes. She made him wash his face to be presentable, prepared him some food in her kitchenette, and gave him $10 for new shoes.

X Narrative Text
___ Informational Text
X Prereading
___ During Reading
X After Reading
X Writing to Learn
___ Reflection
X Discussion
X Vocabulary Development

21. Probable Passages

What is it?

Probable Passages is a prereading strategy that improves comprehension by integrating prediction, summarization, discussion, and vocabulary instruction (Wood, 1988). This strategy provides students with an incentive to read because they read to find out if their so-called probable passage was close to the real story line. When the strategy is introduced for the first time, it is important for the teacher to model each stage, using the think aloud strategy.

How do I use it?

1. Identify important terms and concepts from a story. With students, categorize the terms and concepts according to the story elements of setting, characters, problems, events, and resolution.

2. Have each student write a probable story with words from each category and then share that story with a partner.

3. Have students read the story and then discuss how the actual story compared to the probable story versions they predicted.

4. Have students modify their probable passages so they become summary paragraphs of the actual story.

FIGURE S21.1 ⇢ Probable Passage Organizer

Word List				
Setting(s)	**Character(s)**	**Problem(s)**	**Event(s)**	**Resolution**

Probable Passage Before Reading

1. The story takes place _____ .

2. _____ is a character who _____ .

3. A problem occurs when _____ .

4. The problem is solved when _____ .

5. The story ends when _____ .

Summary Paragraph After Reading

FIGURE S21.2 → Probable Passage Organizer Example

"Singing My Sister Down" by Margo Lanagan

shame, Chief Barnandra, tar pit, into Mumma's arms, Ikky, going down, Mumma, stuck, axe handle, Dash, justice for lost son, wedding, Felly, watch who you love, narrator

Setting(s)	Character(s)	Problem(s)	Event(s)	Resolution
tar pit	Chief Mumma Ikky Felly Dash Narrator	shame watch who you love axe handle	justice for lost son stuck	going down into Mumma's arms

Probable Passage Before Reading

1. The story takes place <u>at a tar pit.</u>

2. Mumma is a character who <u>gets stuck in a tar pit.</u>

3. A problem occurs when <u>Mumma is ashamed.</u>

4. The problem is solved when <u>Mumma uses an axe handle to get out.</u>

5. The story ends when <u>someone jumps into Mumma's arms.</u>

Summary Paragraph After Reading

This story took place at a tar pit. A girl named Ikky killed her husband with an axe handle and brought shame to her family. She was punished and killed by sinking in the tar pit. The family stayed with Ikky the whole time and tried to make the best of it. However, in the end, everyone broke down because they understood that Ikky was gone. The narrator, her brother, went into Mumma's arms and cried.

22. Problematic Situations

____ Narrative Text
X Informational Text
X Prereading
____ During Reading
X After Reading
____ Writing to Learn
____ Reflection
X Discussion
____ Vocabulary Development

What is it?

Problematic Situations is a strategy that activates what students already know about a topic, motivates them to want to read the text, and helps them focus on the main ideas as they read (Vacca & Vacca, 1993). The teacher identifies a problematic situation in a new text that will engage students' interest and require them to gather information to support their ideas and arguments. The teacher provides enough information from the text to form the problem for students to discuss. This strategy provides a clear focus for their reading. This strategy can be used with any text that includes a problem/solution relationship. Mathematics, science, history, and technology materials provide good information from which teachers can create problematic situations.

How do I use it?

1. Before students read the assigned text, design a problematic situation for the content being studied. Provide enough relevant information about the situation so students will be able to focus their attention on the key ideas in the assignment. For example, if students will be reading a text about a company that is facing financial problems, then you can write a problematic situation based on the information in the text and have students discuss their solutions to the question posed before they read the actual text.

> **Merchandising Problem**
>
> Your firm has been selected to design a new package for the Starbar Candy Company. The company is planning to reduce the size of the original bar by 10 percent. The dimensions of the current bar are:
>
> **Length = 6 inches**
> **Width = 2 inches**
> **Depth = 1 inch**
>
> The company must reduce the size to cut costs, but it recognizes that reducing the size may adversely affect sales.
>
> **Teacher-Posed Question for Group Discussion:** How would you design the packaging so that it will minimize the appearance of the size reduction?

2. Have students work in cooperative groups to read and discuss the problem and brainstorm solutions, which they should list. Students state/write why their possible solutions would be good or succeed.

3. Then have the students read the assigned text individually and "test" their solutions.

4. Have groups come back together to compare their solutions with the text. Students may then refine or modify their solutions as they obtain new information from the reading.

5. Have cooperative groups report out on their solutions and hold a class discussion about whether some of the solutions are better than the one presented by the author in the text.

FIGURE S22.1 ⟶ Problematic Situations Organizer

Topic:

Teacher-Stated Problem: **Teacher-Posed Question for Group Discussion:** 	
Possible solution 	*Why is this a good solution?*
Possible solution 	*Why is this a good solution?*
Possible solution 	*Why is this a good solution?*
Possible solution 	*Why is this a good solution?*

FIGURE S22.2 ⇢ Problematic Situations Example

Topic: Illegal Immigration

Teacher-Stated Problem:
The United States is a nation of immigrants. People from all parts of the world have been moving to our shores since colonial times. People have moved to the United States for many different reasons. Throughout our history, our government has passed a variety of laws regulating immigration. Those people entering the country who follow procedures defined by U.S. law are called legal immigrants. Many people enter our nation each year without following the procedures defined by U.S. law. These people are called illegal immigrants. Some citizens believe illegal immigrants are taking advantage of the country by not following the rules. Other citizens believe these immigrants can be an important resource for our nation, even though they did not follow the laws when they moved to the United States.

Teacher-Posed Question for Group Discussion:
What ideas would you propose to the federal government about how to deal with illegal immigrants?

Possible solution The United States could do more to increase the quality of living in Mexico.	*Why is this a good solution?* Citizens in Mexico would have jobs there and want to stay there.
Possible solution People in the United States hire illegal immigrants, so the government should penalize these employers.	*Why is this a good solution?* The people who hire illegal immigrants might not hire them because they wouldn't want to be penalized. Then the illegal immigrants wouldn't come here because there wouldn't be any jobs.
Possible solution Increase border patrol.	*Why is this a good solution?* By having more manpower along the border, the United States could stop people from coming over the border, and then we wouldn't have a problem.
Possible solution Tax all illegal immigrants.	*Why is this a good solution?* Taxing them as citizens are taxed would at least help our economy.

Source: From *Teaching Reading in Social Studies: A Supplement to Teaching Reading in the Content Areas Teacher's Manual* (2nd ed.) (p. 136), by J. K. Doty, G. N. Cameron, and M. L. Barton, 2003, Aurora, CO: McREL. Copyright 2003 by McREL. Adapted with permission.

23. QAR

X Narrative Text
X Informational Text
___ Prereading
___ During Reading
X After Reading
___ Writing to Learn
X Reflection
___ Discussion
___ Vocabulary Development

What is it?

Question–Answer Relationship (QAR) is a strategy for developing four different types of questions—two that are text-based and two that are knowledge-based (Raphael, 1982; 1986). Students who become skilled at this strategy are able to recognize the relationships between and among the questions teachers ask and the answers that are expected. Therefore, they know where to find the information needed for a correct response. Although teaching this strategy can take time, Richardson and Morgan (1994) report that students who learned and practiced this strategy for as little as eight weeks showed significant gains in reading comprehension. Anthony and Raphael (1989) assert that QAR can also help transfer control of the questioning process from teacher to learner. In other words, when students become skilled at QAR, they rely less on the teacher because they are able to generate different types of questions during independent reading.

How do I use it?

1. Introduce the strategy by giving students a written and verbal description of each of the four question types.

2. Assign short passages for students to read. When they finish, ask students one question from each QAR category. Point out the differences between each question and the kind of answer it requires.

3. After students demonstrate they understand the differences among the four QAR types, assign several more short passages. Again, ask one question from each category per passage, provide answers to those questions, and then identify the appropriate QAR type. Discuss why the questions represent one QAR type but not another.

4. Assign short text passages and provide both the questions and the answers. This time, have students identify each question as a particular QAR type and explain their rationale. Repeat the process, but have students work in groups to determine which QAR type each question represents and then write their answers accordingly.

5. Once students are familiar with the strategy, have them read a longer text passage. Provide several questions—though not necessarily one per QAR type. Have students individually determine the QAR types and write their answers. Continue assigning longer passages and questions for students to identify and answer.

FIGURE S23.1 → QAR Question Types

Text-Based Questions

"Right There" questions ask students to respond at the literal level. The words used to formulate and answer these questions can be found "right there" in the same sentence of text. These questions begin with words or statements such as "Who is. . . ," "Where is. . . ," "List. . . ," "What is. . . ," "When is. . . ," "How many. . . ," "When did. . . ," "Name. . . ," and "What kind of. . ." These questions usually elicit a one-word or short-phrase response and have one correct answer. Sample questions are "Who wrote the Declaration of Independence?" and "Name the chemical components of carbon dioxide."

"Think and Search" questions require students to think about how information or ideas in a text relate to one another and to search through the entire passage to find relevant information. These questions may begin with words or statements such as "Summarize. . . ," "What caused. . . ," "Compare and contrast. . . ," "Retell. . . ," "How did. . . ," "Explain. . . ," "Find examples that. . . ," and "For what reason. . ." An example is "Summarize how the individual described in this chapter improves his financial situation."

Knowledge-Based Questions

"Author and You" questions require students to answer with information that is not in the text. However, students must have read the text to understand what the question is asking. A sample question is "The topic of this passage is cloning. In what instances, if ever, do you think cloning should be used?"

"On My Own" questions can be answered with information from the students' background knowledge and do not require reading the text. A sample question is "How do you think your life might be impacted by cloning?"

FIGURE S23.2 ⇥ QAR Example

On May 25, 1961, President John F. Kennedy presented his goal of sending an American safely to the moon before the end of the decade. This goal was in part a response to events from earlier that year. In March of 1961, NASA Administrator James E. Webb made a request to expand the agency's fiscal budget in order to have a moon landing by the United States of America before the end of the decade. Funding was needed to develop the launch vehicles that could support a lunar landing. Unfortunately, the president only approved a modest increase in the budget that allowed for the slow development of launch vehicles.

On April 12, 1961, Soviet cosmonaut Yuri Gagarin became the first human in space aboard the spacecraft Vostok 1. Just a few weeks after Gagarin completed his flight, Alan Shepard became the first American in space as he took a 15-minute suborbital flight on May 5, 1961. Eight years later, on July 20, 1969, the United States spacecraft Apollo 11 successfully landed on the moon. American astronaut Neil Armstrong left the lunar module and became the first man to step foot on the moon.

Since these events, there have been many forays into space. Most have been successful, but a few have been tragic. It is important to note that many wonderful, useful, and exciting discoveries that are now part of our everyday lives came from the research and development that was originally taken on in the quest for space exploration.

QAR Questions

Right There:
In what year did President Kennedy announce his goal of sending an American safely to the moon before the end of the decade?

Think and Search:
Was President Kennedy's dream accomplished by the end of the decade?

Author and You:
How do you think the author feels about space exploration?

On My Own:
How has your life been impacted because of the research and development created by the space program?

X Narrative Text
X Informational Text
___ Prereading
___ During Reading
X After Reading
X Writing to Learn
___ Reflection
___ Discussion
___ Vocabulary Development

24. RAFT

What is it?

The RAFT (Role, Audience, Format, Topic) strategy employs a writing-to-learn approach that enhances understanding of informational text (Santa, 1988). Instead of writing a traditional essay that explains a concept, students demonstrate their understanding in a nontraditional format by writing in the voice of someone else. By taking on a role such as a scientist, newspaper reporter, or factory owner, students can become creative and reflect using different points of view about various concepts they have learned. The RAFT strategy forces students to process information at a deeper level than merely writing surface-level answers to questions, and students are more motivated to undertake writing assignments because RAFT allows for more creative responses to learning. The acronym stands for:

- What is the writer's **role**: reporter, observer, or eyewitness?

- Who is the primary **audience** for this writing: the teacher, other students, parents, community members, the media?

- What is the best **format** to present this writing: a letter, an article, a report, a speech, a poem?

- Who or what is the **topic** of this writing: a famous mathematician, a prehistoric species, reactions to a specific political event?

How do I use it?

1. Distribute a text that is relevant to the current lesson/unit. Use a word classification sort (Strategy 37) to help the class analyze important ideas or information from the text.

2. Explain the RAFT acronym and strategy, and create a four column chart on the board with the headings Role, Audience, Format, and Topic. Write important ideas from the text in the fourth column. Brainstorm and list possible roles students could assume in their writing.

3. Decide who the audience will be and determine the format of the writing assignment (e.g., a spark plug could be writing an informational report to be read by other spark plugs placed in new cars; a farmer could be writing a persuasive letter to the government for or against pending legislation).

4. Model how to write a paragraph using information from the RAFT chart. Then have students write their own paragraphs. Initially, all students could be assigned the same role and format. Once they are familiar with the strategy, offer several different roles from which students can choose.

FIGURE S24.1 → RAFT Assignment Examples

Role	Audience	Format	Topic
newspaper reporter	readers in the 1870s	obituary	qualities of General Custer
lawyer	U.S. Supreme Court	appeal speech	Dred Scott decision
Abraham Lincoln	Dear Abby	advice column	problems with Civil War generals
frontier woman	self	diary	hardships in the West during the 1800s
citizen	U.S. senator	letter	gun control
journalist	public	news release	diminishing ozone layer
chemist	chemical company	instructions	chemical combinations to avoid
cookie	other cookies	travel guide	journey through the digestive system
plant	sun	thank-you note	Sun's role in plant's growth
scientist	Charles Darwin	letter	evolution theory
square root	whole number	love letter	numerical relationship
repeating decimal	set of rational numbers	petition	number sets
Julia Child	television audience	script	wonders of eggs
advertiser	television audience	public service announcement	importance of fruit
lungs	cigarettes	complaint	effects of smoking
Huckleberry Finn	Jim	letter	what I learned during the trip on the river
Joseph Stalin	George Orwell	letter	reactions to *Animal Farm*
comma	ninth-grade students	complaint	misused punctuation
trout	Trout Unlimited members	letter	effects of acid rain

Source: From *Classroom Strategies for Interactive Learning,* by D. Buehl, 1995, Schofield, WI: Wisconsin State Reading Association. Copyright 1995 by the Wisconsin State Reading Association. Adapted with permission.

25. Reciprocal Teaching

What is it?

Reciprocal Teaching is a strategy in which students learn and use the skills of summarizing, questioning, clarifying, and predicting well enough to act as student teacher or leader (Palincsar & Brown, 1985). When students become adept at these four skills, they not only instruct one another but also learn metacomprehension skills they can use while reading independently. Once the four components are learned, students can use them to monitor their reading for better comprehension. The four skills are:

- **Summarizing**: identifying and condensing the most important points of a text.

- **Questioning**: formulating questions about what you don't know, what you need to know, or what you would like to know about the subject of a text.

- **Clarifying**: making sense of confusing text and potential barriers to comprehension, such as new vocabulary terms, unclear referents, and difficult concepts.

- **Predicting**: using information from a text, text structure, reader aids, and background knowledge to formulate a guess about where the text "is going."

How do I use it?

1. Explain the concept of reciprocal teaching—we learn best when we have the opportunity to teach others.

2. Identify each of the four skills students will learn and use to help their classmates comprehend and remember what they read: summarizing, questioning, clarifying, predicting. Point out that learning these skills will also help improve students' own reading comprehension.

3. Choose a familiar text and model how to summarize important points, generate questions, clarify confusing text, and make predictions. After students have practiced each of these skills, begin to shift some of the responsibility for directing class discussion onto them.

4. Demonstrate reciprocal teaching with a four-person group of students in a "fishbowl" format. Designate one student to act as the "teacher" and facilitate discussion among his or her group members. Guide the group through the reciprocal teaching process as the rest of the class observes. For example, prompt the student teacher by asking, "What question do you think a teacher would ask at this point?" Alternatively, have the student teacher begin the discussion with a summary of the passage if he or she is having trouble thinking of appropriate questions. This will help the student summarize thoughts that he or she can turn into questions.

Soliciting advice from the rest of the class can also shift the focus away from you and keep students in control of the discussion.

5. As students become more proficient with reciprocal teaching, have them work with longer passages and alternate roles among group members.

FIGURE S25.1 ⇢ Reciprocal Teaching Walkthrough

Step 1: **Summarizer**. After students have silently or orally read a short section of a passage, a single student acting as teacher (i.e., the student leader) summarizes what has been read. Other students, with guidance from the student leader, may add to the summary. If students have difficulty summarizing, the teacher might point out clues (important items or obvious topic sentences) that aid in the construction of good summaries.

Step 2: **Questioner**. The questioner asks questions to which the class responds. The questions are designed to help students identify important information in the passage. For example, the questioner might look back over the selection and ask questions about specific pieces of information. The other students then try to answer these questions based on their recollection of the information.

Step 3: **Clarifier**. The clarifier tries to clarify vocabulary and confusing points in the passage. He or she might point these out or ask other students to point them out. For example, the clarifier might say, "The part about why the dog ran into the car was confusing to me. Can anyone explain this?" Or the clarifier might direct students to ask clarification questions. The group then attempts to clear up the confusing parts, which might involve rereading parts of the passage.

Step 4: **Predictor**. The predictor asks for predictions about what will happen in the next segment of the text. The predictor can write the predictions on the whiteboard, or students can write them down.

Source: From *Classroom Instruction That Works: Research-Based Strategies for Increasing Student Achievement* (2nd ed.), by C. Dean, E. R. Hubbell, H. Pitler, and B. Stone, 2012, Alexandria, VA: ASCD. Copyright 2012 by McREL. Adapted with permission.

FIGURE S25.2 → Reciprocal Teaching Sentence Starters

Summarizer	**Clarifier**
• To summarize the events in this section. . .	• Here is a word/idea/concept that I would like to clarify. . .
• To summarize the information in this section. . .	• Who else would like a word clarified?
• Who would like to add to this summary?	• Which word or words do we need to clarify?
Questioner	**Predictor**
• Please think about the following question. . . Why does. . . ? What was . . . ? Who did . . . ?	• Based on. . . , I believe . . . will. . .
• What do other group members think?	• In the text. . . Therefore, I predict. . .
• Who has another point of view?	• Who else has predictions about what will happen next?
	• Because of this information, I believe the solution to the problem is . . .

26. Semantic Feature Analysis

____ Narrative Text
X Informational Text
X Prereading
X During Reading
X After Reading
____ Writing to Learn
____ Reflection
____ Discussion
X Vocabulary Development

What is it?

Semantic Feature Analysis is a strategy that helps students discern a term's meaning by comparing its features to those of other terms that fall into the same category or class (Baldwin, Ford, & Readance, 1981; Johnson & Pearson, 1984). When students complete a semantic feature matrix, they create a visual reminder of how certain terms are alike or different. The matrix provides a good summary of concept features and helps students review material and prepare for exams. Creating a comparison matrix (Strategy 6) is the next logical step as students deepen their knowledge of similarities and differences.

How do I use it?

1. Identify a concept that students are currently learning, and introduce the semantic feature matrix template. In the first column, list key vocabulary terms relevant to the concept. Across the top of the matrix, write characteristics and features that are pertinent to the concept as a whole.

2. Have students check individual boxes to indicate which features apply to each term. If students identify the same set of features for more than one word, challenge them to identify a feature that would differentiate those terms.

3. Ask students to explain the rationale behind their markings (to partners, small groups, or the entire class). The acts of explaining their reasons and listening to others' explanations enhance their understanding of the concept.

4. As students become adept at using this strategy, they should use the matrix to analyze more sophisticated or abstract categories such as geometric forms, literary movements, forms of government, economic cycles, or land forms.

FIGURE S26.1 ⇢ Semantic Feature Analysis Matrix

Category: _____

Terms: Features/Properties

FIGURE S26.2 ⟶ Semantic Feature Analysis Matrix Example

Concepts: Polygons

Polygons	opposite sides parrallel	equilateral	equiangular	4-sided	3-sided
Square	X	X	X	X	
Rectangle	X		X	X	
Triangle					X
Rhombus	X	X		X	
Trapezoid				X	

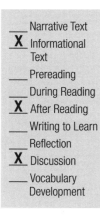

___ Narrative Text
X Informational Text
___ Prereading
___ During Reading
X After Reading
___ Writing to Learn
___ Reflection
X Discussion
___ Vocabulary Development

27. Scored Discussion Protocol

What is it?

The Scored Discussion Protocol is a strategy based on the concept of Collaborative Reasoning (Anderson, Chinn, Waggoner, & Nguyen, 1998). The strategy uses discussion to encourage students' critical reading and thinking about text. These discussions "foster conversation among students that draw on personal experiences, background knowledge and text for interpretive support" (Murphy, Wilkinson, Soter, Hennessey, & Alexander, 2009) This strategy works well with readings that invite opposing viewpoints because students have to use discussion as a means for taking a position on an issue. Talk appears to play a fundamental role in text-based comprehension, but students need to know the criteria of how to have a good discussion. The scored discussion protocol establishes the criteria. Students observe a small group of their classmates carry on a content-related discussion, and then they score their classmates' individual contributions to the discussion. Some effective discussion skills (which contribute to students' scores) include: contributing relevant information, using evidence, asking clarifying questions, making analogies, and encouraging other group members to participate..

How do I use it?

1. Identify and assign a text in which the author takes a position on an issue. For example, students might read an article on physician-assisted suicide in which the author takes a position on the subject. Then ask students the following questions:

   a. What position does the author take on the issue?

   b. Do you agree or disagree with the author's position?

2. Provide enough time for students to write responses and take notes on their rationale. A claim/support outline (Strategy 5) is a good organizational tool for students to use in their preparation for the discussion.

3. Distribute discussion score sheets and clarify the criteria and indicators of a successful discussion with students.

4. Select six to eight students to participate in the small-group scored discussion. Ask each student to be an evaluator for another member of the scored discussion group. For instance, if there are eight students, then there will also be eight student evaluators. Try a practice scored discussion and then debrief with everyone involved to explain how you and the student evaluators scored effective and ineffective discussion skills.

5. Establish a fixed amount of time for the discussion (10 minutes is a good amount of time when the class is learning how to do a scored discussion), and, at the end of that time, have the evaluators provide targeted feedback to the group members.

6. Debrief the protocol, participants' roles, and evaluators' roles and what they learned in this process.

FIGURE S27.1 → Discussion Score Sheet

Student_____

Class_____

Positive/Productive Behavior	Point Value	Non-Productive Behavior	Points
1. Offers his/her position on a topic	_____ x(1)= _____	1. Not paying attention or distracting others	_____ x(−2)= _____
2. Makes relevant comment	_____ x(1)= _____	2. Interruption	_____ x(−1)= _____
3. Uses evidence to Support position	_____ x(3)= _____	3. Irrelevant comment	_____ x(−1)= _____
4. Points out contradictions in another person's statements	_____ x(2)= _____	4. Monopolizing	_____ x(−3)= _____
5. Recognizes when another person makes an irrelevant comment	_____ x(2)= _____	5. Personal attack	_____ x(−3)= _____
6. Develops an analogy	_____ x(3)= _____	**Total Points Positive/Productive Behavior:**	
7. Asks a clarifying question	_____ x(1)= _____	**Non-Productive Behavior:**	_____
		Overall Total:	_____
8. Uses active listening skills (e.g., rephrases or restates what another student says before commenting)	_____ x(3)= _____	**Grade:**	_____

FIGURE S27.2 ⇢ Discussion Score Sheet Example

Student   **Matt Gomez**
Class   **Biology 10**

Positive/Productive Behavior	Point Value			Non-Productive Behavior	Points		
1. Offers his/her position on a topic	2	x(1)=	2	1. Not paying attention or distracting others	0	x(−2)=	0
2. Makes relevant comment	2	x(1)=	2	2. Interruption	1	x(−1)=	-1
3. Uses evidence to Support position	2	x(3)=	6	3. Irrelevant comment	0	x(−1)=	0
4. Points out contradictions in another person's statements	1	x(2)=	2	4. Monopolizing	0	x(−3)=	0
5. Recognizes when another person makes an irrelevant comment	0	x(2)=	0	5. Personal attack	0	x(−3)=	0
6. Develops an analogy	0	x(3)=	0	**Total Points Positive/Productive Behavior:**			21
7. Asks a clarifying question	3	x(1)=	3	**Non-Productive Behavior:**			−1
				Overall Total:			20
8. Uses active listening skills (e.g., rephrases or restates what another student says before commenting)	2	x(3)=	6	**Grade:**			

Letter grade to be determined by teacher's scale

X Narrative Text
X Informational Text
___ Prereading
___ During Reading
X After Reading
___ Writing to Learn
X Reflection
X Discussion
___ Vocabulary Development

28. Socratic Seminar

What is it?

Socratic Seminars are used to promote students' thinking and meaning-making skills along with their ability to debate, use evidence from the text, and build on one another's ideas. When they are designed and implemented well, Socratic Seminars provide an active role for every student, engage students in complex thinking about rich content, and teach valuable discussion skills. It is important to remember that the discussion belongs to the students and the teacher should function as facilitator—the full value of the seminar would be lost if the discussion becomes one in which students simply answer the teacher's questions (Downing, 1997).

How do I use it?

1. Identify a text that is related to the current project or lesson and is also rich with possibilities for diverse points of view. It could be an article from a magazine, journal, or newspaper. It could also be a poem, short story, or personal memoir.

2. Develop an open-ended, provocative question that can be used to begin the seminar discussion. The question should be worded to elicit different perspectives and levels of complex thinking. Encourage students to generate their own questions to discuss with the group.

3. Review the Socratic Seminar ground rules on page 174 with students.

4. Have students prepare for the activity by reading the text and completing a task that will help them build background knowledge they can use during the discussion. The completion of a preseminar task should be each student's "ticket" to participate in the seminar. For example, ask students to use specific text-coding symbols (Strategy 35) as they read. If students have not done the reading and cannot do the preseminar task, then they may observe but they may not participate in the seminar.

5. Facilitate the discussion; at the end of a designated amount of time, debrief with students to review how the discussion went and what content they learned as a result of the discussion.

Alternative Approach (for a large group):

1. Divide students into two groups. One group forms the inner circle and will discuss the text. The other group forms the outer circle and will provide feedback to the inner-circle participants on content, contributions, and group skills.

2. Discuss the ground rules for discussion and criteria for observation, and make sure all students understand them. Members of the outer circle will act as evaluators and be assigned one person in the inner circle to observe.

3. The seminar leader (teacher or students) begins the discussion with an open-ended question designed to provoke inquiry and diverse perspectives.

4. The discussion proceeds for the designated amount of time. When that time is over, the inner group debriefs about the content and their process with one another, and the outer group gives feedback to the inner group about their participation according to the ground rules.

FIGURE S28.1 ⇢ Socratic Seminar Ground Rules

Skills	Comments
Participants respect one another. All ideas are honored and respected.	
Participants are active listeners. They build upon one another's ideas by referencing and developing them.	
Participants stay focused on the topic.	
Participants make specific references to the text and use examples from the text to explain their points.	
Participants ask for clarification. They ask questions to make sure they understand the points that other participants are trying to make.	

FIGURE S28.2 → Socratic Seminar Student Observer Checklist

Did the participant. . .	Consistently	Occasionally	Never
Respond to other participants' comments in a respectful way?			
Listen attentively without interruption?			
Make eye contact with other participants?			
Exhibit adequate preparation for the seminar?			
Use the text to support his/her response?			
Participate in the discussion?			

FIGURE S28.3 → Socratic Seminar Questions Starters and Prompts

A good opening question:

- Arises from a genuine curiosity on the part of the facilitator.
- Has no single "right" answer.
- Is framed to generate discussion that leads to greater understanding of the text.
- Can be answered best by references (explicit or implicit) to the text.

Agree/Disagree Questions: • Has anyone else had a similar thought about. . . ? • Who has a different idea/opinion about. . . ? • I'm not sure I understand. . . ? • Tell me more about. . . ? • Do you see gaps in that reasoning? • Are you taking into account something different from what I have considered?	*Benefits/Burdens Questions:* • What are some of the reasons this would/wouldn't be a good idea? • Would anyone like to speak to the opposite side? • Those are some reasons this would work. What are some reasons it might not work?
Structure/Function Questions: • If that were the goal, what do you think about. . . ? *(action, reaction)* • What were his/her choices of how to. . . ? • Why was he/she doing that? What do you think of that approach? • What better choices could he/she have made? • What rules would we need to make sure. . . ?	*Point of View/Perspective Questions:* • How might he/she have felt if. . . ? • What do you think he/she was thinking when. . . ? • He/She might not like that, but can you think of someone who would? • Can anyone express a different opinion? • Do you have a different interpretation? • Do you have different conclusions? • How did you arrive at your point of view?
Cause and Effect Questions: • Why do you think that happened? • How could that have been prevented? • Do you think that would happen again? Why or why not? • What are some reasons that people. . . ?	*Support Questions:* • Can you give us an example of. . . ? • Where in the story. . . ? • What would be a good reason for. . . ? • What is some evidence for. . . ?
Compare/Contrast Questions: • How are . . . and . . . alike? How are they different? • What is that similar to? • Can you think of why this feels different than. . . ? • How does this (poem, book, incident, etc.) remind you of. . . ?	*Counterexample Questions:* • Would that still happen if. . . ? • What might have made the difference?

Solicit Questions:	Different Situation Questions:
• What are some things you wonder about?	• Can you describe a situation that would. . . ?
• What would you like to know about?	• Suppose. . . Would this still be true? Why or why not?
• Are there questions we should remember now?	

____ Narrative Text
X Informational Text
X Prereading
X During Reading
X After Reading
X Writing to Learn
X Reflection
____ Discussion
X Vocabulary Development

29. SQ3R

What is it?

SQ3R is a versatile study strategy because it engages students during each stage of the reading process (Robinson, 1970). Students preview text material to develop predictions, and they set a purpose for reading by generating questions about the topic. Then, they actively read, searching for answers to their questions, monitoring their comprehension as they summarize main ideas and key points, and evaluating their comprehension with review activities.

How do I use it?

1. Distribute copies of the SQ3R organizer, and model how you would respond to each set of questions or tasks:

   - Survey (one minute)—Model skimming headings and asking yourself questions.

   - Question (one minute)—Model how you can turn headings into questions.

   - Read (time dependent on the length of the text).

   - Recite (one minute)—Model how to answer questions you thought of without looking at the text.

   - Review (four–five minutes)—Model summarizing what you learned.

2. Assign a text passage from the current lesson or unit and have students practice the strategy in pairs or small groups.

3. When students are familiar and comfortable with the strategy, assign additional passages for students to read individually.

4. Bring students back together and have them discuss in pairs or small groups the questions and notes they made for each stage of the organizer.

FIGURE S29.1 ⇢ SQ3R Organizer

Stage	Process	Notes
Survey *(one minute)*	• Think about the title and ask yourself, "What do I know about this subject? What do I want to know?" • Skim the headings and first sentence of each paragraph. • Look at the illustrations and graphic aids. • Read the first paragraph. • Read the last paragraph or summary.	
Question *(one minute)*	• Turn the title into a question. This should become the main purpose for your reading. • Write down any questions that come to mind during the survey stage. • Turn headings into questions. • Turn subheadings, illustrations, and graphic aids into questions. • Write down unfamiliar vocabulary terms and determine the meaning of each.	
Read *(length of time varies)*	• Search for answers to your questions. • Respond to questions and use context clues to determine the meaning of unfamiliar words. • React to unclear passages, confusing terms, and questionable statements by generating additional questions.	
Recite *(one minute)*	• Look away from the answers and the book to recall what you read. • Recite answers to your questions aloud or write them down. • Reread the text for unanswered questions.	

continued

FIGURE S29.1 ⇢ SQ3R Organizer (*continued*)

Stage	Process	Notes
Review *(four–five minutes)*	• Answer the main purpose questions. • Look over your answers and the entire chapter to organize information. • Summarize the information learned by creating a graphic organizer that depicts the main ideas. Draw a flow chart, write a summary, participate in a group discussion, or write an explanation of how this material changed your ideas/opinions or applies to your life.	

FIGURE S29.2 ⇢ SQ3R Organizer Example

Stage	Process	Notes
Survey *(one minute)*	• Think about the title and ask yourself, "What do I know about this subject? What do I want to know?" • Skim the headings and first sentence of each paragraph. • Look at the illustrations and graphic aids. • Read the first paragraph. • Read the last paragraph or summary.	Title: The Beginnings of Ancient Rome What I know: Rome is in Italy. Some democratic ideas came from ancient Rome.
Question *(one minute)*	• Turn the title into a question. This should become the main purpose for your reading. • Write down any questions that come to mind during the survey stage. • Turn headings into questions. • Turn subheadings, illustrations, and graphic aids into questions. • Write down unfamiliar vocabulary terms and determine the meaning of each.	What were the beginnings of ancient Rome? What is a republic? When was ancient Rome?
Read *(length of time varies)*	• Search for answers to your questions. • Respond to questions and use context clues to determine the meaning of unfamiliar words. • React to unclear passages, confusing terms, and questionable statements by generating additional questions.	Plebeian and patrician are new words I don't understand.
Recite *(one minute)*	• Look away from the answers and the book to recall what you read. • Recite answers to your questions aloud or write them down. • Reread the text for unanswered questions.	I had to reread to understand the consul leadership.

continued

FIGURE S29.2 ⟶ *(continued)*

Stage	Process	Notes
Review *(four–five minutes)*	• Answer the main purpose questions. • Look over your answers and the entire chapter to organize information. • Summarize the information learned by creating a graphic organizer that depicts the main ideas. Draw a flow chart, write a summary, participate in a group discussion, or write an explanation of how this material changed your ideas/opinions or applies to your life.	Republic ↓ Senate ↙ ↘ Consul Consul ↓ ↓ Government Military

30. SQRQCQ

___ Narrative Text
X Informational Text
X Prereading
___ During Reading
X After Reading
X Writing to Learn
X Reflection
X Discussion
___ Vocabulary Development

What is it?

SQRQCQ stands for Survey, Question, Read, Question, Compute/Construct, Question. This reading strategy is modeled after the SQ3R approach (Strategy 29) and is intended to help students learn mathematics (Fay, 1965). It is particularly useful with helping students comprehend and solve word problems (Roberts, 2004). Students sometimes rush to the numbers in a word problem without reading the text, and SQRQCQ slows them down so they read and comprehend what the problem is actually asking them to do. The strategy involves previewing, setting purpose, and monitoring success.

How do I use it?

1. Introduce and describe the different steps involved with the SQRQCQ strategy.

2. Model the strategy with a word problem by explaining the steps as you work a problem on the board.

3. Have students work in pairs to practice other word problems.

4. When students are comfortable with the strategy, have them work through word problems independently.

5. Finally, have students discuss their answers and the process with partners, small groups, or the whole class.

FIGURE S30.1 → SQRQCQ Steps

Survey	Students read the problem quickly to get an idea or a general understanding of it.
Question	Students ask questions to identify the information the problem is specifically asking them to find or solve.
Read	Students carefully read the problem to identify the relevant information, facts, and details they need to solve it.
Question	Students ask questions to identify how to solve the problem correctly.
Compute/Construct	Students perform the necessary computations or otherwise construct a solution to the problem.
Question	Students ask questions to see if the solution process they've identified is accurate and if the answer they've computed seems correct.

FIGURE S30.2 ⇢ SQRQCQ Example

Survey	For a certain cell phone company, the basic plan costs $40 per month for the first 5,000 minutes, and each additional minute costs an extra $0.45. Each text message costs $0.20. The prepaid plan is $2 per day with unlimited texts. For a typical 30-day month, if a person spends fewer than 5,000 minutes on the phone, how many texts must that person send before the prepaid plan is the better deal?
Question	This problem is asking me to compare two cell phone plans—the basic plan and a prepaid plan—in order to find out how many texts a person can send with the basic plan before the cost becomes greater than the prepaid plan.
Read	Basic plan cost: $40 (for 5,000 minutes), plus $0.45 per minute after that, plus $0.20 per text. (I think the $0.45 piece of information is not relevant.) The problem states that a person spends fewer than 5,000 minutes on the phone, so the cost is $40 + $0.20 per text. Prepaid plan cost: $2 per day. For a typical 30-day month, that's $2 x 30 days
Question	*What operations must I do and in what order?* First, I need to figure out the monthly cost of the prepaid plan by multiplying the daily rate times 30 days. Then I can create an equation for the cost of the basic plan and set that up as an inequality with the cost of the prepaid plan. Finally, I need to solve that equation for the number of texts. (I wonder what it means when it says that the prepaid plan is a better deal.) It must mean that the prepaid plan will cost less than the basic plan.
Compute	Prepaid Plan: $C1 = \$2 \times 30$ days $= \$60$ Basic Plan: $C2 = \$40 + \$0.2T$ For what value of T is $C1 < C2$? $60 < 40 + .2T$ $20 < .2T$ $100 < T$ A person would need to send more than 100 texts in order for the prepaid plan to be the better deal.
Question	*Were the computations performed accurately, and is the answer reasonable?* 100 texts seem to be a reasonable answer. If a person sends 100 texts, his or her cost for the basic plan is $40 + $0.2 (100) = $60. This is equivalent to the monthly cost for the prepaid plan. If there are more than 100 texts, 120 for example, the cost of the basic plan becomes $40 + $0.2 (120) = $64. Since $64 > $60, the prepaid plan is a better deal for more than 100 texts.

X Narrative Text

___ Informational Text

___ Prereading

___ During Reading

X After Reading

___ Writing to Learn

___ Reflection

X Discussion

___ Vocabulary Development

31. Story Grammar and Story Maps

What is it?

Story grammar refers to a story's structure, literary elements (e.g., character, setting, problem, major events, resolution theme), and their relationship to each other. An examination of story grammar provides students with a strategic plan for selecting important aspects of story information (Short & Ryan, 1984). Alternatively, story grammar can be portrayed in a story map (Beck & McKeown, 1981). Story maps are graphic organizers that map out story grammar information and are helpful in sequencing and explaining the elements of narrative texts.

How do I use it?

1. Review story grammar questions with students. Depending on the grade level, one or all of the questions from each story grammar area may be used.

2. Using a familiar story students have already read, model how to construct a story map outline from the story grammar questions and elements. Story maps do not have to look the same each time because different story grammar questions can be used to construct them.

3. As students read a new story, have partners work together and complete a new story map that mimics the map they have seen modeled

4. Have partners share their maps with other pairs and then discuss the differences.

5. Lead the entire class in a discussion about the information that was included in the story maps.

6. Model how to set up new story maps using different story grammar questions.

FIGURE S31.1 → Story Grammar Questions

Characters	Setting
• Who are the main characters in the story? • Who do you think is the most important character? Why do you think this? • How would you describe the main character? • Who is your favorite character? How would the story be different if that character were not in the story?	• Where does the story take place? • When does the story take place? • Why do you think the author selected this particular setting? • Can you think of a better setting? If so, what would it be?
Problem/Conflict	**Major Events**
• What is the main problem/conflict in the story? • Why is this a problem/conflict for the main character? What impact does this have on the main character? • How do the characters change and what do they learn as a result of this problem/conflict?	• What important events happen in this story? What makes them important? • What new understanding do you have of the main character because of his/her role in these events?
Resolution	**Theme**
• How is the problem solved or the conflict resolved? • What else could have been done to solve the problem or resolve the conflict?	• What is the author's primary message/moral/theme? Why do you think this? • How can you apply this message/moral/theme to your own life?

FIGURE S31.2 → Story Map Graphic Organizer

Characters	Setting

Problem/Conflict

Major Events

Resolution

Theme

FIGURE S31.3 ⟶ Story Map Graphic Organizer Example

"An Occurrence at Owl Creek" by Ambrose Bierce

Characters
Peyton Farquhar
Northern scout
Sergeant
Farquhar's wife

Setting
Owl Creek along
the railroad tracks
in the South during
the Civil War

Problem/Conflict
Farquhar is not able to join the Confederate army.
He is deeply committed to the Confederacy and wants
to be known for doing something heroic for the Confederacy.

Major Events

1. Part One: Farquhar is about to be hanged by Northern soldiers for his attempt to sabotage the Owl Creek Bridge. He is hanged and cut down from the makeshift gallows.

2. Part Two: Farquhar is at home on his front porch with his wife when a "Confederate" soldier rides up. The soldier is really a Northern scout. This soldier tricks Farquhar into believing he will help the South if he burns the Owl Creek Bridge down.

3. Part Three: Farquhar believes he has escaped the gallows and runs home, only to be shot by the soldiers as he sees his wife.

Resolution
Farquhar is actually hanged in Part One, and we learn that
he has a blurred experience between reality and illusion at
the moment of his hanging and his death.

Theme
Putting the desire to be famous
for something ahead of a responsibility
to one's family.

___ Narrative Text

X Informational Text

___ Prereading

X During Reading

X After Reading

X Writing to Learn

___ Reflection

___ Discussion

___ Vocabulary Development

32. Structured Note Taking

What is it?

Structured Note Taking is one of several note-taking strategies that provide students with a visual framework that helps them determine relevant and important information as they read and take notes. Other examples of note-taking strategies are Combination Notes and Teacher Prepared Notes (Dean et al, 2012). Note taking is the process of capturing key ideas from a text for later access. Critical to this approach is a graphic organizer that mimics the organizational pattern of the assigned text. Initially, this organizer should be teacher-prepared and given to students. Eventually, as students practice and become comfortable with this strategy, they should be able to devise their own graphic organizers.

How do I use it?

1. Instruct students in the various organizational patterns authors use (see Strategy 12). Explain that understanding these patterns improves understanding of the text and also provides a structure for taking notes on the material.

2. Once students are familiar with the different organizational patterns, model the process of structured note taking. Give students a short passage for which you have already created a graphic organizer, and walk them through how you would use it for note taking. For example, a teacher might prepare a generalization/principle graphic organizer that corresponds to a text about American Indian removal from 1814–1858. The teacher models how to find examples that support the generalization.

3. Assign a different passage for students to use as they practice the note-taking strategy. Provide each student with a copy of a graphic organizer you have constructed for that passage.

4. Have students share their completed organizers with partners, explaining why they included certain information and justifying its position on the organizer.

5. Continue to scaffold student learning over time by providing organizers without headings and then having students build their own organizers as they read. Demonstrate how to preview text to construct an accurate visual representation of the material; for example, students may decide if the text is in chronological order, in cause–effect order, or in episodic order.

FIGURE S32.1 ⇢ Structured Note Taking Graphic Organizer

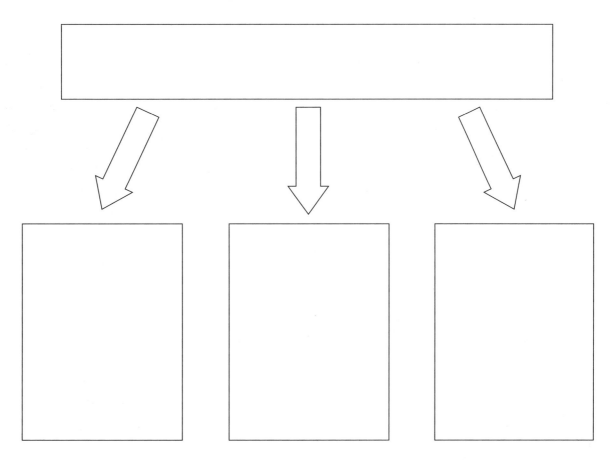

Source: From "Structured Notetaking: A New Strategy for Content Area Readers," by P. Smith and G. Tompkins, 1988, *Journal of Reading, 32*(1), pp. 46–53. Copyright 1988 by the International Reading Association. Adapted with permission.

FIGURE S32.2 ⇢ Structured Note Taking Graphic Organizer Example

American Indian Removal 1814–1858

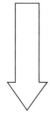

- Andrew Jackson did not want American Indians to hold land in the east.
- Nine treaties were negotiated that took land away from American Indians in the east and gave them land in the west.

In 1823, the Supreme Court decided that American Indians could have land but not hold title to that land.

- American Indians believed in the treaties.
- They agreed to the treaties.
- They adopted White ways.

33. Summarization

What is it?

The reading comprehension skill of summarization affords students the opportunity to capture, organize, and reflect on important ideas they will need to access at a later time in a lesson or unit of study (Piolat, Olive, & Kellogg, 2005). Because students must learn how to decide which information to keep, delete, or substitute, they must analyze the information at a fairly deep level (Dean et al., 2012). Structured summarization strategies such as the rule-based strategy and group summarization are effective means for students to improve their academic performance in reading and writing.

X	Narrative Text
X	Informational Text
___	Prereading
___	During Reading
X	After Reading
X	Writing to Learn
___	Reflection
X	Discussion
___	Vocabulary Development

How do I use it?

Rule-Based Strategy

1. It is one thing for teachers to understand how to make generalizations from research. However, for students to understand and successfully practice summarization skills, teachers must model the appropriate process students should follow.

2. In order for students to effectively summarize a text, they must know and follow the rules below (Brown, Day, & Jones, 1983):

   - Delete trivial material that is unnecessary to understanding.

   - Delete redundant material.

   - Replace a list of things with one word that describes them (e.g., "trees" for "birch, maple, aspen, and oak").

   - Find a topic sentence, or write one if it is missing.

Group Summarization

1. Summaries completed as a class help students review, discuss, and remember information (Olson & Gee, 1991). Class discussion is a key component of the group summarization approach.

2. Have students survey the text passage to identify major topics on which they should focus while reading. They should pay attention to text features such as bold and italicized text, headings, subheadings, photos and illustrations, and graphic organizers. The key terms and ideas students identify from these features should become the topics they will use in their summaries.

3. Divide the board or chart paper into equal sections, and label each with one of the key ideas students identified. These categories will provide students with a clear purpose for reading. For example, a text about soil may have the headings of *description, formation, living things and importance.* As students read, they should look for information about those topics.

4. After students finish reading the text, ask them to volunteer relevant information from the passage that belongs in each of the categories. Record the information in sentence form—not on the group summarization organizer. Be sure to involve the entire class in this step. Class discussion is a key part of the process.

5. Model how students can develop summaries for each of the categories from the recorded information. Write these summaries in the appropriate sections.

6. When students are more familiar with group summarizing, have them work in small groups to encourage more active and involved participation. Remember to have the small groups report out to the entire class, share their summaries, and discuss differences they notice among the group summaries.

FIGURE S33.1 ⟶ Rule-Based Summarization Strategy Example

Original Text

Asteroids are metallic and rocky bodies that orbit the sun but are too small to be planets. Asteroids are considered remnants from the giant cloud of gas and dust that condensed to create the sun, planets, and moons some 4.5 billion years ago. They are sometimes known as minor planets, but asteroids have no atmosphere. They can be as small as a few feet in diameter or as large as several miles in diameter.

Most asteroids orbit the sun in a tightly packed "belt" (a vast ring) between Mars and Jupiter. Four large asteroids—Ceres, Vesta, Pallas, and Hygiea—make up about half of the mass in the asteroid belt.

Asteroids are classified into a number of types:

- **C-type** includes more than 75% of known asteroids.
- **S-type** includes roughly 17% of known asteroids.
- **M-type** includes most of the rest.
- There are also a dozen or so other rare types.

Summary Paragraph

Asteroids are rocky bodies that orbit the sun in a beltlike formation between Mars and Jupiter. Asteroids vary in size. Four asteroids make up half the mass of the belt. There are three main types of asteroids.

FIGURE S33.2 ⟶ Group Summarization Organizer

Topic	

FIGURE S33.3 ⇢ Group Summarization Organizer Example

Description

1. Soil is made up of weathered rock.
2. Minerals and humus are also in soil.
3. There are spaces between the soil pieces.
4. Air and water fill those spaces.

Formation

1. Bedrock is rock under loose material like soil.
2. Bedrock can be broken down into small pieces by weather.
3. Those pieces are called particles.
4. Those particles become pieces of the soil.

Living Things

1. Many tiny organisms can live in or on the soil.
2. Some of those organisms are moss, lichen, bacteria and fungi.
3. When these organisms die they decompose into the soil.
4. Decayed plants and animals are called humus.

Importance

1. Plants need soil to grow.
2. Soil gives plants water and nutrients.
3. Some plants use up nutrients.

Soil	
Description Soil is a mixture mainly containing weathered rock, minerals, and humus. Air and water fill spaces between soil particles.	**Formation** When bedrock is weathered, it breaks down into smaller particles. These particles are further weathered into soil.
Living Things Many organisms live on the soil and in it. Some living things, like moss, lichens, bacteria, and fungi, form into soil through decomposition. Humus is the decayed remains of dead plants and animals.	**Importance** Soil provides water, nutrients, and support to plants. Soil nutrients may be used faster by plants than they can be replaced.

Source: From *Teaching Reading in Science: A Supplement to Teaching Reading in the Content Areas Teacher's Manual* (2nd ed.) (p. 89), by M. L. Barton and D. L. Jordan, 2001, Aurora, CO: McREL. Copyright 2001 by McREL. Adapted with permission.

X Narrative Text
X Informational
Text
___ Prereading
___ During Reading
X After Reading
___ Writing to Learn
X Reflection
X Discussion
___ Vocabulary
Development

34. The Final Word Protocol

What is it?

The Final Word Protocol is a text-based, small-group discussion protocol in which students participate in rounds. During each round, the last person to speak has the final word. All students in the class will have an opportunity to speak, listen, and respond. Individual group members speak about any part of the text they choose, while everyone else listens attentively and doesn't interrupt. This protocol builds students' oral language and listening skills. In addition, all students' comprehension of the text increases as the small group members discuss the text multiple times. This protocol works well with texts that invite opposing viewpoints.

How do I use it?

1. Introduce this protocol in a "fish bowl" environment. Choose four students to model the protocol as you coach them through the steps. When all students are ready to tackle this strategy, organize them into groups of four, review the protocol again, and let them try it.

2. Have students read the text using the text-coding symbols (Strategy 35) you decide are appropriate for the text. Encourage students to identify two or three things in the text they want to talk about.

3. Assign a facilitator and a timekeeper for each group; alternatively, the teacher can facilitate and keep time for the entire class. The facilitator makes sure everyone follows the protocol, and the timekeeper lets everyone know when the time allotted for each step has elapsed. Other students can assume those roles during the round when the timekeeper or facilitator speaks.

4. At the end of the small-group discussions, have each group share three key issues they identified with the whole class.

FIGURE S34.1 ⇢ Final Word Protocol Ground Rules

Preliminary

- Students read a text and identify three things they want to discuss.
- Students form groups of four and count off 1–4.

Round One

- Student 1 begins and speaks about something in the text for one minute.
- No one else can speak during this minute. They must listen to the speaker.
- After one minute, student 1 stops and student 2 has one minute to respond to what student 1 said.
- Again, no one else speaks as student 2 responds.
- After one minute, student 2 stops and student 3 responds to what student 1 said.
- Everyone else listens.
- After one minute, student 3 stops and student 4 responds to what student 1 said.
- After one minute, student 4 stops and student 1 has the "final word" for one minute to respond to what everyone else said.

Round Two

- Student 2 begins this round.
- Repeat all of the steps, ending with student 2 having the final word.

Round Three

- Student 3 begins this round.
- Repeat all of the steps, ending with student 3 having the final word.

Round Four

- Student 4 begins this round.
- Repeat all of the steps, ending with student 4 having the final word.

Closing

- Each group shares three ideas with the rest of the class.

X Narrative Text
X Informational Text
___ Prereading
X During Reading
___ After Reading
___ Writing to Learn
X Reflection
___ Discussion
X Vocabulary Development

35. Think Alouds and Text-Coding Symbols

What is it?

Think alouds help students understand the kind of thinking that is required by a specific task (Davey, 1983). The teacher models his or her thinking process by verbalizing thoughts while reading, processing information, or performing a learning task. Students see how the teacher attempts to construct meaning for unfamiliar vocabulary, engages in dialogue with the author, or recognizes when he or she doesn't understand and then selects a strategy to address the problem.

How do I use it?

1. Explain that reading is a complex process that involves thinking and sense making; a skilled reader's mind is brimming with questions that seek to understand what he or she reads.

2. Select a passage to read aloud that contains ideas students might find difficult, unfamiliar vocabulary terms, or ambiguous wording. Develop questions you can ask yourself that will show what you think as you confront these problems while reading the text.

3. Teach several text-coding symbols students can use to keep track of their thinking as they read. Model how to use them with the appropriate content effectively.

4. Read the passage aloud as students follow along silently. As you read, verbalize your thoughts, the questions you develop, and the processes you use to overcome comprehension problems. Think alouds can include the skills listed in Figure S35.1, but you should also feel the freedom to add to or delete from this list, according to the specific needs of your students.

5. Have students work with partners to practice using think alouds and text-coding symbols as they read short passages of text. Periodically revisit this strategy or have students complete an assessment to make the strategy feel natural.

FIGURE S35.1 → Think-Aloud Skills

Skills	Example Statements
Make predictions or hypotheses as you read.	"From what he's said so far, I'll bet the author is going to give some examples of poor eating habits."
Describe the mental pictures you "see."	"When the author talks about vegetables I should include in my diet, I can see our salad bowl at home filled with fresh, green spinach leaves."
Demonstrate how you connect this information with prior knowledge.	"Saturated fat? I know I've heard that term before. I learned it last year when we studied nutrition."
Create analogies.	"That description of clogged arteries sounds like traffic clogging up the interstate during rush hour."
Verbalize obstacles and fix-up strategies.	"Now what does *angiogram* mean? Maybe if I reread that section, I'll get the meaning from the other sentences around it. I know I can't skip it because it's in bold print, so it must be important. If I still don't understand, I know I can ask for help or look it up in the glossary."

FIGURE S35.2 ⇢ Think-Aloud Assessment

		Not often/ Never	Sometimes	Most of the time	All of the time
Assessing My Use of the Think-Aloud Strategy *While I was reading, how much did I use these skills?* Place a tally mark in the second column each time you use a skill as you read. Notice how many times you use each skill, and put a check in the appropriate column.					
Making and revising predictions	( )				
Forming mental pictures	( )				
Connecting what I read to what I already know	( )				
Creating analogies	( )				
Verbalizing confusing points	( )				

Source: From "Think-Aloud: Modeling the Cognitive Process of Reading Comprehension," by B. Davey, 1983, *Journal of Reading, 27*(1), 44–47. Copyright 1983 by the International Reading Association. Adapted with permission.

FIGURE S35.3 → Think-Aloud Example

The Black Death

Black Death. That sounds frightening. I wonder what it is.

The Black Death was an epidemic of bubonic plague that ravaged Europe in the mid 1300s. Black spots that appeared on the skin of those infected gave this epidemic its name.

Okay. Now I know what it is and how it got its name.

The bubonic plague is carried by fleas on rats. The plague began in Asia and was carried to Europe by merchants and traders. In 1347, it appeared in Cyprus and Sicily. Unsanitary conditions and a lack of knowledge about what caused sickness and disease caused the plague to spread quickly. Major outbreaks were recorded in England, France, and Germany by 1348. By 1351, all of Europe was engulfed in the Black Death. Survival rates for those infected were only one in four. The bubonic plague killed 25 million people in Europe, about 25 percent of the continent's population. The plague killed tens of millions more in Asia.

Engulfed. I think that means completely covered. I better read more to see if my definition makes sense.

I am not sure I understand "survival rates." I should reread this section.

The plague killed millions all over Europe. My understanding of engulfed makes sense.

Black Death had a major economic impact on Europe. As populations fell, agricultural land was abandoned. A shortage of labor created a large demand for workers in towns. Serfs began leaving manors in search of higher wages. This migration of agricultural peasants into towns hastened the end of feudalism in Europe.

I get it. I remember studying supply and demand.

I don't remember what a serf or a manor is. I better look these up in the glossary or go back and reread the earlier chapter.

The epidemic also had a tremendous social impact. The Church lost some of its influence as people witnessed the plague overwhelm Europe despite prayer and worship. Some clergy deserted their infected congregations. Distraught relatives abandoned family members out of fear of catching the dreaded disease.

As fear gripped the continent, people searched for someone to blame. Prejudice against Jews made them a target of terrified and crazed populations. Fabricated allegations that Jews had caused the plague were common. Persecution of Jews spread throughout all of Europe, compounding the tragedy of the plague.

I am not sure I understand why people would blame one group for something like this. I need to ask my teacher about this. Maybe we could discuss this as a class.

I find it amazing and very scary how one disease could kill so many people and change the history of the world so much. I wonder if this is the only time this happened or if epidemics happened at other times and places. Could something like this happen now or do all of our advances in technology, medicine, and science make this unlikely?

The plague returned to Europe over the coming years, but never with the same devastation as the first epidemic. The economic and social consequences of the Black Death induced the disintegration of medieval society.

FIGURE S35.4 ⟶ Text-Coding Symbols

Active Reading	Symbol
Text to Self: This reminds me of something in my life. Text to Text: This reminds me of something else I have read. Text to World: This reminds me of something I've heard in the news.	TS TT TW
I knew that.	√
I didn't expect this, and I don't think I agree.	X
I think this is important.	☆
I have a question.	?
I am confused or puzzled.	??
This is surprising to me.	!
I learned something new.	LN
I need to reread this to understand.	RR

Source: From *Comprehension and Collaboration: Inquiry Circles in Action* (p. 93), by S. Harvey and H. Daniels, 2009, Portsmouth, NH: Heinemann. Copyright 2009 by Heinemann. Adapted with permission.

36. Three-Level Guide

___	Narrative Text
X	Informational Text
X	Prereading
X	During Reading
X	After Reading
___	Writing to Learn
___	Reflection
___	Discussion
___	Vocabulary Development

What is it?

A three-level guide helps students comprehend, analyze, and solve math word problems (Davis & Gerber, 1994). Using a teacher-constructed graphic organizer, students must evaluate facts, concepts, rules, ideas, and approaches to solving particular word problems. This strategy can help students focus on the important facts in a word problem, and it allows students to check the usefulness of a number of approaches, questions, or computations.

How do I use it?

1. Construct a three-level guide according to the following guidelines:

    *   The first level (Part I) should include a set of facts suggested by the data given in the word problem. Students should analyze each fact to determine if it is true and if it will help them solve the problem.

    *   The second level (Part II) should contain mathematics ideas, rules, or concepts that students can examine to determine which might apply to the problem-solving task.

    *   The third level (Part III) should include a list of possible ways to arrive at the answer. Students will analyze these to see which ones might help them solve the problem.

2. Introduce the strategy by showing students a word problem and modeling how to complete a three-level guide. Explain what kind of information is included at each of the levels.

3. Present students with another word problem, and guide them through it. Suggest that they analyze the information in the problem to determine its validity and usefulness in solving the problem.

FIGURE S36.1 → Three-Level Guide Template

Read the problem and then answer each set of questions, following the directions given.

Problem:

Part I

Directions: Read the statements. Check Column *A* if the statement is true, according to the problem. Check Column *B* if the information will help you solve the problem.

A (true?)   B (help?)

_____   _____
_____   _____
_____   _____
_____   _____
_____   _____

Part II

Directions: Read the statements. Check the ones that contain math ideas useful for this problem. Look at Part I, Column B to check your answer.

_____
_____
_____
_____
_____

Part III

Directions: Check the calculations that will help or work in this problem. Look at Parts I and II to check your answers.

_____   _____
_____   _____
_____   _____

Source: From "Open to Suggestion: Content Area Strategies in Secondary Mathematics Classrooms," by S. J. Davis and R. Gerber, 1994, *Journal of Reading, 38*(1), pp. 55–57. Copyright 1994 by the International Reading Association. Adapted with permission.

FIGURE S36.2 ⟶ Three-Level Guide Example

Read the problem and then answer each set of questions, following the directions given.

Problem: Sam's Sporting Goods has a markup rate of 40% on tennis rackets. Sam, the store owner, bought 12 tennis rackets for $75 each. Calculate the selling price of a tennis racket at Sam's Sporting Goods.

Part I

Directions: Read the statements. Check Column *A* if the statement is true, according to the problem. Check Column *B* if the information will help you solve the problem.

A (true?)	B (help?)	
_____	_____	Sam's markup rate is 40%
_____	_____	Sam bought 12 tennis rackets.
_____	_____	Tennis rackets are a good buy.
_____	_____	Sam paid $75 for a tennis racket.
_____	_____	The selling price of a tennis racket is more than $75.

Part II

Directions: Read the statements. Check the ones that contain math ideas useful for this problem. Look at Part I, Column B to check your answer.

_____	Markup equals cost times rate.
_____	Selling price is greater than cost.
_____	Selling price equals cost plus markup.
_____	Markup divided by cost equals markup rate.
_____	A percent of a number is less than the number when the percent is less than 100%.

Part III

Directions: Check the calculations that will help or work in this problem. Look at Parts I and II to check your answers.

_____	0.4 × $75	_____	12 × $75
_____	$75 × 40	_____	40% of $75
_____	1.4 × $75	_____	$75 + (2/5 × $75)

___ Narrative Text

X Informational Text

X Prereading

___ During Reading

X After Reading

X Writing to Learn

X Reflection

___ Discussion

X Vocabulary Development

37. Word Classification Sorts

What is it?

Identifying similarities through word classification sorts helps students "move from existing knowledge to new knowledge, concrete to abstract and separate to connected ideas" (Dean et al., 2012). Students are asked to sort vocabulary terms into different categories, a process that involves students in their own learning. This strategy can be used either of two different ways. In a closed sort, the teacher provides the categories into which students are to assign the words. In an open sort, students group words into categories and identify their own labels for each category. Alternatively, students can be responsible for contributing vocabulary they associate with a particular concept, rather than using vocabulary provided by the teacher. Word classification sorts help students develop a deeper understanding of key concepts, and they also are an excellent method to teach the complex reasoning skills of classification and deduction.

How do I use it?

1. Write a content-area or vocabulary term on the board, and ask students to brainstorm a list of words they associate with that term.

2. For an open sort, have students sort the words into categories and then explain those categories. In other words, how are those words related to one another? For a closed sort, provide the categories into which the words will be sorted.

3. As students become more proficient at classifying, ask them to complete multiple open sorts. Encourage them to identify more than one way to classify the terms. Classifying and reclassifying helps students extend and refine their understanding of the concepts studied.

FIGURE S37.1 ⇢ Open Sort Example

Weather Words

Student-generated list of words: *blizzard, flood, weather vane, cumulus, thermometer, cirrus, tornado, wind gauge, hurricane, barometer, stratus*

Student-generated categories: *tools for measuring weather, cloud types, and extreme weather*

Tools for Measuring Weather	Cloud Types	Extreme Weather
thermometer barometer wind gauge weather vane	cirrus stratus cumulus	hurricane tornado blizzard flood

FIGURE S37.2 ⇢ Closed Sort Example

Geometry Words

Student-generated list of words: *edges, square, volume, prism, circle, adjacent, symmetry, congruent, pyramid, hexagon, cone, rays, cube, area, opposite, perimeter, circumference, cylinder, vertices*

Teacher-generated categories: *parts of shapes, shapes (plane figures and solid figures), measures, relations*

Parts of Shapes	Shapes: Plane Figures	Shapes: Solid Figures	Measures	Relations
edges vertices rays	hexagon square circle	cube cone pyramid prism cylinder	circumference area perimeter volume	congruent adjacent symmetry opposite

_____ Narrative Text
X Informational Text
X Prereading
_____ During Reading
_____ After Reading
_____ Writing to Learn
_____ Reflection
X Discussion
_____ Vocabulary Development

38. Word Problem Roulette

What is it?

Students should discuss and write about the content of mathematics word problems (Davis & Gerber, 1994). Group discussion promotes oral language development and deepens comprehension of text. Word Problem Roulette gives students a chance to collaborate with their classmates, solve a problem, and then communicate their thought processes and solutions in writing. Group problem-solving activities benefit students by allowing them to not only communicate their own thinking but also listen to other students' thinking.

How do I use it?

1. Model the strategy with a small group of students as the rest of the class observes. Coach the small group through the steps, and then debrief how the strategy worked with the entire class.

2. Organize students into collaborative groups, and provide all groups with the same word problem.

3. Explain to students that they should solve this problem orally. They are not allowed to write or draw anything during this step.

4. After students have discussed the problem with their group members and agreed on how to solve it, they should take turns writing the necessary steps with words rather than mathematical symbols. Each group member should write one sentence and pass the solution sheet to the next person, who then adds the next sentence.

5. After the groups finish writing, each group should select one member to read the steps to the whole class. Another group member then writes the symbolic representation of this solution on the board.

FIGURE S38.1 ⟶ Word Problem Roulette Template

Problem:
Students work together and orally solve the problem, agree on the steps, and arrive at a final solution.
Each group member writes one step of the solution and then passes the paper to the next person. No mathematical symbols may be used. 1. 2. 3. 4.
One group member reads the solution to the class.
Another group member writes the solution on the board with mathematical symbols.

FIGURE S38.2 → Word Problem Roulette Example

Problem:
A sale on swimsuits reduced the price of a two-piece suit from $45 to $27. What percent decrease does this represent?
1. The dollar difference between $45 and $27 is $18.
2. $18 is the amount of the discount.
3. $18 divided by $45 is the percent of the discount.
4. The percent of the discount is 40 percent.
$45 - 27 = 18$ $18 \div 45 = 0.40$ The percent decrease is 40%.

39. Written Conversation

What is it?

Written Conversation is an after-reading reflection strategy that engages all students in class discussion at the same time (Daniels & Zemelman, 2004). After everyone has read a specific text, the teacher asks students a question about the text and then has pairs of students write short notes back and forth to each other about the question and the text. This strategy allows students to have variety in their writing assignments, and it has sometimes been called "legalized note-passing" in content areas.

How do I use it?

1. Organize students into pairs, and explain that they will be writing notes to each other about the text. They will be writing notes at the same time, essentially having two conversations at once.

2. Introduce a conversation starter such as the following:

   - What interested you about this article on black holes?

   - Did *The Catcher in the Rye* remind you of another novel? How so?

   - What do you think are the most important ideas in The Bill of Rights?

   - Do you agree with Chevron's position in the article that hydraulic fracturing is important? Why or why not?

   - Did you think the character of Jonas was justified in leaving his community with Gabe? Why or why not?

3. Explain the ground rules of the written conversation.

4. Have students begin the written conversation with each other.

5. After the writing activity is finished, partners may talk out loud with each other about their conversations.

6. Finally, lead a whole-class discussion. Ask a few pairs of students to share a portion of their written conversations as a way of starting the discussion.

7. Decide if you want to collect, read, and assess the conversations.

FIGURE S39.1 ⇢ Ground Rules for the Written Conversation

1. Partners will consider the conversation starter and then write a note to each other for two minutes on that topic.

2. Students should address each other as if they were writing a letter. For example, they should begin their notes with "Dear *X*,"

3. After two minutes, students silently exchange notes. Each student should read his or her partner's note and then take two minutes to respond in writing.

4. No spoken conversation may occur during this time.

5. Students will repeat this process two or three times, as time and interest permit.

40. Zooming In and Out

___ Narrative Text
X Informational Text
X Prereading
___ During Reading
X After Reading
X Writing to Learn
___ Reflection
X Discussion
X Vocabulary Development

What is it?

Zooming In and Out is a strategy that expands on the Frayer Model (Strategy 11) and helps students analyze a concept two different ways (Harmon & Hedrick, 2000). It can be used as both a vocabulary and a text comprehension strategy. First, it helps students examine a concept more closely by asking them to rank important information about the concept and then list what the concept would *not* be expected to do or tell us. Second, students find and think about similar and related concepts and then write a summary statement. When students complete this activity, they make connections with related ideas and articulate specific knowledge about the concept.

How do I use it?

1. Identify a concept that is new or mostly unfamiliar to students. As a class, have students brainstorm what they might already know about the concept. For example, they could brainstorm what they know about archaeological artifacts.

2. Have students read a text and then discuss and decide what information in the text is most and least important (zooming in). For example, in a text about artifacts, students would identify the most important and least important information about artifacts.

3. Students discuss and identify information in the text that is similar to and related to the concept (zooming out).

4. Students then discuss and decide what is *not* related to the concept (zooming in). Again, using artifacts as the example, students would discuss and decide what material from the text is not related to the concept of artifacts.

5. Finally, have students write a summary statement (zooming out).

6. Once students feel comfortable with the process, have them try this strategy in pairs and, eventually, on their own with a new concept and a new text.

FIGURE S40.1 ⇢ Zooming In and Out Graphic Organizer

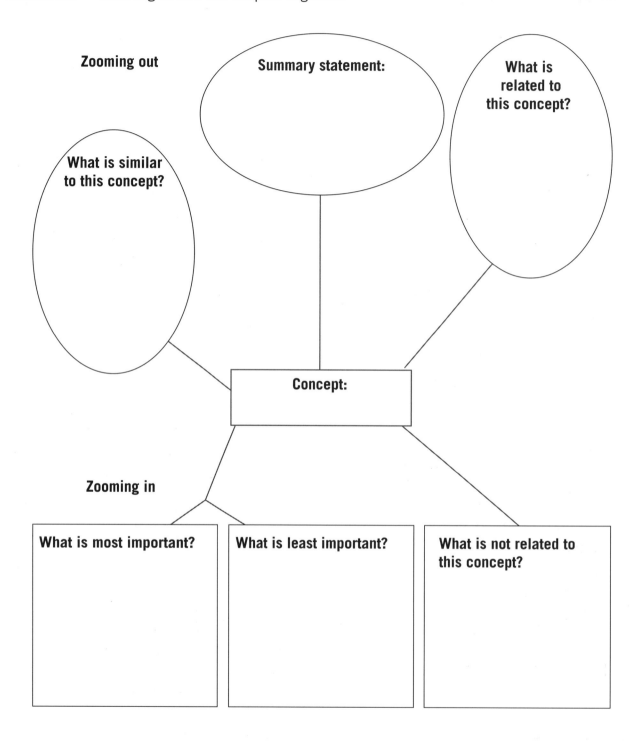

FIGURE S40.2 ⟶ Zooming In and Out Graphic Organizer Example

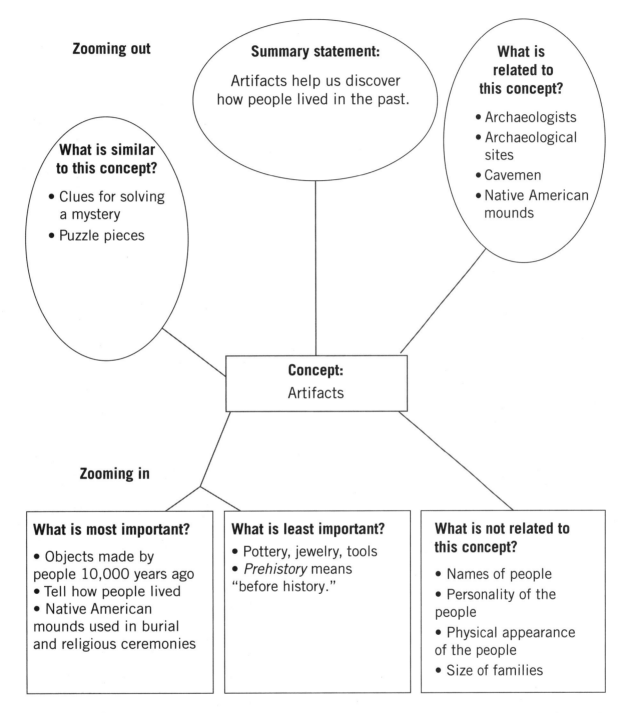

Zooming out

Summary statement:

Artifacts help us discover how people lived in the past.

What is related to this concept?

• Archaeologists
• Archaeological sites
• Cavemen
• Native American mounds

What is similar to this concept?

• Clues for solving a mystery
• Puzzle pieces

Concept:
Artifacts

Zooming in

What is most important?

• Objects made by people 10,000 years ago
• Tell how people lived
• Native American mounds used in burial and religious ceremonies

What is least important?

• Pottery, jewelry, tools
• *Prehistory* means "before history."

What is not related to this concept?

• Names of people
• Personality of the people
• Physical appearance of the people
• Size of families

Source: From "Teaching Ideas: Zooming In and Zooming Out: Enhancing Vocabulary and Conceptual Learning in Social Studies," by J. M. Harmon and W. B. Hedrick, 2000, *The Reading Teacher, 54*(2), 155–159. Copyright 2000 by the International Reading Association. Adapted with permission.

Appendix A
Metacognitive Reading Awareness Inventory

For each question, check as many responses as you think are effective.

1. What do you do if you encounter a word and you don't know what it means?
   - ☐ a. Use the words around it to figure it out.
   - ☐ b. Use an outside source, such as a dictionary or expert.
   - ☐ c. Temporarily ignore it and wait for clarification.
   - ☐ d. Sound it out.

2. What do you do if you don't know what an entire sentence means?
   - ☐ a. Read it again.
   - ☐ b. Sound out all the difficult words.
   - ☐ c. Think about the other sentences in the paragraph.
   - ☐ d. Disregard it completely.

3. If you are reading social studies material, what would you do to remember the important information you've read?
   - ☐ a. Skip parts you don't understand.
   - ☐ b. Ask yourself questions about the information ideas.
   - ☐ c. Realize you need to remember one point rather than another.
   - ☐ d. Relate it to something you already know.

4. Before you start to read, what kind of plans do you make to help you read better?
   - ☐ a. No specific plan is needed; just start reading toward completion of the assignment.
   - ☐ b. Think about what you know about the subject.
   - ☐ c. Think about why you are reading.
   - ☐ d. Make sure the entire reading can be finished in as short a period of time as possible.

5. Why would you go back and read an entire passage over again?

☐ a. You didn't understand it.

☐ b. To clarify a specific or supporting idea.

☐ c. It seemed important to remember.

☐ d. To underline or summarize for study.

6. Knowing that you don't understand a particular sentence while reading involves understanding that

☐ a. you may not have developed adequate links or associations for new words or concepts introduced.

☐ b. the writer may not have conveyed the ideas clearly.

☐ c. two sentences may purposely contradict each other.

☐ d. finding meaning for the sentence needlessly slows down a reader.

7. As you read a textbook, which of these do you do?

☐ a. Adjust your pace depending on the difficulty of the material.

☐ b. Generally read at a constant, steady pace.

☐ c. Skip the parts you don't understand.

☐ d. Continually make predictions about what you are reading.

8. While you read, which of these are important?

☐ a. Know when you know and when you don't know key ideas.

☐ b. Know what it is that you know in relation to what is being read.

☐ c. Know that confusing text is common and usually can be ignored.

☐ d. Know that different strategies can be used to aid understanding.

9. When you come across a part of the text that is confusing, what do you do?

☐ a. Keep on reading until the text is clarified.

☐ b. Read ahead and then look back if the text is still unclear.

☐ c. Skip those sections completely; they are usually not important.

☐ d. Check to see if the ideas expressed are consistent with one another.

10. Which sentences are the most important in the chapter?

☐ a. Almost all of the sentences are important; otherwise they wouldn't be there.

☐ b. The sentences that contain the important details or facts.

☐ c. The sentences that are directly related to the main idea.

☐ d. The ones that contain the most detail.

Suggested answers: 1: a, b, c; 2: a, c; 3: b, c, d; 4: b, c; 5: a, c, d; 6: a, b, c; 7: a, d; 8: a, b, d; 9: a, b, d; 10: b, c

Appendix B
Ten-Point Planning Checklist

	Yes	No
1. Have I identified my objectives for this lesson—what I want students to know and be able to do?		
2. Have I previewed the text and determined key concepts/vocabulary students need to know?		
3. Have I included activities and strategies that will help students develop a clear understanding of key concepts?		
4. Have I selected activities to assess, activate, and build students' background knowledge?		
5. Have I identified the text's organizational pattern and whether it highlights information I consider most important?		
6. If the organizational pattern does not highlight key information, have I determined the frame of mind or pattern I will tell students to use while reading?		

continued

	Yes	No
7. Have I selected a suitable graphic organizer students can use to organize key concepts?		
8. Have I decided the purpose(s) students should keep in mind while reading (e.g., whether they will be using the information in a discussion, performance activity, on a quiz)?		
9. Have I developed questions that will prompt students to employ metacognitive skills?		
10. Have I developed questions and activities that require students to make meaningful connections and deepen their understanding by applying what they have learned?		

Appendix C
Classroom Instruction That Works Strategies Matrix

This matrix connects reading strategies in this book to the nine categories of effective research-based strategies found in *Classroom Instruction That Works, 2nd edition*.

Reading Strategy	Nine Categories of Strategies from *Classroom Instruction That Works*								
	Setting Objectives and Providing Feedback	Reinforcing Effort and Providing Recognition	Cooperative Learning	Cues, Questions, and Advance Organizers	Nonlinguistic Representation	Summarizing and Note Taking	Assigning Homework and Providing Practice	Identifying Similarities and Differences	Generating and Testing Hypotheses
1. Academic Conversation	X	X	X	X	X	X	X		
2. Anticipation Guide	X	X	X	X		X	X		X
3. Chapter Discussion Protocol	X	X	X	X	X	X	X		

continued

Reading Strategy	Nine Categories of Strategies from *Classroom Instruction That Works*								
	Setting Objectives and Providing Feedback	Reinforcing Effort and Providing Recognition	Cooperative Learning	Cues, Questions, and Advance Organizers	Nonlinguistic Representation	Summarizing and Note Taking	Assigning Homework and Providing Practice	Identifying Similarities and Differences	Generating and Testing Hypotheses
4. Character/Historical Figure Comparison Organizer	X	X	X	X	X	X	X	X	
5. Claim/Support Outline	X	X	X			X	X	X	X
6. Comparison Matrix	X	X	X	X	X	X	X	X	
7. Concept Circles	X	X		X	X		X	X	
8. Concept Definition Map	X	X			X		X		
9. Directed Reading/ Thinking Activity	X	X	X			X	X		X
10. Discussion Web	X	X	X	X	X	X	X	X	X
11. Frayer Model	X	X			X		X	X	
12. Graphic Organizers	X	X		X	X	X	X	X	X
13. History Frames	X	X	X	X	X	X	X	X	
14. Knowledge Rating Scale and Vocabulary Definition Card	X	X		X			X		
15. KNFS	X	X		X		X	X		
16. Learning Log	X	X				X	X		

Reading Strategy	Nine Categories of Strategies from *Classroom Instruction That Works*								
	Setting Objectives and Providing Feedback	Reinforcing Effort and Providing Recognition	Cooperative Learning	Cues, Questions, and Advance Organizers	Nonlinguistic Representation	Summarizing and Note Taking	Assigning Homework and Providing Practice	Identifying Similarities and Differences	Generating and Testing Hypotheses
17. Metaphor and Analogy	X	X	X				X	X	
18. Pairs Reading and Summarizing	X	X	X			X	X		
19. PLAN	X	X		X		X	X		X
20. Prereading Predictions	X	X	X	X		X	X		
21. Probable Passages	X	X	X	X		X	X		
22. Problematic Situations	X	X	X			X	X		X
23. QAR	X	X		X			X		
24. RAFT	X	X				X	X		
25. Reciprocal Teaching	X	X	X	X		X	X		X
26. Semantic Feature Analysis	X	X		X	X		X	X	
27. Scored Discussion Protocol	X	X	X	X	X	X	X		
28. Socratic Seminar	X	X	X	X	X	X	X		
29. SQ3R	X	X		X		X	X		X

continued

Reading Strategy	Nine Categories of Strategies from *Classroom Instruction That Works*								
	Setting Objectives and Providing Feedback	Reinforcing Effort and Providing Recognition	Cooperative Learning	Cues, Questions, and Advance Organizers	Nonlinguistic Representation	Summarizing and Note Taking	Assigning Homework and Providing Practice	Identifying Similarities and Differences	Generating and Testing Hypotheses
30. SQRQCQ	X	X	X	X		X	X		X
31. Story Grammar and Story Maps	X	X	X	X	X	X	X	X	
32. Structured Note Taking	X	X	X	X		X	X		
33. Summarization	X	X	X			X	X		
34. The Final Word Protocol	X	X	X	X		X	X	X	
35. Think Alouds and Text-Coding Symbols	X	X		X		X	X		
36. Three-Level Guide	X	X	X	X		X	X		X
37. Word Classification Sorts	X	X	X	X	X		X	X	
38. Word Problem Roulette	X	X	X		X	X	X		X
39. Written Conversation	X	X	X			X	X		
40. Zooming In and Out	X	X	X	X	X	X	X		

References

Alexander, P. A., Graham, S., & Harris, K.R. (1998). A perspective on strategy research: Progress and prospects. *Educational Psychology Review, 10*(2), 129–154.

Alvermann, D. E. (1991). The discussion web: A graphic aid for learning across the curriculum. *The Reading Teacher, 45*(2), 92–99.

Alvermann, D. E. (2002). Effective literacy instruction for adolescents. *Journal of Literacy Research, 34*(2), 189–208.

Alvermann, D. E., Dillon, D. R., & O'Brien, D. G. (1988). *Using discussion to promote reading comprehension*. Newark, DE: International Reading Association.

Anderson, T. H., & Armbruster, B. B. (1984). Content area textbooks. In R. C. Anderson, J. Osborn, & R. J. Tierney (Eds.), *Learning to read in American schools: Basal readers and content texts* (pp. 193–226). Hillsdale, NJ: Erlbaum.

Anderson, R. C., Chinn, C., Waggoner, M., & Nguyen, K. (1998). Intellectually stimulating story discussions. In J. Osborn & F. Lehr (Eds.), *Literacy for all: Issues in teaching and learning* (pp. 170–186). New York: Guilford Press.

Anthony, H. M., & Raphael, T. E. (1989). Using questioning strategies to promote students' active comprehension of content area material. In D. Lapp, J. Flood, & N. Farnan (Eds.), *Content area reading and learning: Instructional strategies* (pp. 307–322). Englewood Cliffs, NJ: Prentice-Hall.

Armbruster, B. B., & Nagy, W. E. (1992). Vocabulary in content area lessons. *The Reading Teacher, 45*(7), 550–551.

Baldwin, R. S., Ford, J. C., & Readance, J. E. (1981). Teaching word connotations: An alternative strategy. *Reading World, 21*, 103–108.

Banks, J. A. (2001). A curriculum for empowerment, action, and change. In C. E. Sleeter (Ed.), *Empowerment through multicultural education* (pp. 125–142). Albany: State University of New York Press.

Barker, J. (2010). Improving instructional practices for English-language learners. *Changing Schools, 61*, 2.

Barton, M. L. (1997). Addressing the literacy crisis: Teaching reading in the content areas. *NASSP Bulletin, 81*(587), 22–30.

Bazerman, C. (2009). Genre and cognitive development: Beyond writing to learn. In C. Bazerman, A. Bonini, & D. Figueiredo (Eds.), *Genre in a changing world* (pp. 279–294). Ft. Collins, CO: The WAC Clearinghouse.

Beck, I. L., & McKeown, M. G. (1981). Developing questions that promote comprehension: The story map. *Language Arts, 58*(8), 913–918.

Beck, I. L., McKeown, M. G., & Kucan, L. (2002). *Bringing words to life: Robust vocabulary instruction*. New York: Guilford Press.

Biancarosa, C., & Snow, C. E. (2006). *Reading next—A vision for action and research in middle and high school literacy: A report to Carnegie Corporation of New York* (2nd ed.). Washington, DC: Alliance for Excellent Education.

Billmeyer, R., & Barton, M. L. (1998). *Teaching reading in the content areas: If not me, then who?* (2nd ed). Alexandria, VA: ASCD.

Blachowicz, C. & Fisher, P. (2000). Vocabulary instruction. In M. L. Kamill, P. B. Mosentahal, P. D. Pearson, & R. Barr (Eds.), *Handbook of reading research, vol. 3* (pp. 503–523). Mahwah, NJ: Laurence Erlbaum Associates.

Block, C. C., & Parris, S. R. (Eds.). (2008). *Comprehension instruction: Research-based best practices. solving problems in the teaching of literacy* (2nd ed.). New York: Guilford Press.

Bolton, M. M. (2010). Pulling together: Brockton High marks 40 years of success. *The Boston Globe*. Retrieved from http://www.boston.com/news/local/articles/2010/11/21/brockton_high_school_celebrates_40th_anniversary

Bransford, J. D., Brown, A. L., & Cocking, R. R. (Eds.). (2004). *How people learn: Brain, mind, experience, and school*. Washington, DC: National Academies Press.

Bransford, J. D., Sherwood, R., Vye, N., & Rieser, J. (1986). Teaching thinking and problem solving. *American Psychologist, 41*, 1078–1089.

Braselton, S., & Decker, B. (1994). Using graphic organizers to improve the reading of mathematics. *The Reading Teacher, 48*(3), 276–281.

Brooks, D. (2011). *The social animal: The hidden sources of love, character, and achievement*. New York: Random House.

Brophy, J. (1992) Probing the subtleties of subject-matter teaching. *Educational Leadership, 49*(7), 4–8.

Broughton, S. H., & Sinatra, G. M. (2010). In M. G. McKeown & L. Kucan (Eds.), *Bringing reading research to life* (pp. 232–256). New York: Guilford Press.

Brown, A. L., Day, J. D., & Jones, R. (1983). The development of plans for summarizing texts. *Child Development, 54*, 968–979.

Brozo W. G., & Fisher, D. F. (2010). Literacy starts with the teachers. *Educational Leadership, 67*(6), 74–77.

Buehl, D. (1995). *Classroom strategies for interactive learning* (Monograph of the Wisconsin State Reading Association). Schofield: Wisconsin State Reading Association.

Buehl, D. (2001). *Classroom strategies for interactive learning* (2nd ed.). Newark, DE: International Reading Association.

Buerger, J. R. (1997). *A study of the effect of exploratory writing activities on student success in mathematical problem solving* (Unpublished doctoral dissertation). Columbia University, New York.

Calderón, M. (2007). *Teaching reading to English language learners, grades 6–12: A framework for improving achievement in the content areas*. Thousand Oaks, CA: Corwin Press.

Carr, N. (2010). *The shallows: What the Internet is doing to our brains*. New York: W. W. Norton & Company.

Caverly, D. C., Mandeville, T. F., & Nicholson, S. A.(1995). PLAN: A study-reading strategy for informational text. *Journal of Adolescent & Adult Literacy, 39*(3), 190–199.

Center for Development and Learning (1997). *Learner-centered psychological principles: A framework for school reform*. Retrieved from http://www.cdl.org/resource-library/articles/learner_centered.php

Center on Education Policy. (2011). *State test score trends through 2008–2009, Part 5:Progress lags in high school, especially for advanced achievers*. Washington, DC: Author.

Collins, N. D. (1997). *Motivating low performing adolescent readers*. ERIC Clearinghouse on Reading, English, and Communication, Digest #112. Retrieved from http://www.kidsource.com/kidsource/content2/low.performing.readers.html

Commission on Reading of the National Council of Teachers of English. (n.d.) *On reading, learning to read, and effective reading instruction: An overview of what we know and how we know it*. Retrieved from http://www.ncte.org/positions/statements/onreading

Common Core State Standards Initiative. (2010). *Common Core State Standards for English Language Arts & Literacy in History/Social Studies, Science, and Technical Subjects*. Washington, DC: National Governors Association Center for Best Practices and the Council of Chief State School Officers.

Common Core State Standards Initiative. (2010). *Common Core State Standards for Mathematics*. Washington, DC: National Governors Association Center for Best Practices and the Council of Chief State School Officers.

Costa, A. L. (1991). Toward a model of human intellectual functioning. In A. Costa (Ed.), *Developing minds: A resource book for teaching thinking*. (Rev. ed.) (pp. 62–65). Alexandria, VA: ASCD.

Costa, A. L., & Garmston, R. J. (1994). *Cognitive coaching: A foundation for renaissance schools*. Norwood, MA: Christopher-Gordon.

Cullinan, B. (1987). *Children's literature in the reading program*. Newark, DE: International Reading Association.

Daggett, W. R. (2003). *Achieving reading proficiency for all*. Rexford, NY: International Center for Leadership in Education. Retrieved from http://www.leadered.com/pdf/Reading%20White%20Paper.pdf

Daniels, H., & Zemelman, S. (2004). *Subjects matter: Every teacher's guide to content-area reading*. Portsmouth, NH: Heinemann.

Davey, B. (1983). Think aloud: Modeling the cognitive processes of reading comprehension. *Journal of Reading, 27*(1), 44–47.

Davis, S. J., & Gerber, R. (1994). Open to suggestion: Content area strategies in secondary mathematics classrooms. *Journal of Reading, 38*(1), 55–57.

Dean, C. & Parsley, D. (2008). *Chapter protocol. Success in sight: Module 3.2.* Denver, CO: McREL.

Dean, C. B., Doty, J. K., & Quackenboss, S. A. (2005). *Research into practice series: Classroom instruction that works.* Aurora, CO: McREL.

Dean, C. B., Hubbell, E. R., Pitler, H., & Stone, B. (2012). *Classroom instruction that works: Research-based strategies for increasing student achievement* (2nd ed.). Alexandria, VA: ASCD.

Dehaene, S. (2009). *Reading in the brain: The science and evolution of a human invention.* New York: Viking.

Denti L., & Guerin, G. (2008). *Effective practice for adolescents with reading and literacy challenges.* New York: Routledge.

Dole, J. A., Valencia, S. W., Greer, E. A., & Wardrop, J. L. (1991). Effects of two types of prereading instruction on the comprehension of narrative and expository text. *Reading Research Quarterly, 26*(2), 142–159.

Donahue, P. L., Voekl, K. E., Campbell, J. R., & Mazzeo, J. (1998). *NAEP 1998 reading report card for the nation and the states.* Washington, DC: U.S. Department of Education, National Center for Education Statistics.

Doty, J. K., Cameron, G. N., & Barton, M. L. (2003). *Teaching reading in social studies: A supplement to teaching reading in the content areas teacher's manual* (2nd ed.). Aurora, CO: McREL.

Downing, J. P. (1997). *Creative teaching: Ideas to boost student interest.* Englewood, CO: Teacher Ideas Press.

Duke, N., & Pearson, D. (2002). Effective practices for developing reading comprehension. In A. E. Farstrup & S. J. Samuels (Eds.), *What research has to say about reading instruction* (3rd ed.). Newark, DE: International Reading Association.

Dweck, C. S. (2010). Even geniuses work. *Educational Leadership 68*(1), 16–20.

Fay, L. (1965). Reading study skills: Math and science. In J. A. Figural (Ed.), *Reading and inquiry* (pp. 93–94). Newark, DE: International Reading Association.

Ferguson, R. F., Hackman, S., Hanna, R. & Ballantine, A. (2010). *How high schools become exemplary: Ways that leadership raises achievement and narrows gaps by improving instruction in 15 public high schools. Report on the 2009 Annual Conference of the Achievement Gap Initiative at Harvard University.* Retrieved from http://www.agi.harvard.edu/events/2009Conference/2009AGIConferenceReport6-30-2010web.pdf

Fernando, A. (2011, January–February). Content snacking—and what you can do about it. *Communication World,* 8–10.

Ficca, T. K. (1997). *Reading college textbooks for meaning and structure* (2nd ed.). Boston: Houghton Mifflin.

Frager, A.M. (1993). Affective dimensions of content area reading. *Journal of Reading, 36*(8), 616–622.

Frayer, D. A., Frederick, W. C., & Klausmeier, H. J. (1969). *A schema for testing the level of concept mastery* (Technical Report No. 16). Madison: University of Wisconsin, Research and Development Center for Cognitive Learning.

Fulwiler, T. (1987). *Teaching with writing.* Portsmouth, NH: Boynton/Cook.

Gavelek, J. R. & Raphael, T. E. (1985). Metacognition, instruction, and the role of questioning activities. In D. L. Forrest-Pressley, G. E. MacKinnon, and T. G. Waller (Eds.), *Metacognition, cognition, and human performance, Vol. 2.* (pp. 103–106). New York: Academic Press.

Gay, G. (2000). *Culturally responsive teaching: Theory, research, & practice.* New York: Teachers College Press.

Gewertz, C. (2011, March 14). Teachers tackle text complexity. *Education Week, 30*(24), 1, 12–13.

Giancarlo, C. A., Blohm, S. W. & Urdan, T. (2004). Assessing secondary students' disposition toward critical thinking: Development of the California Measure of Mental Motivation. *Educational and Psychological Measurement, 64*(2), 347–364.

Goldenberg, C. (2008). *Teaching English language learners what the research does—and does not—say.* Retrieved from http://www.aft.org/pdfs/americaneducator/summer2008/goldenberg.pdf

Goodwin, B. (2010). *Changing the odds for student success: What matters most.* Denver, CO: McREL.

Graesser, A., Ozuru, Y., & Sullins, J. (2010). What is a good question? In M. G. McKeown & L. Kucan (Eds.), *Bringing reading research to life* (pp. 112–141). New York: Guilford Press.

Graham, S., & Hebert, M. A. (2010). *Writing to read: Evidence for how writing can improve reading. A Carnegie Corporation Time to Act Report.* Washington, DC: Alliance for Excellent Education.

Greenleaf, C., Schoenbach, R., Cziko, C., & Mueller, F. (2001). Apprenticing adolescent readers to academic literacy. *Harvard Educational Review 71*(1), 79–129.

Guthrie, J. T., & Humenick, N. M. (2004). Motivating students to read: Evidence for classroom practices that increase reading motivation and achievement. In P. McCardle & V. Chhabra (Eds.), *The voice of evidence in reading research* (pp. 329–354). Baltimore, MD: Brookes Publishing.

Harmon, J. M., & Hedrick, W. B. (2000). Teaching ideas: Zooming in and zooming out: Enhancing vocabulary and conceptual learning in social studies. *The Reading Teacher, 54*(2), 155–159.

Harmon, J. M., Hedrick, W. B. & Wood, K. D. (2006). Research on vocabulary instruction in the content areas: Implications for struggling readers. *Reading & Writing Quarterly, 21*(3), 261–280.

Harvey, S., & Daniels, H. (2009). *Comprehension and collaboration: Inquiry circles in action.* Portsmouth, NH: Heinemann.

Harvey, S., & Goudvis, A. (2000). *Strategies that work: Teaching comprehension to enhance understanding.* York, ME: Stenhouse.

Harvey, S., & Goudvis, A. (2007). *Strategies that work: Teaching comprehension for understanding and engagement* (2nd ed.). Portland, ME: Stenhouse.

Heller, R. (n.d.). *All about adolescent literacy.* Retrieved from http://www.adlit.org/adlit_essentials/priorities

Hill, J. D., & Björk, C. L. (2008). *Classroom instruction that works with English language learners: Facilitator's Guide.* Alexandria, VA: ASCD.

Hill, J., & Flynn, K. (2006). *Classroom instruction that works with English language learners.* Alexandria, VA: ASCD.

Jacobs, V. (2008). Adolescent literacy: Putting the crisis in context. *Harvard Educational Review, 78*(1), 7–39.

Johnson, D. D., & Pearson, P. D. (1984). *Teaching reading vocabulary* (2nd ed.). New York: Holt, Rinehart and Winston.

Jones, B. F., Palincsar, A. S., Ogle, D. S., & Carr, E. G. (1987). *Strategic teaching and learning: Cognitive instruction in the content areas.* Alexandria, VA: ASCD.

Jones, R. C. (2001). *Story mapping history frame.* Retrieved from http://www.readingquest.org /strat/storymaps .html

Jordan, M., Jensen, R., & Greenleaf, C. (2001). "Amidst familial gatherings": Reading apprenticeship in a middle school classroom. *Voices from the Middle, 8,* 15–24.

Kamil, M. L. (2003). *Adolescents and literacy: Reading for the 21st century.* Washington, DC: Alliance for Excellent Education.

Keil, W., Schmidt, K.-F., Löwel, S., & Kaschube, M. (2010). How neurons reorganize in growing brains [Blog post]. Retrieved from http://blogs.physicstoday.org/update/2010/06/how-neurons-reorganize-in-grow.html

Kendall, J. S. (2011). *Understanding common core state standards.* Alexandria, VA: ASCD.

Kolln, M., & Hancock, C. (2005). The story of English grammar in United States schools. *English Teaching: Practice and Critique, 4*(3), 11–31.

Kosanovich, M. L., Reed, D. K., & Miller, D. H. (2010). *Bringing literacy strategies into content instruction: Professional learning for secondary-level teachers.* Portsmouth, NH: RMC Research Corporation, Center on Instruction.

Ladson-Billings, G. (2010). Making the book talk: Literacy in successful urban classrooms and communities. In K. Dunsmore & D. Fisher (Eds.), *Bringing literacy home* (pp. 226–244). Newark, DE: International Reading Association.

Laflamme, J. G. (1997). The effect of the Multiple Exposure Vocabulary Method and the Target Reading/Writing Strategy on test scores. *Journal of Adolescent and Adult Literacy, 40*(5), 372–381.

Lamb, J. H. (2010). Reading grade levels and mathematics assessment: An analysis of Texas mathematics assessment items and their reading difficulty. *The Mathematics Educator, 20*(1), 22–34.

Langer, J. A. (2000). *Guidelines for teaching middle and high school students to read and write well: Six features of effective instruction.* New York: National Research Center on English Learning and Achievement.

Lee, C. D., & Spratley, A. (2010). *Reading in the disciplines: The challenges of adolescent literacy.* New York: Carnegie Corporation of New York.

Lent, R. C. (2009). *Literacy for real: Reading, thinking, and learning in the content areas.* New York: Teachers College Press.

Levy, S. (2007, November). The future of reading. *Newsweek.* Retrieved from http://www.newsweek.com/2007/11/17/the-future-of-reading.html

Manna, A. L., & Misheff, S. (1987). What teachers say about their own reading development. *Journal of Reading, 3*(2), 160–168.

Marzano, R. J. (2003) *What works in schools: Translating research into action.* Alexandria: VA: ASCD.

Marzano, R. J. (2010). Summarizing to comprehend. *Educational Leadership, 67*(6), 83–84.

Marzano, R. J., & Brown, J. L. (2009). *A handbook for the art and science of teaching.* Alexandria, VA: ASCD.

Marzano, R. J., & Pickering, D. J. (2005). *Building academic vocabulary: Teacher's manual.* Alexandria, VA: ASCD.

Marzano, R. J., & Pickering, D. J., with Arredondo, D. E., Blackburn, G. J., Brandt, R. S., Moffett, C. A., Paynter, D. E., & Whisler, J. S. (1997). *Dimensions of Learning* (2nd ed.). Alexandria, VA: ASCD.

Marzano, R. J., Pickering, D. J., & Pollock, J. E. (2001). *Classroom instruction that works: Research-based strategies for increasing student achievement.* Alexandria, VA: ASCD.

Mayer, R. (2003) *Learning and instruction.* Upper Saddle River, NJ: Pearson Education.

McBrien, J. L., & Brandt., R. S. (1997). *The language of learning: A guide to education terms*. Alexandria, VA: ASCD.

McCombs, B. L. & Barton, M. L. (1998). Motivating secondary students to read their textbooks. *NASSP Bulletin, 82*(600), 24–33.

McKeown, M. G., & Beck, I. L. (2009). The role of metacognition in reading and comprehension. In D. J. Hacker, J. Dunlosky, & A. C. Graesser (Eds.), *Handbook of metacognition in education* (pp. 8–24). New York: Taylor & Francis.

McNamara, D. S., & Magliano, J. P. (2009). Self-explanation and metacognition: The dynamics of reading. In D. J. Hacker, J. Dunlosky, & A. C. Graesser (Eds.). *Handbook of metacognition in education* (pp. 60–81). New York: Taylor & Francis.

Medina, J. (2008). *Brain rules: 12 principles for surviving and thriving at work, home, and school*. Seattle, WA: Pear Press.

Meltzer, J. (2001). *Supporting adolescent literacy across the content areas*. Providence, RI: Lab at Brown University.

Merkley, D. & Jeffries, D. (2000/2001). Guidelines for implementing a graphic organizer. *The Reading Teacher, 54*(4), 350–357.

Miholic, V. (1994). An inventory to pique students' metacognitive awareness of reading strategies. *Journal of Reading, 30*, 84–86.

Miller, W. H. (1997). *Reading & writing remediation kit: Ready-to-use strategies and activities to build content reading and writing skills*. West Nyack, NY: The Center for Applied Research in Education.

Moje, E. B. (2008). Foregrounding the disciplines in secondary literacy teaching and learning: A call for change. *Journal of Adolescent & Adult Literacy, 52*(2), 96–107.

Moore, D. W., Alvermann, D. E., & Hinchman, K. A. (2000). *Struggling adolescent readers: A collection of teaching strategies*. Newark, DE: International Reading Association.

Mortimer, E. F., & Scott, P. H. (2003). *Making meaning in secondary science classrooms*. Berkshire, UK: McGraw-Hill.

Moss, B. (1991). Children's nonfiction trade books: A complement to content area texts. *The Reading Teacher, 45*, 26–32.

Moss, B. (2004). Teaching expository text structures through information trade book retellings. *The Reading Teacher, 57*(8), 710–718.

Murphy, P. K., Wilkinson, I.A.G., Soter, A. O, Hennessey, M. N., & Alexander, J. F. (2009). Examining the effects of classroom discussion on students' comprehension of text: A meta-analysis. *Journal of Educational Psychology, 101*(3), 740–764.

Murthy, K., & Weber, S. (2011). School of thought in Brockton, Mass. [Television series episode]. In *Need to know on PBS*. Retrieved from http://www.pbs.org/wnet/need-to-know/uncategorized/brockton-high-proves-that-big-schools-can-be-good-schools/6959

Nagy, W., Berninger, V. W., & Abbott, R. D. (2006). Contributions of morphology beyond phonology to literacy outcomes of upper elementary and middle-school students. *Journal of Educational Psychology, 98*(1), 134–147.

National Clearinghouse for English Language Acquisition. (n.d.). Frequently Asked Questions. Retrieved from http://www.ncela.gwu.edu/faqs

National Endowment for the Arts. (2007). *To read or not to read: A question of national consequence*. Retrieved from http://www.nea.gov/research/toread.pdf

National Governors Association Center for Best Practices. (2005). *Reading to achieve: A governor's guide to adolescent literacy*. Retrieved from http://www.nga.org

National Institute for Literacy. (2007). *What content-area teachers should know about adolescent literacy*. Washington, DC: Author.

National Institute of Child Health and Human Development. (2000). *Report of the National Reading Panel. Teaching children to read: An evidence-based assessment of the scientific research literature on reading and its implications for reading instruction* (NIH Publication No. 00-4769). Washington, DC: U.S. Government Printing Office.

National Survey of Student Engagement (2008). *Promoting engagement for all students: The imperative to look within*. Bloomington: Indiana University Center for Postsecondary Research.

Nix, M. (2011, February 20). Colorado voices: It's old school—and it's the future. *Denver Post*. Retrieved from http://www.denverpost.com/opinion/ci_17417694?source=bb

Olson, C. B., & Land, R. (2007). A cognitive strategies approach to reading and writing instruction for English language learners in secondary school. *Research in the Teaching of English, 41*(3), 269–303.

Olson, M. W., & Gee, T. C. (1991). Content reading instruction in the primary grades: Perceptions and strategies. *The Reading Teacher, 45*(4), 298–306.

Osman, M. E., & Hannafin, M. J. (1992). Metacognition research and theory: Analysis and implications for instructional design. *Educational Technology Research and Development, 40*(2), 83–89.

Palincsar, A. S., & Brown, A. L. (1985). Reciprocal teaching: Activities to promote "reading with your mind." In T. L. Harris & E. J. Cooper (Eds.), *Reading, thinking, and concept development* (pp. 147–158). New York: College Board Publications.

Paul, R. (Ed.). (1990). *Critical thinking: What every person needs to survive in a rapidly changing world.* Rohnert Park, CA: Center for Critical Thinking and Moral Critique.

Perkins, D. (1993, October). Teaching & learning for understanding. *NJEA Review,* 10–17.

Phan H. P. (2009). Exploring students' reflective thinking practice, deep processing strategies, effort, and achievement goal orientations. *Educational Psychology, 29*(3), 297–313.

Pimentel, S. (2007). *Teaching reading well: A synthesis of the international reading association's research on teacher preparation for reading instruction.* Newark, DE: International Reading Association.

Pink, D. (2009a). Dan Pink on the surprising science of motivation. *TED Global 2009.* Retrieved from http://www.ted.com/talks/dan_pink_on_motivation.html

Pink, D. (2009b). *Drive: The surprising truth about what motivates us.* New York: Penguin Group.

Piolat, H., Olive, T., & Kellogg, R. T. (2005). Cognitive effort during note-taking. *Applied Cognitive Psychology, 19,* 291–312.

Pitcher, S. M., Albright, L. K., DeLaney, C. J., Walker, N. T., Seunarinesingh, K., Mogge, S.,. . . Dunston, P. J. (2007). Assessing adolescents' motivation to read. *Journal of Adolescent & Adult Literacy, 50*(5), 378–396.

Plumb, T. (2010, April 8). New focus on reading, writing. *The Boston Globe.* Retrieved from http://www.boston.com/news/education

Pogrow, S. (1993). The forgotten question in the Chapter I debate: Why are the students having so much trouble learning? *Education Week, 26,* 36.

Prensky, M. (2001). *Digital natives, digital immigrants.* Retrieved from http://www.marcprensky.com/writing

Pressley, M., Mohan, L., Raphael, L. M., & Fingeret, L. (2007). How does Bennett Woods Elementary School produce such high reading and writing achievement? *Journal of Educational Psychology, 99*(2), 221–240

Raphael, T. E. (1982). Question-answering strategies for children. *The Reading Teacher, 36,* 186–190.

Raphael, T. E. (1986). Teaching question-answer relationships, revisited. *The Reading Teacher, 39,* 516–522.

Raphael, T. E., Kirschner, B. W., & Englert, C. S. (1988). Expository writing program: Making connections between reading and writing. *The Reading Teacher, 41,* 790–795.

Report of the National Commission on Writing for America's Families, Schools, and Colleges (2006). *Writing and school reform.* Retrieved from http://www.collegeboard.com/prod_downloads/writingcom/writing-school-reform-natl-comm-writing.pdf

Richardson, J. S., & Morgan, R. F. (1994). *Reading to learn in the content areas.* Belmont, CA: Wadsworth.

Richardson, J. S., Morgan, R. F., & Fleener, C. (2009). *Reading to learn in the content areas* (7th ed.). Belmont, CA: Wadsworth Cengage Learning.

Rigsbee, C. (2011, March 16). Reflections of a dance school dropout. *Education Week.* Retrieved from http://www.edweek.org/tm/articles/2011/03/16/tln_rigsbee_dance.html

Roberts, J. M. (2004). *Effective study skills.* Upper Saddle River, NJ: Pearson Education.

Robinson, F. P. (1970). *Effective study* (4th ed.). New York: Harper & Row.

Rog, L. & Kropp, P. (2001). *Hooking struggling readers: Using books they can and want to read.* Retrieved from http://www.readingrockets.org/article/374

Roth, M. (2011, March 20). Why does U.S. fail in science education? *Pittsburgh Post-Gazette.* Retrieved from http://www.post-gazette.com/pg/11079/1133328-84.stm

Santa, C. M. (1988). *Content reading including study systems.* Dubuque, IA: Kendall/Hunt.

Schmoker, M. (2011). *Focus: Elevating the essentials to radically improve student learning.* Alexandria, VA: ASCD.

Scholastic. (2008). *Scholastic 2008 kids & family reading report: Reading in the 21st century.* Retrieved from http://www.scholastic.com/aboutscholastic/news/kfrr08web.pdf

Scholastic. (2010). *Scholastic 2010 kids & family reading report: Turning the page in the digital age.* Retrieved from www.scholastic.com/readingreport

Schunk D., & Zimmerman, B. J. (1997). Developing self-efficacious readers and writers: The role of social and self-regulatory processes. In J. T. Guthrie & A. Wigfield (Eds.), *Reading for engagement: Motivating readers through integrated instruction* (pp. 34–50). Newark, DE: International Reading Association.

Schwartz, R. (1988). Learning to learn vocabulary in content area textbooks. *Journal of Reading, 32,* 108–117.

Schwartz, R., & Raphael, T. (1985). Concept definition: A key to improving students' vocabulary. *The Reading Teacher, 39*(2), 198–205.

SEDL. (n.d.). *Building reading proficiency at the secondary level.* Retrieved from http://www.sedl.org/pubs/reading16/7.html

Shanahan, T. (2010, July 11). *Content area reading versus disciplinary literacy* [Blog post]. Retrieved from http://www.shanahanonliteracy.com/2010/07/content-area-reading-versus.html

Shanahan, T., & Shanahan, C. (2008). Teaching disciplinary literacy to adolescents: Rethinking content-area literacy. *Harvard Educational Review, 78*(1), 40–59.

Short, E. J., & Ryan, E. B. (1984). Metacognitive differences between skilled and less skilled readers: Remediating deficits through story grammar and attribution training. *Journal of Educational Psychology, 76*, 225–235.

Smith, J.A.R., & Martin, C. J. (2007). DNA: Modeling structure and function. *Iowa Science Teachers Journal, (34)*1, 14–20.

Smith, P., & Tompkins, G. (1988). Structured notetaking: A new strategy for content area readers, *Journal of Reading, 32*(1), 46–53.

Southern Region Education Board (2004). *Raise academic standards and get more students to complete high school: How 13 Georgia schools did it.* Atlanta, GA: Author.

Speer, N. K., Reynolds, J. R., Swallow, K. M., & Zacks, J. M. (2009). Reading stories activates neural representations of visual and motor experiences. *Psychological Science 20*(8), 989–999.

Stauffer, R. G. (1969). *Directing reading maturity as a cognitive process.* New York: Harper & Row.

Stedman, L. C. & Kaestle, C. F. (1991). Literacy and reading performance in the United States from 1880 to the present. In C. F. Kaestle, H. Damon-Moore, L. C. Stedman, K. Tinsley, & W. V. Trollinger (Eds.), *Literacy in the United States: Readers and reading since 1880* (pp. 75–128). New Haven, CT: Yale University Press.

Stone, B., & Urquhart, V. (2008). *Remove limits to learning with systematic vocabulary instruction.* Denver, CO: McREL.

Strickland, D. S., & Alvermann, D. E., (2004). *Bridging the literacy achievement gap, grades 4–12.* New York: Teachers College Press.

Sturtevant, E., Boyd, F., Brozo, W., Hinchman, K., Alvermann, D., & Moore, D. (2006). *Principled practices for adolescent literacy: A framework for instruction and policy.* Mahwah, NJ: Erlbaum.

Teaching techniques: Reflective discussion method. (n.d.). Retrieved from http://lrs.ed.uiuc.edu/students/m-weeks/refldisc.html

Tierney, R. J., & Shanahan, T. (1991). Research on reading-writing relationships: Interactions, transactions, and outcomes. In P. E. Pearson, M. Barr, & P. B. Mosenthal (Eds.). *Handbook of Reading Research, Volume II* (pp. 246–280).New York: Longman.

Totten, S., Sills, T., Digby, A., & Russ, P. (1991). *Cooperative learning: A guide to research.* New York: Garland.

Tynjala, P., Mason, L., & Lonka, K. (Eds.). (2001). *Writing as a learning tool: Integrating theory and practice.* Dordrecht, Netherlands: Kluwer Academic.

United Nations Educational, Scientific, and Cultural Organization. (n.d.). *United Nations Literacy Decade (2003–2012).* Retrieved from http://www.unesco.org/new/en/education/themes/education-building-blocks/literacy/un-literacy-decade

Vacca, R. T. (2006). They can because they think they can. *Educational Leadership, 63*(5), 56–59.

Vacca, R. T., & Vacca, J. L. (1993). *Content area reading* (4th ed.). New York: Harper Collins.

Vacca, R. T., & Vacca, J. L. (1999). *Content area reading: Literacy and learning across the curriculum* (6th ed.). Menlo Park, CA: Longman.

Vacca, R. T., & Vacca, J. L. (2005). *Content area reading: Literacy and learning across the curriculum* (8th ed.). Boston: Allyn & Bacon.

van Nimwegen, C. (2008). *The paradox of the guided user: Assistance can be counter-effective.* SIKS Dissertation Series No. 2008–2009. Enschede, Netherlands: Gildeprint.

Wang, L., Conner, J. M., Rickert, J., & Tuszynski, M. H. (2011). Structural plasticity within highly specific neuronal populations identifies a unique parcellation of motor learning in the adult brain. *Proceedings of the National Academy of Sciences.* doi: 10.1073/pnas.1014335108

Willis. J. (2007). Cooperative leaning is a brain turn-on. *Middle School Journal (38)*4, 4–13.

Wolpert-Gawron, H. (2009, April 16). *The importance of a classroom library* [Blog post]. Retrieved from http://www.edutopia.org/classroom-library-importance

Wood. K. (1984). Probable passage: A writing strategy. *The Reading Teacher, 37*, 496–499.

Wood, K. (1988). Guiding students through informational text. *The Reading Teacher, 41*(9), 912–920.

Wood, K. D., & Muth, K. D. (1991). The case for improved instruction in the middle grades. *Journal of Reading, 35*(2), 84–90.

Zwiers, J., & Crawford, M. (2009). How to start academic conversations. *Educational Leadership, 66*(7), 70–73.

Index

In this index the Strategies can be found capitalized, and the letter *f* following a page number denotes a figure.

About the Authors

Vicki Urquhart

As a communications manager for McREL, Vicki fulfills a variety of roles in writing, editing, and producing research-based publications and new products. An experienced presenter, she conducts workshops around the country. She has more than 20 years of experience as an educator, having taught at the secondary and postsecondary levels. Vicki coauthored *Teaching Writing in the Content Areas*, two booklets—*Remove Limits to Learning With Systematic Vocabulary Instruction* and *Using Writing in Mathematics to Deepen Student Learning*—and several articles for *Phi Delta Kappan, Principal Leadership,* and the *Journal of Staff Development,* among others. In 2007, she served on the planning committee that developed the 2011 NAEP Writing Framework.

Dana Frazee

As a principal consultant, Dana works in several areas of McREL's field services group: *Success in Sight* continuous school improvement, guaranteed and viable curriculum development, school audits, and teaching reading in the content areas. Dana has presented at numerous regional and national workshops on a variety of subjects, including teaching reading in the content areas, data-based decision making, writing in the content areas, formative assessment, continuous school improvement, effective instructional strategies, and afterschool teaching strategies. She is a coauthor of *Math in Afterschool: An Instructor's Guide to the Afterschool Training Toolkit.* Prior to joining McREL, Dana taught middle school and high school, served as the principal of a K–8 charter school, and worked as an educational consultant for the Coalition of Essential School and Expeditionary Learning Schools.

About McREL

Mid-continent Research for Education and Learning (McREL) is a nationally recognized, nonprofit education research and development organization, headquartered in Denver, Colorado with offices in Honolulu, Hawai`i and Omaha, Nebraska. Since 1966, McREL has helped translate research and professional wisdom about what works in education into practical guidance for educators. Our 120-plus staff members and affiliates include respected researchers, experienced consultants, and published writers who provide educators with research-based guidance, consultation, and professional development for improving student outcomes.

Related ASCD Resources: Reading in the Content Areas

At the time of publication, the following ASCD resources were available (ASCD stock numbers appear in parentheses). For up-to-date information about ASCD resources, go to www.ascd.org. You can search the complete archives of Educational Leadership at http://www.ascd.org/el.

ASCD EDge Group

Exchange ideas and connect with other educators interested in teaching literacy in the content areas on the social networking site ASCD EDge™ at http://ascdedge.ascd.org/

Online Courses

Common Core and Literacy Strategies: English Language Arts (#PD11OC135)
Common Core and Literacy Strategies: History/Social Studies (#PD11OC132)
Common Core and Literacy Strategies: Mathematics (#PD11OC134)
Common Core and Literacy Strategies: Science (#PD11OC133)

Print Products

Classroom Instruction That Works (2nd edition) by Ceri B. Dean, Elizabeth Ross Hubbell, Howard Pitler, and Bj Stone (#111001)
Reading Strategies for the Content Areas, Volume 1: An ASCD Action Tool by Sue Z. Beers and Lou Howell (#703109)
Reading Strategies for the Content Areas, Volume 2: An ASCD Action Tool by Sue Z. Beers (#705002)
Teaching English Language Learners Across the Content Areas by Debbie E. Zacarian and Judie Haynes (#109032)
Teaching Reading in Mathematics by Mary Lee Barton and Clare Heidama (#310059)
Teaching Reading in Science by Mary Lee Barton and Deborah L. Jordan (#302269)
Teaching Reading in Social Studies by Jane K. Doty, Gregory N. Cameron, and Mary Lee Barton (#310084)
Teaching Writing in the Content Areas by Monette McIver and Vicki Urquhart (#105036)

Video

How to Improve Content Understanding Using Reading Strategies (#607057)
Reading in the Content Areas Video Series (#602029)

THE WHOLE CHILD The Whole Child Initiative helps schools and communities create learning environments that allow students to be healthy, safe, engaged, supported, and challenged. To learn more about other books and resources that relate to the whole child, visit www.wholechildeducation.org.

For more information: send e-mail to member@ascd.org; call 1-800-933-2723 or 703-578-9600, press 2; send a fax to 703-575-5400; or write to Information Services, ASCD, 1703 N. Beauregard St., Alexandria, VA 22311-1714 USA.